HIGH-ALTITUDE
WOMAN

"I've known Jan since her earliest days as an adventurer, traveling to the ends of the Earth to get her story, setting high-altitude climbing and skiing records, making the U.S. Biathlon Team, and even taking a hot air balloon over Everest . . . just to investigate the differences between men and women! Jan never made a big deal out of being the only woman on otherwise all-male teams on these expeditions, fitting in as one of the guys at altitude and an incredibly pleasant companion, friend, and mom at sea level. Fortunately we can just read about her discoveries without hanging off cliffs and falling out of the sky, although that sounds like fun, don't you think?"

BOB ARNOT, HOST OF THE *DR. DANGER* REALITY TV SERIES AND AUTHOR OF 14 BOOKS ON NUTRITION AND HEALTH TOPICS

"Jan Reynolds is an extraordinary athlete who distinguished herself in a high-risk, traditionally masculine subculture, refusing to let her life be constrained by gender. As she explains in *High-Altitude Woman*, "I felt this world belonged to me as much as any man." Following a life-or-death predicament during a solo crossing of a Himalaya, Reynolds muses, "What was it in me that thought always about what I could do and seldom, if ever, about what I couldn't do? Was this a good thing or twisted?" The answer is crystal clear, and it resounds from almost every page of this inspiring, unsparingly honest book."

JON KRAKAUER, AUTHOR OF *INTO THE WILD*, *UNDER THE BANNER OF HEAVEN*, AND *INTO THIN AIR*

"Gripping tales of adventure and feats of endurance make this book hard to put down. Jan Reynolds reveals personal content and behind-the-scenes dynamics that rarely reach the public eye. When women read this memoir, no matter what challenges they are facing, Jan Reynolds's bold and extraordinary experiences will serve as a beacon for looking deeper within for that extra insight and strength that it takes to endure and prevail. The gift this book offers men is an awareness and appreciation of the feminine, leading to the inclusion of the female perspective in all extreme endeavors."

SUSAN GRIMALDI, FORMER VICE PRESIDENT OF
THE NATIVE CULTURAL ALLIANCE, SHAMANIC HEALER, AND
EXPLORER CLUB MEMBER

...ITUDE
WOMAN

From Extreme Sports
to Indigenous Cultures—
Discovering the Power
of the Feminine

JAN REYNOLDS

Inner Traditions
Rochester, Vermont • Toronto, Canada

Inner Traditions
One Park Street
Rochester, Vermont 05767
www.InnerTraditions.com

Text stock is SFI certified

Library of Congress Cataloging-in-Publication Data
Reynolds, Jan, 1956–
  High-altitude woman : from extreme sports to indigenous cultures—discovering
the power of the feminine / Jan Reynolds.
    p. cm.
  Includes bibliographical references.
  Summary: "One of the first female extreme athletes reflects on how her feminine
strengths led to her success in a male-dominated field"—Provided by publisher.
  ISBN 978-1-59477-485-0 (pbk.)—ISBN 978-1-62055-138-7 (e-book)
  1. Reynolds, Jan, 1956– 2. Photojournalists—United States—Biography. 3.
Women mountaineers—Psychology. 4. Success. I. Title.
  TR140.R49A3 2013
  770.92—dc23
  [B]
                                                    2012049047

Printed and bound in the United States by Lake Book Manufacturing, Inc.
The text stock is SFI certified. The Sustainable Forestry Initiative® program
promotes sustainable forest management.

10   9   8   7   6   5   4   3   2   1

Text design and layout by Virginia Scott Bowman
This book was typeset in Garamond Premier Pro with Trajan Pro used as the
display typeface

To send correspondence to the author of this book, mail a first-class letter to the
author c/o Inner Traditions • Bear & Company, One Park Street, Rochester, VT
05767, and we will forward the communication, or contact the author directly at
www.janreynolds.com.

To my boys Briggs and Story,
the men in my life forever.
You have taught me more about men
than anything else.

CONTENTS

ONE OF THE GUYS

I CLIMBED AT HIGH ALTITUDE in the "death zone" and set world skiing records. I consistently shot five bullets, within the size of my thumbnail, at fifty meters. I skydived, scuba dived, and more—always in the company of men. I was one of the guys until I was almost forty. Then, I had a baby. Even when I was pregnant, I was still one of the guys, crossing the Sahara in the first three months on camel back, with snack bars packed in case we ran out of food or got caught out in a sandstorm.

During the next three months of pregnancy I climbed and snowboarded North Africa's highest peak, Toubkal. When I 'fessed up that I was six months pregnant to some of the European guys I shared a hut with at the base of the peak, one exclaimed, "Voilà, I knew pregnancy was not a sickness." I had made the summit that day. These guys didn't. In my final months of pregnancy I was in the Himalayas in the Everest Region shooting a video on a "use it or lose it" grant. My climbing buddies, who were going in and out to climb peaks through the Khumbu in northeastern Nepal, were telling me to go home. I could have the baby any time. But I knew all my Sherpa friends were born right there.

I did eventually go home to our little shack in Vermont, with only a woodstove, little insulation, and a very leaky roof, to have a beautiful home birth with a competent midwife. At this point my life changed in ways I never imagined. Having a new, bouncing baby boy to care for wasn't as life changing as the response, or lack thereof, of my male companions. In their minds it was almost as if I had died. I

1

was no longer someone they called, rode bikes with, hiked with, had a beer with, or did anything with. My self-view hadn't changed since the onset of motherhood, but the way the men viewed me had. To add to this confusing injury, my male friends would call for my husband and ask to speak to him without so much as a howdy-do to me, or would ask point blank, "Hey, Jan, can Jay come ride with us?" Why not ask me to go?

That was almost as bothersome as not being asked to participate in the fun, being treated as if I held the keys to my husband's freedom. It was as if nothing should change for my husband, Jay, now that he was a father, unless I held him back for domestic and family reasons. To the men, I had suddenly turned into the bad guy. They saw me as having the power to say no to their fun. But weren't they saying no to me when I wasn't invited? What was I, chopped liver?

I felt confused, rejected, and down, even though all I had done was have a baby, one my husband and I created together. I had often been the only woman on expeditions and had carried the same loads while climbing the same peaks. I had set the same skiing records; I had raced the same endurance triathlons; I shot the same targets in biathlon. But now that the tables were turned, it appeared the men didn't see themselves as carrying the same load in what they considered a woman's world. Women's work was left for me alone, by their determination.

I felt cheated. No one had told me the rules would change. I pulled my weight, and sometimes more, while living in the man's world of expeditions. Why didn't this work in reverse? Shouldn't a man be expected to pull his weight and more in the woman's world of the home and child rearing, the world they told me was mine, whether or not I agreed? Don't get me wrong. I reveled in motherhood, nursing, and caring for my newborn. I had found a love I never knew existed. My life was joyous—except for this rejection and label as fun killer by my male ex-companions.

Forced from the fraternity I began to assemble a new life of adventure on my own. Before my son, Briggs, was even two months old I had us on a mountain bike trip in the backcountry of the Czech Republic. The baby rode in a special one-wheeled trailer hitched to the back of the bike, to roll him through the tight, single track in the woods. We went on to ride in northern Europe, the Caribbean, and North Africa this way. I suppose I was still one of the guys, considering I was with my son and my husband. I was inspired to write a book, *Mother and Child: Visions of Parenting from Indigenous Cultures,* to describe how indigenous mothers had always taken their babes in arms everywhere with them, whether on camel back, yaks, horses, you name it. I was merely carrying on the way mothers had throughout time before the advent of bottles, cribs, baby gates, playpens, monitors, and all that other unnecessary paraphernalia that just weighs you down and separates you from your child.

But an amazing revelation occurred to me when I was home, writing between trips. I realized the power of women. Because I had for the most part spent my life admiring men—their motivation, sense of daring, and physical prowess—and had watched with uncertainty as women headed to the ladies' room in packs and kvetched for hours, I never realized just what women had in them. I was more of a guy than the guys. Now I found myself at playgroups and playgrounds, kvetching myself over coffee with all the other moms. We shared information. We passed on tips about how to handle anything from croup to cranky husbands to how to please our bosses, or be bosses, at work, while not sacrificing time with our new families. These women were super; they did it all, in the man's world and the woman's world. Men, I found, were more limited.

In general, if you'll forgive me for gross generalizations, from my own experiences, as well as studies and statistics, I've learned that men use language to create hierarchy and to compete; women use language to bond and support. Men are naturally more aggressive, assertive, and competitive; women focus on relationships and connecting. Men live with a sense of entitlement; women live with a sense of harmony.

How had I been so blind? I had been so focused on climbing higher, running faster, and becoming stronger, like the guys I was with, I never stopped to notice that the women all around me were setting up networks of support, working their way into important jobs while having families. By the time I had my second son I gave up on trying to connect with the men for fun and found women to hit the trails with, often with little ones on our backs, or with tiny ones in tow. And yes, although we may have been considered fun killers, we sometimes left the children with their fathers while we went out for an adrenaline rush of our own.

Over time the men participated more in the child rearing, freeing us women for work and play. Things were shifting, worlds were merging, and they still are. I do feel men and women are so much more alike than different, but the subtle differences in our makeup are worth taking a very close look at in order for us to understand one another better, to create greater harmony. We have much to learn from each other, without changing each other. There is symmetry and balance to our ways as men and women when working in tandem. But it is through understanding these differences that we will be empowered to take advantage of them and put them to good use.

I went from being raised on a dairy farm with a Catholic ethic to traveling to the Himalayas and immersing myself in the Buddhist culture, setting me up for a profound shift in view. Life seen as black and white transformed into life with an incredible number of shades of gray. No longer was what you did as important as what you were thinking when you did it. Buddhism went deeper into motivation. Intention became more important than the result. My worldview of ethics was turned upside down. Once my mind was shaken loose from my formative foundation, I opened to the myriad ways older cultures expressed their human spirit. With no one, or any group, to condemn, I was free to feel the similarities in us all as a human family. This was a gift.

It all began to come together for me, several years BC (before children), when I set out to cross the Himalayas solo with National Geographic in support. I wondered, as I was sick and alone for days in my tent, out of fuel and food, before I was taken under the wing of a band of Tibetan salt traders, if many women would have chosen this venture. I was again one of the guys. But I thought, even if another woman's dream differed from mine, it would still be important for me to lend her support through what I had learned: women can do anything when they receive the positive validation they deserve. When a woman is praised for a job well done or encouraged for her positive contributions she will have the same confidence level as that of a man. My own experiences had proved this to be true.

These Tibetan fellows treated me as another trader when I was back on my feet, bartering tsampa for me to eat in exchange for my scarves and even my fingernail clippers. They brought me to their homes on the other side of the Himalayas to meet their wives and children, where I could explore their daily lives and rituals. Again I realized the importance of passing on what I learned from my experiences with these older cultures I lived with: that we are one human family with many ways to express the same human spirit. As a collective species we need to recollect the ways to live in connection and conjunction with our natural world and each other.

Following this solo Himalayan expedition, I traveled the world living with an indigenous group on each continent, experiencing their lives, rituals, and celebrations with them, dancing and singing a heri (song) of thanks with the Yanomami, spinning prayer wheels with the Tibetans, eating rancid whale blubber with the Inuit, drinking fermented mare's milk with the Mongolians, painting up to dance dreamings with the Australian Aborigines, and so much more. I saw and felt the commonalities among us all. I felt compelled to live a life of service in support of women and in support of the cultures and landscapes in peril of vanishing from our world. Yet it took immersing myself in the realm of women in my own culture and reflecting on my own adventures with men, indigenous and otherwise, to realize just how capable and wonderful women are worldwide. In our collective human family I feel men and women have so much to learn from each other across cultures. And if you care to listen, I will tell you what I know.

CHAPTER 1

SOUTHERN CROSS EXPEDITION

"YOUR LIFE IS WHAT YOU MAKE IT, and the world is what it means to you," drifted through my mind as I lay on my bed, stalling before starting my homework. I remember being twelve years old, lying on my bed with these thoughts running through my head. I was starting to get the feeling that I should really explore this human experiment before my time was up; I should make my life compelling. Somehow, early on, I was able to cut through dogma and predetermined roles. Being a human, living on this planet, is an incredible sociological experiment, and none of us get out of here alive.

Ten years later a growing, heavy, wet mass of snow was racing down with unrelenting speed on my climbing partners and me. The avalanche had just dropped off the heights in the heart of the New Zealand Alps. After a thunderous vertical fall it had hit the slope above us as we slogged upward together, Ned Gillette, Allan Bard, Tom Carter, and I. There was only a moment, which seemed to expand effortlessly in time, in which to make a decision. Allan, in the lead, made the call.

"Ladies and gentlemennnnn." He drew out the *n* as he deliberated which way would keep us from being swept away. "Move left!" Allan had a flair for fun. "Red-lining the fun meter" he called it. He swung his arm to the left, and we all post-holed desperately in that direction, out of the path of this freight train of snow. The avalanche had been rushing dead on, only its varying width determined which direction would give us the best chance of escaping its pressure and turbulence.

From where I stood, down the slope, it appeared to me too that left was the best option. Support and agreement makes any choice easier, no matter what the stakes. After the passing wind and wet from the avalanche slapped our faces, we stared at the rubble left behind, almost detached, then looked up and carried on our slog upward. Adrenaline was easing out of our systems, and in its place lactic acid was building in our muscles. We had returned to our familiar rhythm. Ned had told me before this trip that "expeditions can be short periods of joy and glory, interspersed with long periods of monotony and nastiness." He was right on.

This trip was the equivalent of getting my master's degree in adventure. I met Ned Gillette the day I led our university ski team to a relay victory and the NCAA championships at the Trapp Family Lodge in Stowe, Vermont. I skied right over and asked Ned for a job to teach skiing because I was graduating soon. The next winter not only did I get the job, I got the boss's attention and a spot on his climbing roster for the Southern Cross expedition set in New Zealand.

Completing the New Zealand roster were Tom Carter and Allan Bard, inseparable, beautiful, blond buddies from California who also taught skiing for Ned. Tom and Allan, some of the best rock climbers, had logged time in Yosemite, honing their craft. Ned had drawn together many people to create a colorful cast of characters to work for him at Trapp's. Ned's crew called themselves "the unemployables." For these characters life was too large to be lived in any controlled or contained way. Most of the crew worked for a little cash, then split for parts unknown to climb, ski, kayak, and push the edge of what was possible.

Ned, Allan, Tom, and I had come to ski the heart of the New Zealand Alps on a route that hadn't been done before and to push the possibilities of Nordic skiing. We would begin at Mount Cook National Park and head up the Tasman glacier and beyond. Skiing this line, which included a series of huts, had been done in stages before our trip in 1979, but our ambitious route had never been knit together as one long ski. We were also the first to be doing it on metal-edged cross-country skis with free-heeled leather boots. Each boot was held to the ski by three-pin toe bindings, with a metal bale clamped down on the rim of the boot's toe, which is why Nordic telemark skiing came to be called three pinning. Parts of our route had only been done on heavy ski mountaineering gear—wide, stable skis and big plastic boots with locked-down heels. At the time we were stretching the limits of cross-country ski gear.

After the avalanche we continued to climb up the white wall in front of us, scoured by the high winds and engulfed in a whiteout. We heard the low buzz of an engine cutting the silence. Gavin Wills, a wonderful, wild man who ran the alpine guiding service for the Mount Cook area, had managed to find a tiny hole in the angry weather to fly in and search for our party. Gavin, accompanied by Merv Falconer, a chief pilot for Mount Cook Airlines, flung something small from the plane and banked a turn, heading out of the weather pressing back in on us. Attached to a small rock were a map and a note describing where treasure lay! On the Rangitata Col above us, our last big hurdle before completing the traverse, was a box Gavin had pushed from the plane with food, delicious food.

We had been dividing bouillon cubes four ways for days, trying to ration the last bit of nourishment we had as a storm kept us in our two-man tent for days—the four of us lying like sardines, head to foot. Preparing and drinking that lukewarm, watered-down bullion not only hydrated us but also broke up the monotony while we waited out the weather. At the outset of our trip Gavin had advised, "You've got to start thinking of travel in these mountains differently. Miles are nothing. It is weather and vertical that will give you a run for your money." These mountains were his occupation, and he knew what lay in store for us. What we had thought would take days had now taken us a month.

The weather was insidiously gorgeous when we began this Southern Cross traverse the last week in August, winter Down Under. We adhered our climbing skins to our skis before heading up the Tasman Glacier underneath the bluest of skies. We didn't disbelieve Gavin's words, but it all seemed so straightforward on the map, and the weather couldn't get any better. We started off if not naive then overly optimistic. Years of ski training and racing had programmed me into a comfortable, sliding rhythm, roped for glacier travel. Ned and I were one rope team, Tom and Allan on the other.

The first day out was long; the sun was brilliant but draining. We each carried a pack of forty to fifty pounds. We had been determined to keep the packs to forty pounds, because, without our heels locked down on our cross-country gear, we felt more weight would just throw us around on the downhills. We were right, we learned, as we skied with our heaviest load on the first day, lurching over hummocks and through dips of snowy terrain. The packs pushed us down slopes and pulled us back going up, in a sort of go-stop-go motion, like a car lurching onto the highway in the wrong gear. Eventually we began to smooth out.

Clear views of the amazing Alps, crowned by Mount Cook, were spectacular under perfectly clear skies. Our only weather worry was sunburn. Our two rope teams kept to themselves. Something was off; all the levity during our time of preparation seemed to have dissipated. No one seemed to be talking. I wasn't sure what was up, so I kept to myself. I was left to my own imagination most of the day, broken up by occasional water and food breaks. Our seven-mile day ended with a steep climb to the hut and festering blisters on our heels.

The two rope teams had seemed awfully distant to me, not physically, but quite separate from each other. We weren't one cohesive group. Ned and I were a couple; we had been seeing each other after working together all winter. Tom and Allan were an inseparable pair of comic twins. One would start a story, and the other would finish his sentences. I'd never met a couple of guys that were closer; they seemed to share the same brain waves. In hindsight it probably would have been good to change rope partners each day, but I don't think Allan or Tom fancied roping up with me.

The huts on our traverse varied in size, sleeping from four to thirty persons. They were set in precarious places, so as not to be shifted by glaciers or slammed by avalanches, and fastened to bedrock with cables and turnbuckles. Even so, one hut had been ripped from its moorings by violent weather and thrown to the valley below. None of the occupants had survived. Absolute safety in the mountains can be an illusion. We slept our first night undisturbed by wind, avalanche, or shifting glaciers. We were being lulled into thinking this would be a simple affair.

Allan and Tom were good camp cooks. For breakfast they whipped up some batter and poured it out as eyes, a nose, and a smile in the pan, frying up faces for us to eat. These two guys could make anything fun and games. What amazed me was that they did everything as a duo. But the mood began to dim as we prepared ourselves for our day's work. I made the big mistake of asking where we should go to the toilet.

Now, of course I have no trouble doing my business in the wilds. I had guided canoe trips in remote Canada, climbed glaciers in Norway, and worked as a camp guide in the European Alps. But to me this hut was "civilized." To my way of thinking, if many people were using this hut, you'd want to have a designated toilet area outside to keep the mess in one place. No one wants to melt snow for water and find out the chunk that you brought in is yellow, or worse, brown underneath. Well that was all Tom and Allan needed to hear to start rolling their eyes and say patronizingly, "You just go outside"—intimating I was a nincompoop and inexperienced to be looking for an actual toilet area.

I had worked with these two all winter and could Nordic ski them into the ground if I had too, so I didn't think there would be any problems with my being a female on the trip. As a matter of fact, when I was first asked to go on this expedition I had said no, but they badgered me to go. I wasn't sure if they knew the extent of my previous outdoor experiences, but I felt it would be inappropriate to go on about my work as a guide and a wilderness rescue team member overseas. This toilet response was the first sign to me that they were looking for ways to find me inadequate. They had given me the impression that they felt the "girl" on this trip was too inexperienced to know what to do.

I didn't bother to explain or defend myself. I just went out far from the hut and returned to pack up in relative silence. Doing is better than speaking. I figured I'd just keep up the pace and the effort, and their attitudes might ease up. I wondered, would a man, in my position, have been more likely to tout his past accomplishments to impress his mates?

Do men need one-upmanship to feel more confident in their abilities and those of their teammates? Is spreading those brightly colored feathers necessary for all male species? Do they find comfort in speaking this same language, whether or not it is threatening? It is well documented that men tend to compete and women to bond. Would I have been less suspect if I had blurted, "Man, I have to take a dump!" and then stomped out to dig a hole wherever I pleased?

We headed out of the hut and roped up two by two. Scant clouds were blowing in from the west, otherwise all was still very clear. But the air hadn't cleared between the rope teams; tension permeated the air. Ned had confided in me that he felt that Allan was resenting his leadership on this trip. With this New Zealand traverse, Allan's second expedition with Ned, Allan's role had increased in scope. He had been organizing gear for the trip while living and climbing in Yosemite earlier this summer. Ned felt as if Allan had adopted the attitude of a teenager, rebelling against Ned's authority, and perhaps Allan felt he should have more authority because he felt more responsible for making things happen this time around.

Ned had raised the money for the trip through the sole sponsorship of Kastle, a ski company. A personal friend in the company had agreed to give Ned the funds. In return the company expected him to document the trip in words and photos, and that responsibility rested heavily on Ned's shoulders. Because Ned came from blue blood on both sides of his family, he had a good financial management background. He wanted to show that he could do the job and be held accountable. It would have crushed Ned to come back without the promised documentation, personally even more than professionally.

Allan, on the other hand, was younger and perhaps freer in attitude. His southern California attitude was max out the fun, don't worry, it'll all come together. Allan wasn't irresponsible in any way, just less intense. His approach might not have been as thorough as Ned's from a business perspective. But it was apparent that Allan felt Ned's approach wasn't thorough enough from a mountaineer's perspective. These higher profile expeditions are a mix of mountaineering and business or, rather, mountaineering as business. Ultimately I think Allan saw himself as a mountaineer and guide, and Ned saw himself as an adventure businessman. Rather than settling into complementing each other's strengths, it started to look as if they were beginning to chafe about each other's potential shortcomings.

~~We were again on skis with skins attached,~~ monotonously yet pleasantly moving forward. The rhythm of the legs and arms can be lulling, almost meditative. Perhaps part of the problem was that there was too much time to think, to dwell in one's own perspective. The day was slipping by, punctuated by bouts of eating and drinking to fuel our bodies. Weather was holding, and we were still frying under a beautiful sun.

Tom toppled into a crevasse; nothing much, he fell to his waist. We were all roped and prepared, but a first fall is always a good wake-up call and keeps everyone alert. It is easy to become lax when rocked by the skiing rhythm and comforted by good weather. Ned and I skied right over to Tom and Allan as they had stopped moving. In all the excitement Tom let it slip to me that "Allan has seen you and Ned dead a few times!" referring to the times Ned and I had moved unroped in territory that we felt was safe.

It was coming into focus for me now. Allan thought Ned and I were negligent. He felt Ned was unsafe, made inexperienced choices, and was not fit to be a climbing leader. But Ned felt Allan was taking an immature approach to working together by expressing anger rather than trying to communicate and was not fit to be an expedition leader. The two teams had each been revolving in their own worlds as we traveled during the day, not venturing to see what the other team was thinking. To Ned and me it appeared as if Tom and Allan wished to be their own separate entity. But I felt this wondering about what the others were thinking, the lack of communication, was causing minds to create adversities that were, perhaps, unfounded.

So where did that put me in all this? Because Ned had chosen me to be an expedition member I fell subject to the California blond boys' scrutiny, day and night. And because I was Ned's partner I took the brunt of his frustrations with Tom and Allan. Ned was often on edge, becoming curt with me. Seeing myself as the expedition dumping ground for disgruntled males, I adopted a "nose to the grindstone" mind-set. Just get the job done. So this is what high-profile, sponsored mountaineering expeditions were like?

I had experienced comradeship and teamwork as part of a wilderness rescue squad in the frozen north of Norway looking for lost persons. My being an American woman on the crew was no problem for that team of males. I had led canoe trips on wilderness rivers in the area of James and Hudson Bays in Canada, and my abilities hadn't been questioned or challenged by the males with whom I had guided. The dynamic on this expedition was new to me. Could it be that the pressure of a sponsored expedition had soured attitudes?

The day was winding down; our tiny hut for the night was in sight. Our blisters were under control as they had been taped up first thing in the morning. There were no worries about them becoming infected, although we had a good medical kit with us full of painkillers, antibiotics, and a lot more. Physically we were doing well, making good time and feeling all right two days into the trip. Mentally we were down.

This next, small, silver hut was a squeeze; we couldn't even fit our packs inside. Tomorrow we would have a wild ride on the Murchison headwall. We would ski the 35-degree headwall where the Tasman Glacier tops out, and then drop to the next glacial system, the Godley Glacier. This descent would be comparable to that of the famous Tuckerman's Ravine on Mount Washington in New Hampshire. Our collective focus was on the skiing to come, which was a welcome relief.

Again, great weather honored us as we individually summoned our strength and skill through a web of nerves in preparation for riding the headwall. Tom and Allan expressed their jitters by teasing each other and howling with laughter while they dared each other to do amazing feats on the way down. Ned released his tension by paying great attention to equipment details and checking to make sure we all had our peeps—electronic devices that send a signal in case anyone of us got buried in an avalanche—switched on.

I made sure my peeps was tucked well under clothing, nestling the device between my breasts so that it wouldn't be ripped from me in the event I tumbled and was snowed under. It felt like an electronic heartbeat resting on top of my own. I was just plain quiet. My nerves were drawing me inward. I tied my long avalanche cord to my waist, which would be trailing behind me, hopefully in full view above the snow if I was covered by an avalanche. At the time this was state-of-the-art gear for locating bodies beneath the snow.

Ned, physically the strongest of us all, opted to go first. Allan had always said he had never seen a stronger skier than Ned. He had been on the U.S. Nordic ski team for years and could manage a heavy pack well on the most precarious downhills. We looked out onto an amazing mountain range, sharp peaks underscored by rippling, gaping crevasses, as the glaciers folded around the mountains. Although the slope was steep, the snow was good; it had not blown or avalanched off and was a blessed knee-deep powder. In a sense, this was a skier's dream come true. It was just that no mistake can happen this far out; immediate rescue isn't possible. You'd be spending days dragging yourself out to any kind of aid. Skiing these steep slopes with free heels and nearly fifty-pound packs on our backs, which tried to shove us forward onto our noses, was the biggest challenge to overcome. We were pushing our gear beyond what it was designed for.

I could sense Ned's nerves as he threw himself into the fall line. Nerves are good when they activate adrenaline to access additional strength. Ned pierced downward, bent low on one knee, and swooped out of the falline, in a beautiful, large, arcing telemark turn. He turned far enough to come around to a stop and encouraged us all to go for it. "It's fast but quite doable," he shouted up with excited conviction. Tom Carter pushed off and tried a couple of hopping parallels, difficult in deep snow with a fifty pound pack on, as opposed to sinking low into telemark turns. He pulled it off but bent over his poles to catch his breath after the initial exertion.

Allan was on Tom's heels, telemarking beside him. I didn't see too much more of the men's exploits because I shoved myself off. I was the least experienced on the downhills, being a Nordic ski racer not a big-time alpine skier. It would take all my skill and strength to keep my pack from burying my face in the snow at the speeds I would be descending, considering the sharp angle of slope. This descent was like genuflecting at a rapid rate, from knee to knee, while carrying a boulder on your back and going who knows how many miles an hour.

I turned and crashed and burned, many times. Success and failure every other attempt. My nose was so stuffed with snow by the bottom I could only breathe through my mouth. And even at that I had to time my breaths so that I wouldn't choke on snow. I wasn't a pretty sight, but I was unscathed, careful, and solid. No crazy spills, just slow launches over the fronts of my skis when I couldn't hold the pack weight back as my heels lifted up.

The men's spirits were extremely high at the bottom of the slope. They were still wallowing in the adrenaline rush. They had had the occasional fall, but it wasn't the overshadowing element of their descents. It was an odd reaction on my part, I'll grant you, but it rankled me to see them so buddy-buddy now, when all their lead-dog testosterone had previously made them into the bicker brothers. With hot adrenaline flowing they were bonded. I, on the other hand, would have related better to support, a more feminine response, which seemed to be lacking. This feminine response may be why women statistically live longer than men, because they tend to give other women support. Women alleviate stress through bonding, while men may experience more stress because they tend to compete with each other.[1]

More relieved than elated, I adhered the skins to my skis to carry on over the distance to the next hut. I wasn't going to be a spoilsport, but I did find these guys annoying. I chose to push on quietly, alone. Allan noticed I wasn't screaming and shouting like he and the others were. To his credit, he let his sensitive side show. Although he heard no complaints from me, he sensed something was paining me, and it wasn't my body. When he turned his attention to me, I let it ease out in front of everyone that I thought there were "vultures in the air." We really weren't all together in spirit, and this was causing me to lose my spirit. I had skied alone, behind the guys, in silence—not in protest but to travel in peace.

I think all the excitement of the headwall pushed me into revealing my true thoughts, instead of holding back as I had been and just watching the interpersonal dynamics unfold. For the men the rush did just the opposite; they could bury their feelings deeper and rally around a high peak of excitement. Men and women run on different chemicals, and it becomes more apparent in times of stress or high action.

We left early the next morning to tackle the Classen Saddle, which we dubbed the popover. I felt a solid esprit de corps now. I wondered if my outburst about not being together in spirit, after skiing the headwall, had hit home. When we reached the saddle, skiing it was easier than we anticipated; the snow was good, and two-thirds of the way up Gavin buzzed us in his plane. The low flight and wing dip of a Super Cub close overhead took us suddenly out of our moving meditation in the mountains and brought us back to society and friends. Although we had felt quite removed, we realized there were those keen to track our movements and share in the adventure. So far things were coming together—the weather, the route, and, finally, our team spirit.

On the other side of the saddle we had a long descent over snow-covered moraine, which didn't look very skiable. Getting down was a comic, slapstick effort, like that of an old movie. It was tipsy travel over frozen avalanche debris, which looked like giant popcorn one to two feet around, followed by moraine slogging and then crashing through brush. We were slip sliding away in our clumpy leather boots covered by cloth overboots. Hops and jumps on foot over wet, icy rocks, with skis sticking out of your backpack, can be pretty funny, provided you don't slip a leg between a couple of hard spots and snap it.

The guys made it look smoother than I did, but we hit the bottom, each of us in one piece. I noticed my legs were shaking, but no one mentioned anything. So I thought, hey, with guys, this isn't something you discuss; it's something you ignore or act like it doesn't exist. I don't think guys like to talk about, or even acknowledge, weaknesses, or maybe I was the only one affected? It didn't matter; I was happy to carry on, and it wouldn't separate me from the boys or leave me open to criticism if I never mentioned it. I was beginning to realize that, on a long expedition, relief was the emotion I more commonly experienced, rather than the joy or high excitement of accomplishment.

The day seemed long probably because it was my first day of menstruation, which usually causes me to have less oomph. I wasn't fazed with this timing, and it helped explain why my legs had been shaky. But even without my hormonal changes the effort had been pronounced. Our descent, then our ski over the moraine, could be likened to hours of one-legged squats with fifty pounds on your back, followed by balancing on a skateboard for several more hours while carrying that same weight. I suppose that might make your legs shaky with effort. Some women stop menstruating under physical strain and weight loss. That has never been my case. My hormonal system seems determined to continue churning out those chemicals.

We were on the Classen Glacier, about a mile from the pool of glacial water at the end of the moraine rubble. Weather was acting up a bit, so we grabbed our light snow shovels and all began to dig. In minutes we had scooped out home for the night, about eight feet wide and four feet deep. We had beautiful blue Gor-Tex bivouac sacks made for us by The North Face for this trip, and we were more than glad to use them. It had begun to snow. We lay head to foot in the hole so that we could all fit in. We said our good nights, pulled our heads in like turtles, sealed the Velcro strips at the top of our separate bags, and independently drifted off into our own dream worlds.

We slept an uninterrupted twelve hours that night. The next morning we emerged from our bivy sacks puffy eyed and slow, as though waking from hibernation. As we punched out of our cocoons from under two inches of snow, I realized that yesterday had been a long day for the guys as well. I then knew I wasn't off their mark and felt like I was indeed in the ballpark for this endurance event. Sleeping out all night had made me feel more animal-like. I was self-contained, carrying my home on my back, as I moved through these majestic mountains. Sleeping out in the elements can be such a treat, although it might have been an interrupted sleep if we'd gotten two feet of snow instead of two inches on top of us.

I'd spent the past summers living outside in a hammock with a tarp, a small tent, or a bivouac sack while being a canoe guide in Canada, guiding in the Swiss Alps, and climbing and skiing on the glaciers in Norway. I was accustomed to watching the moon change, drinking in sunsets, catching the sunrise, and feeling the weather change. To me this was the good life, while so many of my college buddies would party hardy, working at resorts in the summer, making good cash. They thought I was a little coo-coo. Here in the Alps, bivying out, waking to snow covering me, was what I lived for.

We moved along the glacial lakeside, some by ski and some on foot, had an easy lunch together, and all seemed smooth. We had returned to flatland after skiing up the Tasman Glacier to about 8,000 feet, down the Murchison Glacier, back up to the Classen Saddle at about 7,000 feet, and down the Classen Glacier. We'd reached terra firma and the wide glacial spread of the Godley River. After the past five days of hard work and, of course, wearing the same garments day and night, we were getting a little overripe. You could smell it.

We had to cross the great Godley River and some tributaries a few times, and the temptation overtook me for a bath in the icy, milky, glacial waters. I stripped completely and lay in the rushing torrent. After a bit I rose out of the water tingling, as if an electric current coursed through me. It felt delicious, wild, and sensuous. I suppose I shouldn't have been surprised, but Ned had been photographing my bath. Cameras were always clicking on this trip for any new event or condition. We had a sponsor and a duty of sorts, and this was journalism transpiring. There would also be expedition lectures in need of illustration. But my bath! C'mon.

I've come to learn that personal hygiene is something people want to know about when I give lectures. Ned's experience with "expeditions as business" told him that this illustration of bathing, if done discreetly, would prove useful in many ways, in many different venues. I understood. Candid photos are part of the job description as an expedition member. I shrugged it off. But when Ned smelled himself with disgust and jumped in, I didn't hesitate to grab my camera to record the event.

The boys went ahead of Ned and me to the Godley Hut, which was a short piece away. Ned and I ambled along, enabling me to drink in my surroundings. We were in the wilderness, yet there was no imminent danger of avalanche, crevasses, or falling on your face. The world around me was glowing in the sun, and I was still glowing from my icy plunge. Life was radiant and relaxed for a change.

Once at Godley hut we welcomed the two days of rest offered to us by the storm outside. We spent our time slowly repairing gear, dozing off, and doing equipment checks. Life on an expedition is unlike the corporate world. When nature is your CEO life can be quite random. Inside the hut were various ebbs and flows of energy and activity. Something like a tide or current would run through the hut, exciting one, then the other, until we all were drawn to converse, then we'd gently drop out to our own thoughts, only to slide back in later and complete the circuit of energy and conversation. We easily wove in and out of each other's verbalized thoughts, while nothing in-depth occurred. We were getting low on food, but we knew we had a cache buried one day's march away, which had been air-dropped before we set off on the trip.

I slipped out to recharge myself with a snow bath. The dip the day before had been so invigorating, I was enticed to throw off the complacency of a relatively warm hut and no physical exertion or miles covered. I'd already repaired small items and washed my socks and long underwear, so why not me? It is possible to stay relatively clean, neat, and tidy on an expedition. You just need to be prepared to use water in any of its various forms, regardless of how fast or slow those hydrogen and oxygen molecules are oscillating.

Back in the hut Ned and I were talking about sponsor obligations, what the ski company that footed the entire bill was expecting of us. In a sense we were reassessing what needed to be done by the end of the trip. Allan drifted into the conversation, and it progressed between Ned and Allan, as I listened. It evolved to Ned asking Allan if he felt exploited or ripped off. Ned was the sponsor liaison and stood to gain the most exposure and potential monetary return from the trip by writing articles and more, or obtaining further sponsorship for his ideas. But Ned was also working the hardest to record events.

Tension permeated the room. I was quite surprised Ned faced the question head on. I caught myself holding my breath, waiting for a response. The air changed; Allan stiffened and after a couple of moments replied, "Exploited, not ripped off." To me it appeared that Allan had given this some deeper thought. He felt used by Ned, but he hadn't felt cheated. These are two very different things. Although on previous expeditions with Ned, Allan had received recognition for the great mountaineer he was, it was clear that Allan now felt Ned was coasting on Allan's talents and expertise.

It seemed to me that this was perhaps a natural progression for natural-born leaders. Both Ned and Allan were leaders of their own sort. I couldn't see any way around this. Allan really needed to run his own show. It would always be upsetting to him to sweat for someone else. He needed to pursue his own ideas and dreams, or he would feel he was contributing too much of himself for something that didn't have his own signature on it and didn't promote his own work. This did smack of corporate hierarchy, even though we seemed far from the corporate world.

At least feelings were clearly out in the open now instead of mysteriously smoldering around us. Allan felt like second fiddle, and Ned was treading lightly around Allan's moody rebellion. We were still only about halfway to our goal, distance wise, so I wondered if this conversation would cause camaraderie to improve or deteriorate for the rest of our expedition. No course of action was determined; both men had just expressed a point of view.

In most cases a conflict between only two of a four-member team can be diffused by interaction with the others not in conflict on the expedition. But our case was a bit atypical in that the other guys considered me Ned's girl, and therefore I wasn't really in the offing to be a rope partner with the others. It would have been fine with me, but I don't think that they would have consented. Tom connected most and best with Allan. "Hey AB," short for Allan Bard, was the start of most sentences for Tom. With two distinct teams and no mixing, the conflict between Allan and Ned became everyone's conflict.

Fortunately, as the storm blew itself out later that evening, we had a stove calamity. Allan became the master technician after we all gave the thing a try. Too much fuel was getting through, and huge flames would shoot out, nearly incinerating our faces, which were all too close from the effort to get the darn thing to spark. This stove fiasco was a good thing, because there was nothing to prove, no competition; we were all just hungry and thirsty and anxious for the stove to work properly. This eased all tensions with roof-high fireworks, laughs, and Allan becoming the hero of the evening.

Tom was inspired to carry on with fire. We all had lit candles to read and eat by, and Tom began making obscene faces, holding his candle under his chin and creating long, strange shadows over his distorted features. That's all it took to get us all going. Here we did compete, to see who could look the most bizarre. With tongues out, noses pushed up, and eyes pulled down, or vice versa, we launched into our own interpretation of gurning with the use of fingers. It felt therapeutic to just be foolish, outlandish, and ridiculous. We could look as evil and ugly as we wanted to each other, and it was only hilarious. I was happy to know this is the way we could be and this is the way we should be. We needed to remember what a gift it was to live these days simply, in these mountains.

The next morning we faced the Terra Nova pass at 6,850 feet. Though 1,000 feet lower than the Tasman Saddle we'd already crossed, this pass looked considerably steeper and more threatening. The pass earned the distinction of becoming the Terror Nova. It would be a long, maybe eight-mile day heading to our next hut. We would travel across the frozen, glacial lake at the base of the Godley Glacier, up the glacier, over the Terror Nova, down St. Winifred's Glacier, and along St. Winie's River to St. Winie's Hut. Whew!

We were back to gorgeous weather. We stripped to our waists, rolled our knicker socks down, and slapped on zinc oxide. Yes, what the boys did, I did too. I stripped down to my waist, but my suspenders holding up my knickers held my breasts largely in place, for comfortable ski travel. There were no audiences out in these wilds, and we'd seen it all before, so nothing really mattered to us, no proper protocol expected, no one to offend.

After hours of bright, sunny travel over ice and snow, we'd slogged our way up toward the excitement of the Terror Nova. The buzz of an engine told us we were going to have a visitor. With no place to land, of course, Gavin's Super Cub appeared, as if ascending out of the pass, did some theatrical flying, and dropped four packages from the plane. We counted as they flew out, anxious not to miss a thing. We hadn't expected to be tracked so well on our route; perhaps Gavin was having fun playing with us as we traveled in his well-known backyard. Digging up the gifts we found ice cream, homemade cookies, and gin—things you just don't normally find this far out!

We allowed ourselves the ice cream and cookies but carried on with our business of climbing over the pass. The snow was better than expected, so we didn't put on our crampons. We did rope up for a tight col to avoid a bad slide if we lost an edge. Ned wanted a shot of Tom on top, holding up his skis in celebration of making the ascent, so just the way the timing worked I ended up above Allan giving him a top-rope type of belay when Tom untied for the photo. As Allan untied at the height of the pass, I got the feeling that he saw my efforts as merely an annoyance. I let it go. We were all up with no problem; that was important.

Down the other side Tom took a twenty-footer, a slide of no real consequence as he didn't hit anything and it was arrested early. But still, it reminded us that we were all fallible. It began to look as though the day would draw to a close before we'd reached the hut. We'd done river crossings already, but doing them in the dark was taking it to the next level, especially when the guys felt taking the plunge was challenging in normal circumstances.

I had done my share of river crossings. When I was guiding in Canada, I'd had to recover canoes wrapped around large rocks, in heavy current, using lines and whatever man power was available. No easy feat if you calculated the mass of water pressing the boat onto the rock, waiting to crush you if you got in the wrong place during the extraction. When we were on wilderness canoe trips I'd have the clients hiking and portaging in bathing suits in the rain to keep clothes and gear dry. As long as we were moving we were warm, and this way, when we stopped, we'd have something warm and dry to put on when we cooled down. Mountaineering and river travel have commonalities; body temperature management is crucial for both. With this experience behind me, jumping in these rivers was simply a refreshing dip.

I decided to strip from my waist down to keep my clothes dry while crossing the river. When I got to the other side and was waiting for the fellows, I just jumped in. My earlier river bathing experience had intrigued me; instead of bone chilling, I had found it bone thrilling, exciting, and refreshing, and holding on in the current was a blast.

Tom took my plunge as a challenge—somehow my splashing around challenged the guy's manhood, I guess, and he went for it. I had to laugh. For all of Freud's ranting about women having penis envy, that little thing became much smaller in the cold, glacial waters. I imagine my extra female fat layer probably gave me a slight edge of comfort Tom didn't have. Veins popping, eyes bulging, he ran out hooting and stepping as if he were on hot coals. He'd just lost the feeling in his feet.

Skies were dimming; rock hopping across streams was getting dicey. It was difficult to discern depth and height correctly, and it was very easy to misstep or jump inaccurately, slip, and crash with your pack slamming you onto the rocks or holding you down in the river. We started to pass our packs up to one another, with skis slid into the side pockets, when we had to maneuver up onto higher rocks. This worked. Then it really got dark. We still hadn't made it to St. Winifred's Hut, built some distance away, perhaps to avoid flooding waters. We began slashing through thick vegetation with ski poles, climbing rocks, and thrashing over tree branches.

We thought we were close and decided to dump our loads. I know I was parked on the packs to be the foghorn because I was the female in the group, but so be it. I didn't feel I had to compete or prove myself; someone had to do it. Soon I heard a holler, and I'd hoot out, bringing them back to where the gear and I stood. It took some time, but eventually after a few trajectories were tested, the hut was located. All guys returned to the packs, we hoisted loads, and we were in for the night.

St. Winifred's River led to the Havelock River, with St. Winie's Hut located near this confluence. We had only two simple miles to travel the next morning along the rocky Havelock River to our next shelter, Veil Bivouac. It wasn't labeled a hut, but a bivouac. We stopped 250 yards from Veil Bivy to eat lunch in order to stretch out our travel time. The mood ran from silly to foolish, and the day was conducive to play. Tom had this ridiculous side to him, and now and then he'd have me laughing so hard I was speechless; no sound would come out as I doubled over in the pain of silent laughter.

Tom started with food shows as he chewed his lunch. We all remembered these from grade school. I tried desperately to one up him, without success. We sat there living this life of relative luxury—no imminent danger, our hut within sight. We still had food from our cache near the Terror Nova, enough so that we left some staples of rice and more back at St. Winie's. We couldn't imagine what lay ahead of us as Tom carried on trying to gross us out. Ned and Allan had begun to converse together a bit more, and so Tom and I were sharing the frivolity of base humor more regularly.

Veil Bivy reminded me of a telephone booth and the common joke of determining how many people you can fit in it. There were two bunks and just enough room to swing your legs around and put them on the floor to sit, barely. It was basically two narrow beds in a box. We amused ourselves shooting ridiculous photos to show just how tiny this place was. Ned and I took the bottom bunk together but fit best sleeping head to foot to avoid falling onto the floor where Tom was lying. Allan was on the top bunk with the ceiling right in his face. For an overnight, this would be fine.

We got slammed by a four-day storm. Winds and snow prevented any movement. We had a cache one long day away but just couldn't get there, or back to St. Winie's for that matter. These storms, like the one we experienced at the Godley Hut, were tenacious. Again, as at Godley, Allan became the chef. He created a sort of biscuit cooked on a kerosene stove, and we ate a gruel of watery rice and sipped tea all day. This could be the next miracle weight-loss diet we joked, thinking we'd make a fortune sending people to huts like this and locking them in for days.

In times like this, one comes to appreciate the tastes in literature of your climbing mates. Every chapter completed, or less, gets torn off and passed around so that we can all read at the same time. We had intense and ludicrous book club discussions in our close proximity. Maybe we could begin a trend for "lock in" book clubs along with our weight-loss plan. We hadn't brought much along for reading as we didn't want to be carrying the extra weight. We would have been better served carrying more food. However, I had some C. S. Lewis with me, which seemed to suit about everyone in one way or another. He can be interpreted any number of ways, so we had plenty to let our imaginations work with.

Books people choose to read and how they interpret them tend to elucidate their characters. Ned was more serious and literal, Tom was absurd and hilarious, Allan had depth, and for me the devil was just in those details. Four days of discussions along with the typical fart and burp humor of guys and the odd dirty joke that hadn't been told yet, and we got through our time. Yes, let's face it, we were doing time. A short break in the weather on the fourth day let Ned and I charge back to St. Winie's Hut and gather up the flour and rice we'd left behind to splurge on in the evening. It felt good to unfold my body and make sure it could still move. It was so delightful to travel without a forty-pound backpack. With the weight off I felt like I could float or bounce.

Next morning the weather was clear enough for travel. We had quite a distance to cover, but we'd have the lure of cake, brandy, marzipan, cheese, salami, and more in our food cache buried in the Garden of Eden, a gorgeous glacial arrangement of ice towers, runnels, and sculpture made by water in its varied frozen forms. We were a little shaky but certainly robust enough to carry on through an almost twelve-hour day of hard work.

As we climbed we traversed avalanche slope after avalanche slope. We dug a pit to analyze the snow layers, but predicting slides is as much an art as it is a science and perhaps as much instinct as anything else. If there is a weak layer of snow, perhaps crystal-like and dry with a lot of air space, below a heavier layer of snow, like the wet slop that had been falling for days, the weak layer cannot support the weight above, and there you have an avalanche in the making.

If the slope is ready to let go, the smallest vibration—a footstep, a sound—can break the surface tension and set it off, causing an avalanche of great force. We all knew this, yet we knew that the layers looked good enough. And who knew how long our good weather window would last? We were hungry, and there was food waiting for us at the other end of our day. Besides, if we waited, maybe the avalanche danger would get worse! The weather was unstable.

We stuffed our skis in our packs and climbed straight up, post-holing in thigh-high snow. It was steep enough that my belly was almost touching the slope as I moved up. If this slope had been icy, we would have been roped and using crampons. Post-holing is laborious and energy draining, especially with heavy packs. Lifting each leg high with every step and then sinking down in is more effort than trying to run up a sand pit. I know because I used to run pits to train for cross-country ski racing.

Once over the saddle we saw what we were in for. We had been told that this part of our planned route had not been done before. One look and we understood why. It was doable, but with iffy weather and funky snow, it was a frightful sight, with fracture lines here and there waiting to break away and send tons of snow cascading down. We could work our way around most of the fracture lines, but there was one short slope we had to cross. We could smell our food cache in our minds, and we certainly didn't want to retreat back to where we'd just come from. Allan moved forward and volunteered to cross under the fracture line without any encouragement from us.

Tom was a bit short with Ned in their conversation as they readied themselves and their avalanche beacons, exposing Tom's concern for Allan. We were all concerned. Allan turned to us after he'd moved out under the fracture line itself and said with a grin, "Tell Janet I love her." Although he was trying to be funny and sound dramatic, I know he really meant what he said. In case anything happened to him he wanted his girlfriend back in the States to know how he felt. But the Allan who red-lines the fun meter wasn't about to get too sentimental on us. As the female on the trip it would be welcomed if Tom and Allan expressed their feelings. It wouldn't make me think they were any less of a mountaineer. They would actually impress me as being stronger mountaineers if they could communicate their emotions without fear.

The snow held. We all ventured out, one at a time to avoid stressing the slope any more than we had to. We knit our way along the ridges of the peaks for half a mile at about 6,500 feet in elevation until we came down upon the Garden of Eden ice plateau. Thrilled, stressed, and exhausted, we began to dig for our food cache like pirates for buried treasure. We struck gold, edible gold. The brandy went straight to my legs, just like a beer after a bike race. I felt the anesthesia of the alcohol in my stressed muscles.

The marzipan I had stashed in the cache provided more sugar to go with the alcohol, pushing up my rapidly ascending blood sugar. My body was used to watery rice, and it was having a manic reaction to these high-glycemic-index foods. Yeeeha! This added to the party atmosphere. We were all buzzing around laughing and eating like starved people at a banquet. We had our tent cached as well and put it up in hyper speed as darkness surrounded us. We were beyond the hut system; we were in the Garden of Eden.

We all played on our skis in the garden the next beautifully sunny day. Incredible ice towers and blocks littered the glacier. We climbed on top of some, put on our skis, took funny photos, and then came careening down. The snow was loose and very skiable, provided you didn't ski into a crevasse sliding off a block. We had food with us, but no packs, which was delightful. The pack becomes the new skiing norm on an expedition, and without it you feel like you're getting away with something forbidden, a hand-in-the-cookie-jar kind of feeling.

Ned and I skied up to the peak we had so carefully crossed under the day before, as evening began to show signs of descending. The sun was low, and a white moon was high. The moon, just shy of full, began to glow as the sun went lower and threw bright shades of luminescent orange and pink across the blue sky covering a distant blue ocean.

Sometimes you can't believe the beauty in this world. You find yourself in a place where you couldn't have imagined this artistry surrounding you. Trite as it sounds, it takes my breath away; my heart pounds, and this feeling expands inside my chest, a lot like that loving feeling you have for another person. It can be overwhelming.

We were moments away from the very summit, so I kicked and glided with alacrity, wanting to go as close to that big, round moon as possible. Ned was shooting photos, ever-ready journalist that he is. I couldn't resist completely absorbing where in the world I was. Every hardship of this expedition had melted away, and only this glorious moment was alive in my psyche. I theorize this is why some people go back on expedition after expedition; they easily forget the strain of the trips and remember the joyous moments in great detail.

Ned and I saw clouds of moisture from below, rising. We turned to ski back to our tent camp. Before it was completely dark we were engulfed in a whiteout. This was my first time in one. It was hilarious, although it can be quite dangerous because one is totally sensory deprived. We couldn't see more than a couple of feet in front of us, if that. I could barely make out my skis underneath me. Consequently I couldn't tell if I was going down, or if I'd turned too far and was going back up, so my balance was thrown off completely. One minute I'd almost fall forward onto my nose because I'd overturned and was skiing up the hill and had come to an abrupt stop, then I'd almost fall on my butt by turning straight down without knowing it, my skis taking off out from under me. I couldn't really tell how fast I was going or where I was going.

We heard Allan hooting us back to the tent site. We called back to him, and he became our foghorn to help us locate our home for the second night. Hot drinks were waiting when we arrived. These simple pleasures are deeply appreciated when living so simply. Allan and Tom had explored the area together and had discovered an abandoned snow cave. Mountaineers had most likely come up the lower glacial system, the way we were heading out, and made themselves at home in this wondrous place. They hurried off to the snow cave for the night after we ate together, and all was well. But, as the weather would have it, not for long.

We had come to understand Gavin's point, "The Southern Alps present more difficulty per square mile than almost any other mountain area in the world." We had been lulled by good weather at the onset of our trip into thinking this expedition might be easier than it really would be. We woke at about 1 a.m. to the sound of frozen pellets hitting the tent in a forty-mile-an-hour wind. Ned and I considered making a break for the cave the boys were in, but our down bags coaxed us to curl up instead of uprooting at that hour. Fortunately our tent was still standing when the sun rose, instead of wrapped around our faces.

When Tom and Allan ventured forth from their ice palace to come to the tent for breakfast, they were astounded at the ferocity of the storm. Inside their insular cave they had no indication as to what had been transpiring all night long. After eating we bundled up everything, shoved it in our packs, and moved into the ice cave. This roundish, white hole was big enough to stand in, near the cook shelf, which had been fashioned waist high. As the ceiling rounded down we had wide snow berths on which to sleep. Inside a cave the cold air sinks, so one wants to sleep up off the floor of the cave. We had a tunnel entrance, and of course this was lower too so that the cold air could sink and flow outward.

We did some house designing with our little avalanche shovels, improving spaces to sit and sleep, then hung a line to dry socks, mitts, and hats over our small camp stove on the kitchen shelf. This hole was becoming downright cozy, but it was a little dark, seeing as it was a cave. Allan made some makeshift candles by twisting gauze tightly into wicks, melting a little hole in our tins of ski wax, and inserting the gauze wicks in the holes. It worked, and there was light. And there we were, the four of us squished in together for another two days while the storm raged.

Although our food cache was getting thin on the real food—nuts, dried fruit, salami, cheese—we still had rations of oatmeal and rice, our staples, with dried milk. Four big people holed up in a snow cave after days of physical labor can put a dent in any amount of food. Eating becomes a focus, because it is the only way to punctuate the day. We had our books and our stories, but we'd been through them all once by now. If the weather had been cooperative, we would have been almost out of the mountains. My mind began to wander a bit. I lay there thinking about how all of us on this trip were coming from different places and philosophies.

I was living the life of the most basic ski-and-climbing bum. I'd graduated with my teaching degree, but I just couldn't stay still, or indoors. I'd spent the past several summers never sleeping indoors. I was too blinded by the wildness and beauty of the world to see deep enough into my future to worry about security. I'd have to say Tom and Allan were similar in many ways. They were superhot rock jocks, doing some of the hardest climbing Yosemite had to offer, and were very relaxed about social conventions and expectations.

Ned was about ten years older than the rest of us. He was the director of the ski schools at Trapp's in the East and Yosemite in the West. He owned a house. He had a foot in both worlds of responsibility and income and communing with the hardest core climbers and skiers living the basic life for their sport. Ned had the best of upbringings and went to the best private schools, and his parents saw him becoming a well-paid professional, perhaps a successful businessman like his father. Ned, in a way, was conflicted. He always carried his parents' expectations with him, as he did the expectations of his sports-bum friends. His identity fluctuated in a somewhat unconscious manner depending on his company.

We periodically crawled out the tunnel exit to relieve ourselves and to shovel out the opening, which kept blowing in with snow. On the third morning Tom and Allan reported seeing a crack of sun after going out for their morning constitutional. We hustled around and got all the gear outside to dry on lines hung from ski poles. Our down bags and clothing, even our bodies, felt moldy. We ate, keeping an eye on the weather with the highest of hopes that we would move on to the Garden of Allah by noon. We'd been out twenty days on this trip, and about half of them were storm days. But the storm started back up, slowly at first then gaining speed to its normal velocity by noon. We retreated to our cave after having worshipped the sun while we could, just long enough to get the moss out of our armpits.

The next day the weather was good, and we traveled from the Garden of Eden, over the end of the Garden of Allah, and on to the Lambert Glacier. We didn't stop to explore the Garden of Allah and chance getting trapped by weather. We went as far as we could on our designated route. There were no huts on our route, so our stopping point was completely up to us. Travel was hard, as we hadn't had much physical activity or food in our cramped snow cave for three days, but the skiing was straightforward—nothing extraordinarily technical, thank goodness. Miles were the mandate, not exploration or play, although the scenery was magnificent.

The men had seemed fine during our snow cave period, but as soon as we were engaged in the effort of movement, tempers seemed to flare. Perhaps they had been stewing while at rest, and now all seethed out as we ventured forth. Angry spirits loomed in the air, and Ned seemed to take the affront of the boys out on me by being short and snapping at my efforts. I felt like a real loser. The boys thought of me as Ned's possession, and Ned thought of me as his scapegoat. So where did that leave me? Just a loser on all accounts. I was getting pretty tired of their bad moods.

We set up camp near the base of our last two cols, or passes, before we were to exit our route on the Lyell Glacier to the Lyell Hut on the Rakaia River and the airstrip pickup. We could almost smell the sheep farms on the other side of the ridge and all the comforts that come with them: warm houses, good food, and other human company. But why break tradition of being stormed in instead of breaking camp? When we woke the next morning inside our round, yellow bubble of a tent, we were slammed with violent storms again, denying any travel. It would be dangerous to attempt any movement, and seeing as we'd all made it this far, why do something foolish now?

I'd packed a small portable chess set and had it stashed in our last food cache. So far no one had been driven to distraction enough to play with me. I knew everyone was getting to the end of his rope when each man played with me—once. I don't consider myself a good chess player by any stretch, but after winning a game over each of the guys they all refused to play with me again. I found this interesting, because I am very beatable. Wouldn't you think one of the men would take the challenge of improving his game and carry on to while away the time? But, no. Nor did they venture to play with each other. It all smacked of the fear of failure to me. Personally I do attribute this trait to testosterone, along with the fear of showing emotions.

Ned's alarm clock went off. As we roused ourselves from our bags, preparing to make tea, scooping up snow from outside the tent, we realized it was very dark. Ned rechecked his watch. It said a little after 1:30 a.m., not the 6:30 he thought he had set it for to begin our day, hopefully, of travel. We all laughed and decided to have a midnight snack instead. The weather wasn't looking good at this point, and we knew we had plenty of time to sleep, so why not eat? After pooling all food sources from different packs, we realized we had between us one breakfast, one dinner, and two lunches consisting of either freeze-dried or gruel-type foods for the remainder of the trip.

When we awoke hours later we were engulfed in another whiteout. Weather and wind had toned down some, but we couldn't see more than a few feet in front of us, leaving us no way to navigate. We'd venture out of our yellow bubble, a dome of about six feet in circumference and only chest high at its highest, to shovel snow away that had been pressing in on it. The snow had been mounting up fairly quickly. We decided to build a bit of a snow wall around the tent for protection.

The boys had worked out a way to avoid going outside into the storm to pee: one guy would open a side vent, and then while another pushed him from behind, he would arch his back, molding his body to the round sides of the tent, and relieve himself out the vent. I, on the other hand, always had to dress up, go out, bare my butt, and face into the wind as I squatted, so the wind would blow everything away from, instead of into, my snow pants. My plumbing was just not as convenient as the guys. We had enough gas for our stove to melt snow for water and shared one tea bag until the liquid didn't change color, so we had fluids to drink but food was slim.

We spent three days and four nights in our yellow dome. Even though the storm raged outside, inside the tent was a sunny day. The yellow fabric was a little bright to our eyes, we needed to wear our sunglasses throughout the day. We looked as if we were beachcombers reading with sunglasses on. And still, with all this down time, not one single guy would play a game of chess with me. I was amazed at how the time did pass, abbreviated with fluffing up bags at one end of the tent to make a roll to lean on as our couch, then a little later making hot water and divvying our last bouillon cube four ways, followed by book discussions and outside work to repair the wall, then inside for a little more hot water, and so on. We had finished all our food.

It was puzzling, but pleasant, that as long as we were stormed in people were more congenial, even jovial, which was good, considering we had no food. But when we would actually move on our route, moods disintegrated and sometimes tempers would flare. I would have guessed it would have been the opposite. Active men with strong egos holed up in a tiny bubble for days on end? Because we were spending much more time stormed in than moving, it was wonderful that we could all just relax. Tom could always make me laugh; he could really be ridiculous, and I just thought it was hilarious. I kept thinking, "How many times in your life do you spend days on end trapped in a small space with three other interesting people with no food?"

We were all becoming quite sodden and a bit slimy, so when there was a slight change in the weather we decided to dash. Visibility was low and at times nonexistent. Guesswork was needed to find the route. The wind kicked back up, and the snow pellets felt like little icy arrows stinging your face. It was preferable to look down at your skis, and then occasionally dare a look up, to peer into the encompassing whiteness to locate the other rope team. It really did seem silly to me to be out in this weather, but a bit of a break had come, and there were hopes that better weather would follow. But only worse weather followed.

We managed to gain the elevation needed, but the ridge we needed to traverse was ice encased, and the wind was blowing up to sixty miles an hour. The heavy backpack made it difficult for me to stay on my feet. I was in danger of getting literally blown down when my pack was pushed off my center of balance. We could see we were traversing a slope, which was quite steep, but we couldn't see its total length or steepness. At any moment we could all be blown down and over.

Allan took a fall but didn't slide any distance. He called to Tom up ahead to alert him so that Tom wouldn't fall over as well when their rope went taut between them. A short wait and all was righted. After seeing, or rather not seeing, where we were and where we needed to go, we decided to retreat and set up our tent again in its old spot, down away from the high winds. This was no time to make a foolish mistake. We all knew we needed to wait out the weather, like it or not. We would need suitably good weather to make it over Lambert and Rangitata Cols; none of this shot-in-the-dark attitude would be safe.

That evening we'd gotten so chilled and wet and without any food as fuel for our bodies I found it impossible to go to sleep. My feet were so cold that sleep eluded me. Then Ned did something I'll always remember with great affection. Because we were sleeping head to foot, he unzipped the bottom of my damp, limp down bag, put my feet under his armpits, and pulled his bag up and over as best he could. Eventually some semblance of warmth returned to my feet, and I slept, wonderful sleep. Maybe we couldn't eat, but it was heaven to sleep. We spent the next day trying to dry out everything as we'd gotten even wetter trying to get ourselves over this last hurdle of a ridge and failed.

When we looked out the tent door the next morning the wind had swept the slopes clean of snow, leaving ice behind. We took this small opportunity to put on crampons this time, instead of skis, while the winds were somewhat lower, and climbed to the ridge to see what lay in store. We took no packs; we intended to move quickly and simply to reconnoiter our route and judge its steepness and perils, hopefully while this weather window lasted. Upon reaching our first col, Lambert, we could see the ridge was traversable and the slopes on the sides were steep but not death defying.

Allan and I even sat on our butts and slid down on our way back to camp to give our weakening legs a break and to just simply have some fun. Now we knew our route, knew about how long it would take us to get over, and knew what lay on either slope edging down from the ridge. We were in good position now, provided we got decent weather, to move fast with all our gear on our backs and finally get up and over this ridge. From there it was less demanding to move down off the Lyell Glacier onto the Rakaia River bed and out.

The next morning brought conditions marginally suitable for travel. Ned was irritable, and Allan was terribly out of sorts. Allan immediately hopped on my case saying, "The map-reading tactics you used in Norway were fucked." I realized I wouldn't be able to comment on routes without severe criticism; certainly he wouldn't listen. And because Tom would take Allan's position without question, it wasn't looking like I was going to be included in any map discussion today. The others appeared to me to revel in feeling nasty. I didn't enjoy it. Perhaps because I don't lash back I've become a good venting target? Maybe my extra, subcutaneous fat layer was giving me a certain resiliency these guys didn't have, after being so low without food these past days.

We pulled down our half-buried tent, again, and shook it out to pack it up, again. Once loaded we headed up, again. We heard a low buzz through the light snowfall and slight wind. It was Gavin and Merv in a beefier Cessna airplane. They had slipped through a window in the weather. When they caught sight of us they launched something out of the plane. They knew our route and food supplies and that we had been fairly immobile for the past two weeks. Or if we had tried to move they knew we could be in big trouble. They'd come to check on our status.

It was truly amazing to be tracked like this. It was nothing we had planned on before our trip. Curiosity and kindheartedness had kept Gavin on a lookout for us. He provided a safety buffer of which we had no idea that we would have the benefit. We never found that first drop; it was buried somewhere in the snow away from our searching eyes. A second circling brought a second drop. We raced to it and found a "You've skied the Tasman Glacier" certificate attached to a rock. It informed us to stamp out F if we needed food, L if we were all right, and H for a helicopter.

These guys knew the score. In case we didn't want any interference with our plans, L, which, let's say, meant "Leave us alone," would suffice. They knew what else we'd want or require and had simplified communications by putting it in to the graphic letters F and H. Ned dashed off without a word and immediately tramped out a large F for food, three times the size of himself, into the snow. Allan was irate because there was no communication before Ned's actions. Tempers stewed while the plane disappeared, but there was no explosion. Ned defended himself by saying that he knew the plane had only a moment to get an answer if they had any prayer of making it back to drop food to us before more bad weather shut them out. Ned assumed that this was the obvious "right" answer, and no discussion was needed.

Apparently his action epitomized the problem. Ned felt the responsibility of being in charge. Allan felt he was being slighted, that the leadership should be shared more equally. As we made our way onward, I whispered to Tom, "The atmosphere is bad jazz around here. Let's see if we can change it." This was something I perhaps should have done long ago. Tom and I shared a sense of humor, and maybe if I had tapped in to this connection and tried to enlist him sooner rather than see him as Allan's sidekick then we might have had a better effect earlier.

Tom picked up on my desire to shift the milieu and said something to Ned on his way by. I assumed it to be something about Allan's mood. Allan had seemed sharp tempered at the onset of the day as we broke camp. Perhaps Ned would take Allan's words less to heart if Tom coached Ned on Allan's reactions. Tom knew Allan better than anyone else on the entire planet, I would guess. At just about this point we spotted the avalanche pouring down on us. Allan made the call to step left to avoid this wet, heavy freight train of snow. With the rush of fresh adrenaline in their veins, these guys bonded, and all was well again, just as had happened at the base of the Murchison Headwall. Testosterone mixed with adrenaline appeared to me to create a state of mind that superseded any previous emotion and replaced it with a jovial, fraternal connection. Go figure!

I was coming to the conclusion that if you ever wanted to change a guy's mind, give him a real scare and he's a clean, open slate. Jump into the excited state with him and make your move. You might just have him bond over the thrill and agree to whatever you want. Maybe politicians around the world should start cliff diving and bungee jumping together to facilitate their compromises.

By the time we resumed our climb Gavin and Merv returned. They dropped a message with a map of where they'd pushed out the food, at the top of 6,400-foot Rangitata Col. Clouds were knitting together; the plane had to bank and leave immediately. We lost visibility to about fifteen feet and kept moving toward the col.

At the height of the pass we dropped our ropes, split up, and began to search for the treasure the map had indicated. Mouths were watering in anticipation. We'd spent our last three days sharing our last eleven tea bags and fifteen bouillon cubes. We'd had food caches put in for this trip, so we felt no real loss of pride to have food dropped to aid our way along this final stage of our route. We were feeling quite dejected for the twenty minutes we'd been looking. Where was it? The whiteout was continuing to close in. Then Ned spied a small crater in the snow and began to dig. "Oh frabjious day, caloo calay!"

We feasted on pancakes with peanut butter and honey, still warm from the stove. We had apples, carrots, and cabbage that crunched as we tore into them and more. It had been about a month since we'd experienced anything that crunched in our mouths. The sound was so loud in our heads! We could tell how much experience Gavin had in the wilds; he knew just what one would be craving after days with no food. Most people would have dropped canned or packaged food, but not Gavin. He'd probably made the pancakes himself, or enlisted his wife, Vicky, to whip up something for the hungry Yanks in the mountains.

By the time I'd put the whole cabbage down that I'd been taking bites out of, I realized the wind was kicking up. We needed to get off the Ragitata Col and down to safety very quickly. We packed up our banquet and the letters from home included in this package of very special air delivery and tromped down the backside of the col onto the Lyell Glacier. We dug out a platform, popped up our tent, and snuggled in for the night. It didn't take much to fill our shrunken stomachs, and we laid ourselves flat to extend our full bellies while we read letters from loved ones at home in the States. I felt like a bloated coon who had just raided the best garbage can he'd ever found.

The next day we dragged ourselves through the gorgeous, exciting, icefall wonderland of the Lyell Glacier and morainal debris over the next mile to the Lyell Hut. But I was lifted in spirit as I felt set free. No more anger to contend with. During the storms there was no separation, and while moving roped up there was no separation, but now I was at peace moving alone. I felt satisfied carrying the tools of my trade for the past month on my back. I enjoyed watching the terrain change and the traces of life unfold before my eyes, which couldn't exist in the barren mountains. I sang to myself and was content with my own company.

The Lyell Hut was very welcoming, situated on the rise of the Rakaia River. But I dumped my pack instead of entering, trotted back to the stream, and stripped off my clothes. It was heaven for me to scrub myself and my second skin, my long underwear. It was as if I were washing away everything undesirable before standing, naked, to look back on our route of ninety miles covered in thirty days, with a fondness and an admiration for the beauty in all the wildness of these mountains.

Of course the weather threw frozen slush at us the next day. It was hypothermia weather. We couldn't move out to the makeshift airstrip on the river flats where we had prearranged for a pickup by plane; the cloud ceiling was too low for any smaller plane to land. Next morning blossomed into a beautiful day, and we moved out in search of the airstrip Gavin had told us about. Ned was angry. He usually vented on me, but today he seemed to keep to himself.

I knew from reading the map, which the guys would never let me carry, that the Rakaia River would be breaking up into several long fingers. We could easily get separated from one another if we didn't stay together. It's easy to track one another in the snow, but down here on rocks, it isn't. Ned and I exchanged hand signals as he was ahead of me. I'd tried to run in my heavy Kastinger climbing boots, but to no avail; I couldn't catch him.

Tom and Allan were ahead of Ned, and I sensed Ned didn't want anything to slow him down and keep him from being up in the front of our group finishing our big project. It wasn't a good feeling. I waved, he waved. I beckoned to him, and he pointed ahead, turned from me, and proceeded. I watched Ned round the bend and go out of sight. Later I followed Ned's tracks across the river once again, then the tracks vanished over the rocks. I continued on late into the day, not seeing hide nor hair of anyone. And of course I didn't have the map, which should never have happened.

So I sat, before moving on, wondering if the airstrip we had all agreed that we were heading to this morning was nearby. By my estimation, it should be. I thought it best to take my bright yellow sleeping bag out, hang it from my skis, and wait, thinking anyone would spot me from any direction. I didn't want to head too far downriver and out to the first road head, maybe four or five miles away, and receive criticism for not waiting at the airstrip. As it was getting dark I walked back to a little clickety-clack cabin I had spotted and sat out in my sleeping bag under the stars until my eyes kept closing, then went inside to sleep.

At sunrise the next morning I went back downriver, thinking I'd spy our tent somewhere propped up by some odd means, as I had the tent poles. I did come across the airstrip, but no guys. I was puzzled. There had been no plane, and this was the area we had agreed to travel to at our last conversation. If they had made it before me, why weren't they there now? I felt quite comfortable alone; I had food, there was plenty of water, but this wasn't making sense at all.

It had started to rain, so I humped back to another cabin I had spied after we had all been separated. Perhaps they had holed up there for the night, because the tent was funky without any poles. No one was there. There was no sign that anyone had been there recently. It was still raining, so I made a fire for tea and began to dry out my clothes. I was very hungry, so I put on a pot of rice and raisins. I was closest to the airstrip here, so I waited. Why move in the rain, especially when I felt like I was where I was supposed to be?

The weather cleared, and I opened my bright yellow sleeping bag wide to catch the eye of anyone on land or in the air. I could walk out to the road head, but I still was leery of being accused of not following the last directive. Who knows how we would find each other then? I was going to give this sleeping bag signal one last try. Shortly, the low buzz of a plane could be heard in the distance. All I could think was, What'll I tell Gavin when he sees there are no men with me? I had no idea what had become of them.

I was waving in great humor as the plane landed, when to my big surprise out jumped Ned, angry of course! "We thought you were dead," he shouted. I just kind of went blank. These guys take off, they were in a huff, I'm where we agreed to meet, and I'm getting yelled at? Go figure, again. Ned had caught up to Allan and Tom. I surmised this was important to him to be up in the front as we made our way out. They went right by the airstrip, never found it, and carried on to the first sheep station and were taken in and given a meal and a bed. You'd think I'd be tweaked because I was left with no map and no idea the game plan had changed. I was the one that was ditched. Did I get angry? No.

I was just relieved. We'd finished. I wasn't sure I really still had a deep trust in Ned after his actions and reaction. I had to admit, as much as I didn't want to, that I felt Ned was afraid to have Tom and Allan ahead of him, afraid to be separated from them, and if it meant leaving me it was worth it to him. I knew I was branded a failure by the men, but I also knew, regardless of what story they told, I was where I was supposed to be, and that's how they knew where to find me.

I leaned on my old philosophy I created at the age of twelve, "Your life is what you make it, and the world is what it means to you." We are all dealt a hand of cards in life—our looks, strengths, weaknesses—but how we play this hand is our choice. We become the sum of our choices. I have had difficult choices to make in life, but it has rarely been difficult for me to make a choice. After that, all of life is point of view, how you choose to express or internalize the ramifications of your choices. I chose to let go of the way our trip ended and take the point of view that I'd just been through an incredible experience with some very incredible people. My life was exciting, and the world was full of adventure.

CHAPTER 2

AMERICAN
FRIENDSHIP EXPEDITION

AT THE END OF THE SECOND SEASON of teaching skiing at Trapps and following our ski trip to Harbin in northeastern China with *Ski* magazine to coach skiing under communism, Ned headed to the Karakoram in Pakistan. I headed to Colorado in an old, beat-up pickup truck with a friend of mine to meet up with some geologist friends. They were logging off beetle kill for cash. Trees destroyed by beetles had to be cut and hauled away, and loggers were being hired quite easily and making quick cash. A lot of experience wasn't required to do the job. This was attractive.

We shacked up at this big, old mountain house with several other youth who were logging to get by while skiing and climbing some beautiful lines in the backcountry. Life felt simple, true, and pure to the core. All that really was required was some muscle, the ability to handle a chain saw, and a whole lot of enthusiasm, and you could join the crew. These guys were intent on making money to begin a small company geared toward remote geological exploration and make some great climbs along the way, of course.

We drank cowboy coffee any time of day by dumping coffee grounds into boiling water; a little roughage was good to drink. We had no furniture save for a basketball hoop at one end of a large room with a vaulted ceiling, a hammock, and an old wire spool as a table, just far enough away from the hammock to require swinging in the right rhythm to grab your coffee mug for a swig and then return it to the table on the back swing. My basketball skills improved here, as did my taste for coffee, which hadn't interested me before. We had our sleeping bags, a kitchen, good attitudes, and great company, so life couldn't be better.

Getting a little scraped up on the job was a minor occupational hazard. We were still hard-core ski bums looking for powder, not hardcore loggers looking for Saturday night fight action. We maintained this distinction despite encouragement from the loggers to join their culture. After two years of teaching skiing and a couple of international ski trips, I had become acutely aware of skiing as an occupation in its own right. For the culture of deeply committed skiers, skiing was your focus in life; everything else was done in support of this endeavor. I was enamored by this way of life.

As I hitched down the highway on a day away from logging to meet up with some U.S. Demo Ski Team friends, I was picked up by a large, athletic guy with a heavy Austrian accent in a rather disheveled, somewhat rickety van. His leg muscles were bulging out of some overly tight, plaid Bermuda shorts, probably borrowed from a friend with a more average body type. His pectoral muscles were bursting out of an overly tight, striped shirt, small enough on him to reveal his belly button. The stripes and plaid in combination added a humorous touch.

I liked this guy, who introduced himself as Franz Webber. He was dressed so bizarrely for a tennis club requiring whites that I started giggling, imagining he could probably crush anyone challenging him on the court. When I introduced myself, it was his turn to laugh at me as he told me that we were going to climb and ski a peak together in China. The world of true climbing and skiing bums was so small, so very small. Ned and Galen Rowell, before departing for the Karakorum trip, had already asked Franz, who had just won the speed-skiing trials at Silverton, Colorado, going two hundred kilometers an hour, if he was interested in skiing a major peak in China on a record-breaking expedition with us.

Soon I got word Ned had just returned home from Pakistan. He was alive but didn't sound completely well. He sounded a bit low. The trip had been very physically demanding. They carried heavy packs as well as towed plastic sleds behind them as they skied to have enough provisions on their remote route of more than 285 miles of linked glaciers. As a result of their physical exertion, "their capacity for emotional response was near zero," as a writer had explained in an article written just after they finished this trip.

Ned wanted me back in Vermont to partner with him on the China expedition, now dubbed the American Friendship Expedition. He needed to have support, and our relationship tighter, for him to get himself up and running again. Although I had intended to stay in Colorado for some time, I changed my tack, returned to Vermont, and threw myself into the organization of our climb and ski of 24,757-foot Muztagata Mountain in the Chinese Pamir Range, a sort of northern spur off the Himalayas and the Karakoram Range, where Afghanistan, Pakistan, the former Soviet Union, and China all came together like the hub of a wheel.

National Geographic magazine had anted up, paying all expenses for the seemingly countless barrels of food and equipment that had assembled at Galen's house in Berkeley, California. Ned and I flew to Galen's in late June 1980. Dr. Cameron Bangs arrived from Portland, Oregon, to be our climbing medical expert, and Dick Dorworth, past world-speed-skiing champion and expert ice climber, rounded out our team, replacing Franz, who had unexpected competition commitments. Without Franz, I was again the youngest expedition member by more than ten years. Galen's girlfriend, Jo Sanders, who worked in the travel industry, would accompany us on this venture. This was my first sponsored trip with another woman along.

When we arrived, Beijing was a symphony of sounds with all the insects humming and creaking in the moist, humid air, audible as soon as we deplaned. Last winter, when we came to China to coach skiing, all was cold and somewhat barren, but now this corner of China was green and lush, pulsating with life in air so thick it felt like warm, wet cotton around my body. Gear prep had been my responsibility on this expedition, so I was relieved to locate our ski bag and a couple of missing barrels at the airport. I hoped this gave the men confidence that I had a head on my shoulders. I self-consciously felt that, because I was female and much younger, I needed to prove, again, that I was one of them. Perhaps (with the feminine tendency to be under-confident) I needed to prove to myself that I could hold my own with the men.

Of course there was a big banquet to welcome us back, and being familiar with Chinese banquet customs from our last adventure in China, I was ready to *gan bei,* bottoms up, with the best of them. We all went into the evening ready to warmly connect with our Asian counterparts and came out crawling on our hands and knees. Mountaineers in any culture can be an expressive, excessive bunch. In many ways mountaineers create a culture unto themselves, regardless of country of origin. We had so many toasts that when Cam, our doctor, pulled out the largest pair of basketball sneakers Nike had ever made and gave them to Wang Fuchou, a small, unassuming official in the Chinese Mountaineering Association (CMA), everything broke loose.

Wang put the sneakers on looking like Bozo the clown and walked around the table while we snapped blurry photographs. Cam's wild sense of humor was pouring through. I thought everything was grand until the next morning when I came in from the run I had taken to shake my hangover. Jo let me know she thought I should cover up, shut up, and stop being an embarrassment to the team. I didn't know what to say, so said nothing. She was upset over the banquet behavior. I was unsure why I was the target. When all the men were toasting, I was feeling like one among them and did the same. I didn't consider a different protocol for myself.

No matter, my head was largely filled with images of people I had seen practicing t'ai chi in the gray mist during my early morning run. Jet lagged, I had been up before dawn to watch the day come into light and unfold. Those slow-moving figures, in common Mao clothing, practiced in unison, making motions that defied time. Some groups had wooden swords, lunging and turning extremely slowly, with great control. It was as if a button had been pushed, slowing down the speed of life across the city for the first hours of the day. Those practicing seemed to notice me running by, but paid no particular attention, as if my running speed was in a dimension other than theirs.

Older China and younger China were already separating in my

mind. This giant country was teetering on the brink of great changes. China had already broken through a communist system and was charting new territory for its people. I wondered how much of the old ways they would keep and what new ways they would create. So much of China's ancient culture had literally been obliterated by the young army of the Communist Red Guard and through "reeducation" that it appeared these older philosophies were no longer commonly known or practiced by the youth. I felt inexplicably drawn to a more ancient Asian point of view, to the philosophies of the old China.

The next morning Ned and I rolled out of a warm bed for another early-morning run to absorb the beauty of t'ai chi being performed in the fog of daybreak. This run would also help us to clear out toxins from too much drinking the night before. This time Ned and I bumped into Galen and Dick as they headed out the door to do the same. It was refreshing to speak with comfort in a nonjudgmental group as we jogged along. These guys seemed at ease with me. I was still puzzled by Jo wanting to close me down while she accepted the men's behavior. Truthfully I was concerned that Jo would continue to think I should have more decorum, but I didn't feel I needed to cover up (my body or my personality) more whether I was running or dining. The men had worn their everyday clothes at the banquet, and I had felt entitled to do the same.

This reminded me of a study I had read about in which an essay was given to two groups to rate for quality. Each group, consisting of both men and women, received the same essay. For one group, Joan T. McKay was listed as the author, while the other group got the same essay with John T. McKay listed as the author. Interestingly enough, Joan was rated as having written an essay of lesser quality than John, even though it was the very same essay, and it was the females who often gave Joan the lower rating.[1] Perhaps Jo rated me lower than the men because I was a woman? It is a natural tendency for women to support each other as women, but when circumstances are murky, both men and women tend to think that men are more experienced and accomplished, which means we use different standards to compare women to men and therefore can have different expectations. This needs to change for us women. I decided it was time to carry on and leave this behind me. I needed to put my mental energies to better use.

That afternoon, our whole crew flew to Urimuchi, barrels, bags, and all. We had a couple of days to stretch our legs, adjust to a bit of altitude, and photograph this area at the base of the Tian Shan, or the Celestial Mountains, about three-fourths of the way across China, before moving on to the Pamirs. We had Chu Ying Hua, known as Lao Chu, as our liaison officer from the CMA with us, and our interpreter, Wang Wei Ping. These two were wonderful men, just loveable and real characters. They weren't vanilla or chocolate; they were more like spicy ginger and hot pepper.

Out of Beijing we were a little freer to move around as we saw fit. Both Wang and Lao Chu were more relaxed away from their superiors and were easy about anything we wanted to do. Lao Chu was just glowing to be out of the city of Beijing and back in the mountains. The word *lao* means "old"; it was a title of honor he had earned by being one of the top Chinese mountaineers when in his prime. Chu was in his forties, and I noticed he walked with an odd staccato gait.

Chu told us that he had climbed Everest, which he called Chomolungma, meaning "Mother Goddess of the Earth." We had heard that the first ascent from the north, in Tibet, had been done by three Chinese men in 1960, but the world mountaineering community had been skeptical. There was no one outside China, or even outside those three men, to verify this. China had been largely closed and out of communication with the rest of the world during that time. The three men who reached the summit had also been beyond the view of their climbing mates.

I felt solid with Chu. We struck up an immediate liking for each other. I would believe anything he told me. He was just that sort who seemed truthful, honorable, and tougher than hammered nails. It seemed to me he couldn't be bothered to tell a lie. He couldn't possibly live a charade.

Our interpreter, Wang, must have been barely thirty, if that. Wang was ready to reform all of China single-handedly. He would often say,

"I fear nothing," when the rest of us would cringe and think he should perhaps play it a little safer and bow to the political big brother.

Ambling at the base of the Tien Shan Mountains we came into contact with a group of Kazaks herding their cattle. Wow, this was China? Until now, on both this trip and my first ski excursion into China, I had only been in contact with the Han Chinese, the ethnic group associated with the stereotype of China. The Kazaks were wild, nomadic horse riders, herding their animals, living in yurts, in this clear, evergreen forest area.

As a matter of fact, the Kazaks are divided between China and the former Soviet Union. The border between these two countries might have moved a bit one way or another, but the Kazaks carried on with their traditional life, not paying too much attention to being labeled Chinese at one point then Russian soon after. The Kazaks knew who they were regardless of political boundaries; they dressed and looked more Mongolian, had round eyes and high cheekbones, and wore no government-issue Mao clothing, preferring their high boots and skin jackets to ward off the elements. My definition of China shifted.

We were here only today and off tomorrow, so I went looking to find a nugget of Kazak life to savor. Becausee Ned and Galen were often photographing furiously, sometimes creating a hectic tension, I found it better to slip off on my own, independently, and see what presented itself. I took out my wooden instrument, a recorder, and began to play some folk tunes in a meadow alongside a lake as the sun was coming up. We had gotten an early start to explore the area, because morning light is wonderfully rich for color photographs. A horseman drifted by to listen. After a bit he motioned behind him and gestured for me to hop on the horse. I didn't hesitate. We took off like a shot; I think he wanted to impress or borderline scare me with his skills. I'm convinced that if I were a man, he would never have lifted me up to his saddle; if I were Ned or Galen, he would want to compete with me, but as a woman I was someone he'd rather connect with. Like guys everywhere, I think he wanted to woo me with his prowess.

As I held tightly around the horseman's waist trying to stay on, bouncing on the rump of the horse, the fellow began to laugh. The Kazaks were often the hired fighting men for the variety of emperors and conquerors who had reigned over this area throughout history. This man's horsemanship was what had made the Kazaks so famous, and so feared, along this area of China's ancient trade route. In this area, Wang had told me, there is a proverb that goes, "The eagle has his wings, the man his horse."

It had been awhile since I had had a thrill like that. We'd only been traveling and jogging and banqueting; although there had been some really good times, nothing had gotten my adrenaline going for several days now. Suddenly I felt life in my veins, over my jet lag and clear-headed without the regular mao-tai at night. The horseman brought me back to a sense of adventure on our galloping tour. When we dismounted I played another tune for him while he did a little makeshift jig. I laughed and did one myself. Music is a common language for all people. I think we had a better time not speaking with each other, only gesturing, laughing, and responding to the music. I was glad I'd brought my simple instrument with me.

I wandered back to our site for lunch, feeling invigorated. The men and I went for a run, once more, the last before boarding a forty-eight-seat, twin-engine prop plane for Kashgar the next day. We were anxious to arrive, as this signified the real beginning of our climb and ski. No foreigners were allowed to fly into this area along so many sensitive borders, but we were, because we had to, in order to get into the area for our expedition. We would pick up some foodstuffs here and then drive the remaining seventy-five miles to the Pamir Mountains and Muztagata, our destination. Cameron would be just getting into his element here, to our surprise. We thought we'd seen his humor, but it had apparently been just warming up.

No one knew Cameron before this trip. He had contacted the team wanting to be the doctor for the expedition at just about the time our original team doctor realized he wouldn't be able to participate. With little time to search for a licensed doctor who could, at a moment's notice, leave for three months and who could climb and ski, at high altitude no less, we decided to invite Cam without any recommendations. We considered ourselves lucky indeed to have someone to act as our medical expert on this potentially risky venture.

Cameron was a doctor, and he assured us he was a mountaineer, but we had no way of knowing he was such a jokester. Here we were, more than 2,000 miles from Beijing on the borders of Afghanistan, the former Soviet Union, and Pakistan, once known as East Turkistan, with Cameron walking down the streets with his arms spread wide and a local crowd pressing in on him as he shouted, "These are my people!" Was he kidding, or did he mean it?

In Beijing we would get stares; in Harbin, the past winter, throngs had gaped at us. But nothing prepared me for the reaction of all the different ethnic groups in Kashgar. Here, along this western border of China, are fifty-five different minorities: some grow hair on their faces, some don't, some have almond eyes, some round, some have white skin, some yellow or darker. It was an amazing array of Tajiks, Kazaks, Kirkiz, Uygur, and so many more.

Looking out on Kashgar one would see women in close-fitting, brightly colored dresses over stockings or loose-fitting pant-type bloomers with colorful scarves wrapped around their heads and long braids often hanging below their waists. Many men wore vests and buttoned shirts. The main mode of transportation was a two-wheeled cart, often pulled by a donkey, but for heavier loads it might be a horse or a camel. There were many bicycles in use, and the occasional state-owned olive-green truck would rumble by. The streets were full of people going every which way.

Young boys were swimming naked in the irrigation streams flowing beside the streets, which were quite deep at junctions and controlled by wooden dams, operated by simply turning a metal wheel. An older man rode by on his donkey very slowly, and I noticed the Chinese script written in paint on the mud brick wall and right beside it something written in Arabic. To me both scripts looked like artwork. I wondered if the long-bearded man with the tight-fitting, embroidered cap could read either.

Houses lining the streets were mostly single story and made from mud brick. Often there would be a latticework of vines over an open, two-walled porch on the side of the buildings. The streets were dirt, and dust was in the air. There were power lines along the road among the tall trees, but power was not readily available. At the end of the street I could see a one-hundred-foot-tall statue of Mao, maybe a mile or so away, with his hand raised high over this biblical, mud brick city in the distance. I had seen this same giant statue in Harbin. It appeared so strange to see this sculpture, looking very out of place in this ancient, culturally diverse setting.

The people of Kashgar did not act or look like the Hans in Beijing or Harbin. Their mannerisms were very direct, lively, tactile, and vocal. Cameron got a kick out of the masses of people following him down the street, touching his hair, his face, his clothes, his camera, anything they could get their hands on. We were all being followed. The attention was not unfriendly; it was just a much more interactive curiosity. In Beijing the activity on the streets would quietly carry on as people stared at us; here, people would yell, shout, wave, and run after us. And this was all the same country! This was all China.

Xinjiang Province is the heart of Central Asia, with thirteen million people in an area twice the size of Texas. Here borders and boundaries have morphed time and again throughout history, encasing perhaps the most diverse population to be found anywhere on a world map. This wild west of China was exciting, open, and living in the ways of an era gone by, compared to most of the rest of the world. About the time the Islamic muezzins began singing from their towers to call the devoted to lie down on the ground in prayer—wherever they were on the street—I knew I wasn't in Kansas, or even Beijing, anymore.

It is truly embarrassing to confess how little I knew about the world's cultures at this time, but I feel compelled to express my ignorance in order for new generations to understand how ethnocentric we and our process of education have been in the United States. I was an honors student and college graduate. Yet Asia, containing half the world's population and an array of deep, varied cultures, was such a mystery to me. Now, finally, halfway around the world I could add Allah into my mental mix with Lao-tzu and Buddha.

The Han Chinese historically called this area the Thirty-Six Kingdoms, which also included lands from the present-day nations of Iraq, Iran, Afghanistan, Pakistan, and the former Soviet Union. This area of Xinjiang Province has only been firmly under China's control since just before 1900. But interestingly enough, today Chinese school-children learn that this ancient trade route, once called the Fur Route, the Jade Route, and now most commonly the Silk Route, was initially opened when Han Emperor Wu Di in 139 BCE sent explorer Zhang Qian out to the edge of these kingdoms to find the famed, large horses said to sweat blood.

Kashgar was a key oasis on that ancient route, a loose network of trails that crossed the mountains and deserts of Central Asia to connect East Asia with the Mediterranean. This historical world trade route was at its height about 200 BCE to 1400 CE, before many of the major sea routes were explored. It wasn't hard to envision Kashgar in its heyday as one of the most cosmopolitan areas on Earth as Wang told me that things hadn't changed greatly in this area since that time. At first this sounded like an exaggeration, but when I thought about it, Marco Polo was believed to have led his caravans on the Silk Route only about seven hundred years ago.

The following day when we went to the weekly market I sensed an absence of time passing. A throng of hot, sweaty people pulsated past the vendors, who simply sat with their wares spread on blankets or material. Livestock and fruit were for sale, along with different crops and dried, hand-powdered spices. Giant piles of melons avalanched into the crowd, adding to the excitement. The smells of food and manure, fur and feathers was beautiful, pungent, and disgusting all at the same time. The sounds of braying, shouting, laughing, mooing, cackling, and clanging and of carts being unloaded, bags and barrels thudding to the ground, filled the air. The summer temperatures were in the nineties, with the dust being kicked up and stirred into the air.

This scene could have been from ancient history. There were no signs of technological advances; all was brought in by hand and made by hand, including most saddles, clothes, food, or equipment. People brought their own glass bottles, if they were lucky enough to have one, to hold their purchased or bartered oil. Both men and women worked the market, although men had more hard goods for sale while the women were more likely to be preparing and selling food. To me those men and women who connected with the most customers were not only better merchants but also more likely to be mentally androgynous and as a result could connect with everyone.

As I was pressed into the hot, sweating crowd, often shoulder to shoulder, trying to photograph this ancient bazaar, the men would slap my butt or squeeze me close on their way by. I wasn't really frightened that this would spin out of control. I just persistently carried on, wondering if this had occurred to women in the bazaar for centuries before me. In a way, if that was true, I should be complimented that I was being treated as one of the many here, not something other.

This trade route, by any name, silk or otherwise, was also essential for the passage of new ideas and numerous religions and philosophies. Buddhism came up from India, and Islam from Arabia, while Taoism moved out. Along with glass, cinnamon, and lapis came forms of metal-working, lacquer work, and other such techniques, which passed back and forth over the route. Cultural exchanges of foods and their preparation traveled the great distance from ancient Rome to eastern China. All trails creating the Silk Route ran through the bottleneck of the Pamir mountain range, connecting east with west, making Kashgar an oasis at the base of the mountains, a home for anything strange and exotic. Nothing, no matter how rare, seemed out of place here.

A giant, stinky, diesel bus parked outside our guesthouse to take us up 12,000 feet into the mountains. Wow, was this what we negotiated for in Beijing? Of course not! You'd think it might be some rugged four-wheel drive military vehicle. We all sat in the front, anticipating the best views and avoiding the bounce of the back that we all used to love as kids. We were heading out on the dirt Karakorum Highway, a famous portion of the ancient Silk Route, headed to the Pamirs, where the Himalayan, Karakoram, Tian Shan, and Kunlun Mountains all come together. We were on our way to the Roof of the World, on a bus!

At first we drove by fruit groves full of plum trees and fields full of all types of melons. Fifty kinds of fruit were said to be grown here: pears, apricots, peaches, pomegranates, plums, white apples, and on and on. One field had a bunk bed with a man sleeping in it. He was stationed among the melons most likely to protect his crop, day and night, from pilfering.

Wang Fuchou, the climber who had worn the huge Nike basketball sneakers at our Beijing banquet, had been with Chu to this area in 1959 to do the second ascent of this peak as training for their Everest climb of 1960. One of Wang's fondest memories was of all the fruit grown in this region. While in Beijing he would tell me again and again how sweet these melons would be and that I have never tasted the likes of them before. Wang was right; I'd been eating them daily, and their vine-ripened sweetness was acute.

Outside our bus windows we could see child labor going on. I'd seen young boys working with blacksmiths in Kashgar, pounding and hammering metal, learning their trade. But now I could see little girls by the roadside, often with older women, very grandmotherly looking, pounding bigger rocks into smaller rocks for the "highway" we were driving on. With basic hand labor all people could be employed under communism, including older women. This idea had indeed reached the communes here on the western front. I was just surprised to see children working too.

After my first trip to China, I looked into more information about Mao's "liberation" of women. One of the significant changes Mao brought about was registering all women for work under the slogan, "Women can hold up half the sky." Mao knew he was using only half his total workforce before he enlisted the women. Wang had clarified some of the history for me. In many ways 1949 was an important year for China's women because of the promulgation of the marriage law, which protected the rights of women. Previously women had been more exploited and oppressed: they received almost no schooling, were forced into arranged marriages, were restricted to the home, and their feet were often bound. Infanticide of girl babies was not unusual. But in '49, for example, women who had previously been forced to be prostitutes were registered and treated for disease, received job training, and had a chance to marry and hold respectable jobs.

In 1950 equality between men and women in a marriage relationship and freedom of choice concerning marriage were established. An article was added to the Constitution of the People's Republic of China in 1954, which Wang translated as saying that "women have equal rights with men in all spheres of political, economic, cultural, social, and family life. Men and women enjoy equal pay for equal work, and women shall marry of their own free will. The state protects marriage, the family, and mother and child. The state advocates and encourages family planning." Wang told me women did not have to have the man's consent for abortions, which were done at clinics and hospitals.

Although in 1949 Mao's women's liberation still had more to accomplish than we had to in the United States, changes happened almost overnight, in contrast to our long, gradual process of suffrage and liberation and the ongoing battle for equality. The suffragettes won women the right to vote in the 1920s (after seventy-five years) and we had the slow-moving effects of the feminist movement in the 1960s (our Equal Rights Amendment didn't get too far), but Mao's move to employ all women was swift and radical by comparison. Instantly Mao doubled his workforce, perhaps his main motive. So much had to be done by hand labor in China that now, having two times the workforce, he could speed up economic output considerably.

Wang was free with his opinions, which I thrived on. He liked having women in the workforce and having opportunities to work with them rather than with only men. He felt women's lesser physical strength did not put off men and that people were often placed in jobs that best suited them anyway. He felt what these laws really did was free women, opposed to giving them equality: "Laws change overnight, but attitudes take time." Before liberation, he said, "women had no public work to do. They did everything for their husband and children. Their feet were bound to keep them home and dutiful." Now, more than fifty years later, women were fully integrated into the workforce at all levels, and good day care was provided by the government.

I suspected many of the minorities living in this region of China had always had their women participating in their nomadic and farming lives, children as well. I wondered how much being brought into China's fold had changed their lives, for better or worse. They were under China's umbrella but were still, perhaps, somewhat autonomous. Wang had interpreted for one Uyger farmer we had spoken to earlier who said, "Before liberation each family here lived from the harvest of a small plot. Four landlords owned almost all the land around our village. Then, after liberation, the people were gathered together and provided with more free land to grow crops together."

These people went from growing crops for the landlord to growing for the government. This fellow felt he had more ownership of the property, and this, I thought, seemed to please him. He didn't say, but he seemed happy with China's communist arrangement. I assumed his life was improved, but it was often difficult to know for sure. We were learning people felt safer giving the party line, saying what they believed the government wanted to hear.

We were beyond the great oases and irrigation now. We had to open the windows because of the heat, but this let all the dry, air-borne particles in, and silt and sand were whirling around us like the insides of a vacuum cleaner. My hair was getting coated enough with grit that it started to stiffen and stand out. I tied one of my scarves over my face and wore my sunglasses to protect my eyes. The men tied cloth or scarves over their heads like pirates when their hair started standing up stiff. Dick and Ned already wore glasses, so their eyes were okay, but their big, dark, thick beards were gathering dirt. Galen and Jo put on hats and face scarves. We looked like banditos who had overtaken our bus.

By this time we were feeling a bit like Ken Kesey of the beat generation. In many ways the party had begun when we boarded the bus. Now, as with all expeditions, we were creating our own world. We belonged to no government in a sense. There were no rules and regulations, just a striving for harmony within our small group, this far away from the rest of the world. In a way this has always helped me to have a less opinionated and hopefully more objective view of what I see and experience as I shed my own expectations of lifestyle or culture.

We reached a small settlement called Gez, about our halfway point, thirty-five miles out. There was a phone switchboard just put up. We could see poles for telephone lines just going in. We stopped to see the switchboard, to stretch our legs, and to eat and drink. I discovered we had no water, just wooden cases upon cases of Tsingtao beer in large, green bottles, about quart size. Dick explained that while gathering supplemental food in Kashgar he realized there was no bottled water to be had. We had camp stoves for melting snow into water on the mountain, and below that elevation at a base camp we'd probably find a stream, so until then it was beer, and lots of it. We were all parched, so the party rocked on.

Inside the plain cinderblock building was a Uyger man wearing his traditional white cap with black embroidery on it, with headphones on over that. He was laughing while plugging and unplugging the metal ends of flexible black cords, which appeared to us as haphazard guessing, trying to make a connection. To whom, we wondered; certainly not Beijing! The phone lines were not exiting out of the building and up the valley we were headed, so we knew this was the last chance to make a phone call. Well supposedly. I'm not sure we could have connected with anyone from here just yet.

But this scene put things in context for me. We were now really on our own, regardless of having a huge diesel bus. We had exceeded communication. We had exceeded any form of electric power. Although this area was under Central China's control, it certainly wasn't in direct communication. Beijing didn't really know what went on here. Did all those negotiations in Beijing really matter? We doubted it. Beijing made sure we paid for it, though. Travel at this time in China was exorbitantly expensive.

Back on the bus, moving forward, we saw that the area was becoming drier and drier, and it made more sense that the sand blew in from over this landscape. We knew the word *pamir* meant "high, wide, grassy valley between mountains," but this terrain looked very bleak, brown, and mostly a dirty gray. We had climbed to 11,000 feet, with our hypoxic bus sucking wind as we lurched along. The road finally seemed to be flattening out, and outside our windows a horseman appeared, galloping beside us. It was evident that he was racing us, as he urged his horse on.

This man, dressed in a black cloth coat; a black, curly, sheep's wool hat; and tall black boots, was grinning yet intent. The sun was shining brilliantly, yet it would be cool soon when the sun dipped at this elevation. The horse seemed to manage well in the thin air, and after a short pause of riding right beside us as we all hung out our windows cheering him on, the horseman left us behind, waving with one hand, his other on the reins, as he directed his horse like a polo pony. "That's an auspicious beginning," Ned said, sliding back into his seat. When I queried him why, he said something about the way man and beast had bettered modern machinery; the horse beat the bus. In this place maybe climbing, which is physical and elementary, would be respected and accepted, and we would fit in with the people. Let's hope so, I thought.

Then as we crested a small rise, a meadow as beautiful as anyone's imagination could create spread out before us. Small yellow, red, and purple flowers wove through the thick green grass on a flat plateau bisected by a clear stream. At the sides of the meadow rose barren hills dusted with dunes, and then behind them rose glorious, white, glaciated peaks. The colors and textures of water, sand, rock, grass, flowers, and ice had me awestruck. Not a road or powerline broke up the wholeness of this place. The Pamir mountain range was not named for the rocky peaks but for the most inviting, pretty meadows laced between the peaks. These meadows were the Pamirs.

Marco Polo is said to have reported that "a lean beast grows fat here in ten days," when referring to these Pamirs. These meadows have been legendary and a safe haven and goal for many a hard-pressed trading caravan. I suppose it had been uttered in many languages in many different eras: We'll be fine when we reach the Pamirs; if only we could reach the Pamirs in time; when we reach the Pamirs the worst will be behind us, we will survive. Although the valley felt timeless, our entrance was of the modern era, in a carriage powered by fossil fuel. We had no real appreciation for what past caravans had gone through to reach this famous bottleneck, through which all groups must pass, on the ancient Silk Route.

The bus dumped us, our foodstuffs, and our equipment off and departed. I'm sure our driver was anxious to head back at least as far as Gez that night. Maybe the phone lines would be connected by then! We looked right up at our peak, Muztagata, the highest of the peaks, whose name means "Ice Mountain Father." We'd be climbing just shy of 25,000 feet to the summit for an almost 10,000-foot descent on skis. Now that's a ski run. We were most concerned about the ski conditions, what type of snow we would find up there. There is a reason why the Inuit have more than one hundred different words for snow; it comes in as many forms, and most of them are disastrous for skiing.

As placid and peaceful as these meadows were in summer, we'd heard they were blown by ceaseless winter winds, known to be the cruelest outside the polar regions. With winds like that high up on the mountain it would be typical to have harsh, frozen conditions, like sastrugi for example, which are sharp little ice peaks, or maybe death cookies, small breakable pieces. Then of course there's the usual avalanche and crevasse danger to look out for while skiing. We came expecting nature's grooming, not mechanical grooming, on the slopes of Muztagata.

After quickly setting up camp, Dick and I lay in the grass, drinking beer and writing in our journals in those last gorgeous rays of late afternoon sun. Who knew what the official time was, as all of China runs on Beijing time, regardless of how far west you are. We were several time zones away, so we stopped bothering with the clock, and as it should be, we tuned in to the sun.

The next day while out playing Frisbee, trying to run a bit as we acclimatized to 12,000 feet, three men came up and just sat watching us play. We thought we must look ridiculous to them as they sat shoulder to shoulder, almost motionless in the grass. I beckoned for them to join us. I persisted in motioning to them as I played. Eventually they got up and started running around with us, leaping for the plastic disc. So I guess, as the old saying goes, "People who play together, stay together." These guys stuck around.

When we opened up our ski gear to mount some bindings these fellows—who we affectionately named Hear No Evil, Speak No Evil, and See No Evil—were intrigued by the mechanical workings of the bindings. They handled the skis and looked with amazement when we gestured to the peak and then stepped on the skis to indicate we'd be sliding down their mountain. They looked as though they weren't sure if they should laugh at us or honor us. We were so far from their concept of reality. We threw things around and slid down mountains. How strange was that for animal herders who wore the very same skins of the animals they herded.

The three men began to motion down the valley and encouraged us to come with them. We assumed that they lived in the yurts that we had passed just a few miles down the valley before the bus unloaded us here. Their homes, which they called *aq ui,* Turkic for white dwellings, were made of bent saplings and covered with pressed wool felt. These people were Kirkiz, known for their animal husbandry. The man who had raced our bus with his horse on his way home was a Kirkiz from this community.

As we looked down the valley something exciting appeared. A herd of camels was loping up toward us. Someone was with them. Could this be a real caravan still on the trade route? Were we hallucinating? As they got closer we figured it out. Ned was humorously surprised as he said, "Well, in Beijing I negotiated for yaks. I guess this is what happens when there is no communication between Beijing and the Pamirs." All of us came together and circled the camels, Wang did a bit of translating through a variety of languages and patched this much together. These Asian Bactrian camels were for us, and they could hold up to seven hundred pounds each. Ned knew a yak couldn't carry that much and was pleased with the mistake.

Because all payments had already been made in Beijing, all we had to do was say, "Thanks, and how the heck do you drive these things?" We took turns hopping onto their covered humps and trying to steer them while someone on the ground was nearby to grab the lead if need be. The leads were attached to wooden dowels that pierced their sensitive noses. Galen and Ned had plenty of wilderness experience between them, but none with camels, although they were both quick to announce that camels spit awful-smelling green stuff and bite.

The camel driver hung around long enough to be entertained and let us know we needn't ride if we didn't want to; we could load the camels' backs and walk beside them, holding the leads. Then he knelt down to the ground and prostrated himself in prayer, as he always did, five times a day. The Kirkiz wore muslin caps underneath their black, curly, sheep's wool hats. Like the hats, outwardly these people appeared to be Kirkiz, but underneath they were influenced by the major religion of the region; they loosely practiced the Islamic faith. All clocks may be set to Beijing time, but here we were into the deep rhythms of East Turkistan, Central Asia, and the Middle East.

We still had more gear to prep and sort out, and we felt we could use another day acclimatizing before we moved up to our base camp on the mountain's moraine at about 15,000 feet. We decided to stay an extra day, and Ned, Galen, and I asked Wang to accompany us the next day on a walk down to visit the Kirkiz in their yurts.

When we got our cameras and walked down the valley to the village the following day, we were recognized as we approached. To my surprise the women circled around me, while the men were drawn to Galen, Ned, and Wang. I so seldom see myself as something other than part of the group, not as "the woman." These women were not dressed in Mao clothing like the women of Beijing but wore brightly flowered, long-sleeved dresses and scarves wrapped around their heads. I must have looked odd to them, wearing a short-sleeved shirt and shorts like the men on our team. Even the Kirkiz men wore pants. However, they looked at me only curiously not judgmentally. I think they wanted to make sure that I was indeed a woman first, and my obvious breasts were a dead giveaway.

We were ushered in out of the blazing sun and sat on the floor of the yurt on one of the many beautiful handwoven blankets and rugs. There was a tin stove with a pipe running out the top of the yurt. I imagined they fired up the stove for the nights, which were much colder than the days, with temperatures in the thirties. The men left to photograph, which left just us girls. Once we were alone there was a bond— laughter, earring exchanges, and goodwill in the air. I found the women to be so tactile with me, feeling my hair, fingering my clothes, and such. Galen and Ned, outside with the other men, were not having close to the same warm experience I was.

When the men returned we were served flatbread, goat's cheese, and yogurt. There was no furniture per se in the yurt, just stacks of folded textiles, making an incredible display of color, handwork, and artistry. Again Wang amazingly patched together words from a few languages— the Kirkiz Turkic dialect, Han Chinese, a little Uyger, and so forth— and we were told a story and asked a question. I got the feeling there had been some discussion among them about this subject before we arrived. The man who seemed to have some authority and was well respected, Turdi Beg, said that he had been told by his grandfather, who had been told by his grandfather, and so on, that "there is a beautiful, sacred garden on top of Muztagata, and this garden is tended by spirits wearing white robes. These spirits live in peace and harmony." Then he peered at us intently and asked, "Will you tell me if this is true when you reach the top?"

At first I didn't realize the magnitude of the question; this was culture-altering material. There was perhaps some mythical importance to the story, and it shouldn't be dashed by some renegade climbers looking for a good ski. What would we tell them upon our return? Maybe we would never make the top, or these spirits would make sure we didn't, to keep their garden sacred and secret. At any rate Ned dutifully agreed to come back and report what we saw from the top of the mountain. All the people from this cluster of about five yurts, sitting in and around Turdi's yurt, seemed nervously excited and satisfied with the answer.

Reluctantly we had to get back to our expedition preparations and made our way through the sheep, goats, mules, and horses milling around. Some cheeses were being set out to dry on the yurt roofs, wool was being spun on a hand spindle, and some of the animals were getting an afternoon milking. The scene was very pastoral and peaceful. Young children ran after each other and splashed in the stream. Parents seemed content with their work.

Wang was settling negotiations for something with one of the Kirkiz men as we departed. I didn't pay much attention to it as I was amused to see Wang still had our *National Geographic* map of China sticking out of his pants. He'd shoved the treasure just under his belt to keep it secure but constantly within reach. There were no maps readily available for the Chinese people. Perhaps this was another way to keep a population more easily in control. Wang was more than thrilled to have his own map and poured over it regularly to understand the physical extent of his country. Something our schoolchildren take for granted, like a map, was a treasure in China. Wang truly felt invincible now as the owner of perhaps the world's most current map of China

When we reached camp Chu came over in his unbalanced gait to talk to Wang. As their heads were bobbing in agreement, I asked what was up. Wang and Chu looked at each other. Then while Chu sat to take off his black cloth Mao shoes, Wang told us a story about Chu's ascent of Everest. Many had climbed Muztagata in 1959, on the first Chinese ascent of the peak, following the very first Sino-Soviet ascent in 1956. Of those from the Muztagata training climb in 1959, Wang Fuchou, who loved the melons and wore the Nike basketball shoes at our banquet, and Chu were selected to be part of the first Chinese group of climbers to attempt Everest.

By this time Chu had gotten his shoes off, and we looked, spellbound, to see that Chu had what amounted to blocks of flesh for feet. He had no toes; his feet ended at the base of the toes, making a flat, blunt ending to each foot. His straight-legged gait made sense to me now. He couldn't rock forward as others do when they walk, or he would risk tipping over. Perhaps Lao Chu hadn't shown us this before, not wanting to appear unable to do his job as our liaison officer in the rugged outback.

Wang continued with the story. Chu, Wang, and another climber were the only three still capable and climbing at what is called the second step, a solid rock wall close to the summit of Everest, the last real hurdle to the top of this magnificent peak. Because they couldn't use ice tools to climb this obstacle, as it was rock, Chu eyed a tiny crack and envisioned a way to success. I had sensed this guy was tough, but this next decision showed him to be of undeniable character as well as hardcore.

Of the three, Chu decided he would be the one to take his insulated climbing boots off and expose his bare, sockless feet, so that he could get his toes into the tiny crack and lead the climb up the second step. Once on top with a rope he could belay and even haul up the other two. The three men summited and made it back down to base camp before Chu was incapacitated by his frozen feet. Most likely Chu's toes never thawed out until he was down from 28,000 feet onto level ground, at about 17,000 feet. At this point he couldn't walk; he had to be carried out and driven back for medical care, but he survived any complications from the amputations.

Rather than fail, Chu decided that he would sacrifice his toes in order for them all to reach the summit, showing incredibly strong character, selflessness, and rugged determination. This is how Lao Chu earned the Lao in his name and how he had earned a high-ranking position in the Chinese Mountaineering Association. When the People's Republic of China sent Chu and his group to Everest, it was under the mandate "Succeed or die trying."

Chu took this very literally. He also knew if they did succeed, his life, even without toes, would be secure in terms of his job, finances, and honor. Apparently Chu was willing to make this gamble and trade his toes for the summit. I later saw old black-and-white photos of Chu being carried out of base camp. I believe every word of his story.

Yesterday Wang had discussed with the Kirkiz the use of a donkey for Chu, who would ride it to base camp set at 14,850 feet, where Chu had camped about twenty-five years before. The next day Chu, on his tiny donkey, so low to the ground that his feet dragged over the gravel, led our caravan of giant camels with huge loads as he sat upright with his old, trusty, rusty rifle slung over his shoulder. You'd think we were going snow leopard hunting or warding off the Mongols by the look on Chu's face. But instead we looked like a caricature of ourselves and not at all like the stalwart camel caravans during the time of Marco Polo, ready to brave all elements. With sunglasses, bandannas, bottles of beer, and skis sticking out everywhere, we were on the move, led by the little donkey. We were a climbing carnival caravan.

We reached base camp where Wang and Chu set up the kitchen right away. Great smells hit us while we pitched camp. We were just beginning to realize that Chu really knew how to travel in style. He'd put a lot of thought into this trip. He would be residing at base camp with Wang and Jo for who knows how long, while the rest of us climbed. He had his gun for fresh meat if he could find it, and he brought plenty of vegetables that would store well, like root vegetables and lots of sausage—real food. As they dished up their meal it was served on real china. I imagined Chu was the envy of all his comrades in the office in Beijing. He was out of the city and on a mountain, not pushing paper. Perhaps his past heroic efforts gave him the seniority for these privileges.

Others had looked up from this very base camp as far back as 1894 when well-known Swedish explorer Sven Hedin made four attempts and failed each time to reach the summit. In 1947 British explorers Eric Shipton and H. W. Tilman also failed. Only the Russians and the Chinese were successful on Muztagata much later, in 1959. We would have the third ascent and the first ski of the peak, provided we were successful.

It began to spit snow, so I hurriedly put up a yellow dome tent for the camel drivers to let them know they were more than welcome to stay the night and drive the camels farther the next day if that suited them. For these guys this was an adventure, to sleep in a tiny cloth dome instead of their larger, warmer yurt and to explore what their animals were capable of. For me this trip was becoming a real adventure too, to explore, like the camels, what I could do. We would be spending the night at the highest elevation I had ever been to, just shy of 15,000 feet, higher than the New Zealand, European, and American peaks I had been on.

Upon waking the next morning in freezing temperatures I felt queasy and woozy. There was a vague headache throughout my head, and I didn't feel too relevant to the world; instead I felt quite spacey. I felt unmotivated and sluggish, and if I didn't know better I'd think I was coming down with the flu. So this was what acclimatization felt like. I was coached to drink to excess, and now we were drinking water so I could drink copious amounts. If I had been drinking that much beer, this feeling could easily be attributed to a hangover. So all those gan beis, bottoms-up toasts were training for mountaineering at high altitude, in a twisted sense. They got me used to functioning well enough while still hungover.

I walked with the camels and laughed to see these Kirkiz drivers wearing the blue nylon Nike sneakers we had given them as they negotiated the tough moraine. It wouldn't have been my choice of footwear for this effort, but they were very proud of their new shoes. We had a variety of clothing, food, and drink sponsorships; Dick had even gotten Harold's Club Casino in Reno to ante up for photographing their banner as high as possible. We all thought this was a hoot. Consequently we got banner shots in many funny scenarios with camels and donkeys, just for our own entertainment. Although we were here with *National Geographic,* we still had American commercialism along for the ride.

The drivers were beginning to pull on the nose dowels via the lead ropes as they neared 17,000 feet. This seemed to be the ultimate elevation for the camels. Still, these animals had brought our gear 2,000 feet above base camp, which was something just short of a miracle. This would allow us to move the expedition along at a much better rate, because now we would only be carrying loads over snow using skis, which is much easier than struggling over shifting rock and debris on foot. The camel drivers dumped our loads right at the base of the snow line, proud of themselves and their animals as they sat to roll up some tobacco for a smoke and admire the view. These guys were tough. Smoking?

We returned to spend a couple of days at base. Galen was feeling some food gollywobbles and stomach rumblings, and he didn't want to go up until he felt better. Dick had had some troubles acclimatizing before and felt going too high too fast wasn't in his best interest. Ned, Cam, and I hemmed and hawed trying to decide whether to go up; the weather could be unstable, but Ned thought we had a window clear enough to walk up what amounted to about three hours of moraine slogging. Ned was antsy to be active, and from our higher camel camp we could have great skiing. We could ski all day while acclimatizing, climb high, shush down, and sleep low at camel camp. We would hump loads up before our descents and get things moving forward for everyone.

On July 12, we left at 3:30, which sounds late, but this was Beijing time, about four or more time zones east of us, and arrived at about 6:30. It began to spit snow; our timing was good. But what we thought was an innocuous decision apparently caused a huge communication gap. Although we didn't require the others to go up if they chose not to, apparently the two at base thought we should have stayed below. Those at base began wondering why we three went up, and suspicion crept in. Meanwhile we just wanted to ski. Ned thought going up was an option and asked who wanted to go, no pressure.

Cam felt quite at home with Ned and me, and now he began to unload thoughts and feelings. Maybe there are similarities of character in those from the Northeast and the Northwest, maybe the hard winters we contend with make us no-nonsense characters. Cam had a simplicity of life view, a love for his family and his grown children, and a disregard for monetary rewards. "Thank God it rains in Oregon so we don't get the weirdoes from Berkeley," he laughed. He struggled a bit with the California attitude, which he thought was self-obsessed. Cam saw himself as a team player, not self-centered.

I noticed I wasn't feeling as strong; my stomach was churning. I assumed it was food or water foreign to my system; maybe I had a version of what Galen had. In these distant parts where one finds the enticing mountains one also finds exotic bacteria, germs, and what-have-you.

Even that delicious Kirkiz yogurt had cultures my insides had never known before. To fall prey to illness when great strength is required is every mountaineer's nightmare.

With my load and rumbly gut I was fully aware that Cam and I were evenly paced. I had been pushing myself to hike faster than the men, most likely to overcompensate. I was hiking, feeling inadequate, underestimating my ability, and Cam was happy as a clam to be marching along with me, as I'd been out in front previously. Same pace, two different mind-sets. Both thought processes are self-generated and superimposed. Women tend to underestimate their abilities, which could be a result of the men having a tendency to overestimate theirs, thus making the women appear less confident.[2] There is a certain symmetry to that. I could see in myself an ever-ready eye of comparison, not with competition in mind but to make sure I was never holding anyone back.

I decided to *shu shi*, or take a rest, on a knoll top. We'd adopted this Chinese phrase for our own little pauses. Pleasantly, the men decided to take the load off too. My pulse was up. I had been monitoring my pulse, the weather, and temperature since we hit base camp. Normally, when I was training for running and skiing, I would work to get my pulse down to thirty beats per minute at rest, in the early morning upon awakening. This is when the body is at its most relaxed. For years I had kept detailed daily journals to evaluate my training and performance.

My pulse was in the 70s now, working under a load just below 17,000 feet. By the time we reached camel camp my pulse was 75 at rest. When I woke in the morning my pulse was back down to 61, but the queasy, headachy feeling was back. I was starting to get the hang of this acclimatization thing, I thought, as I kidded myself. Pulmonary and cerebral edema will kill you. But my first impressions of acclimatization were that hydration and rest were key. This was all like athletic training on a condensed scale, changes in your condition occurred daily as opposed to monthly.

Upon arrival at base my pulse went up and a bad morning followed, but things improved. The same occurred again at camel camp: pulse went up followed by a bad morning, but I assumed I'd improve and I did, with plenty of water and rest. We expected to see Galen and Dick arrive in the afternoon. We intended to climb higher and return to sleep at camel camp, but we all decided to stay put and sort through gear, organize food into meals, work on ski bindings, that sort of thing.

After another night, Galen and Dick appeared on July 15. We caught wind that they were feeling misled about ascending to camel camp. They had wanted to stay below and weren't so sure why we three went up. Oh boy, it was all much simpler than they thought; we just wanted to sleep high and get on with preparing gear. It pretty much amounted to Ned being restless at base and wanting to make the best of any weather window; waiting doesn't come easy for him. He'd been on too many mountains to think that one can climb when one wishes; one climbs when lady weather allows. Ned never intended to move camp up farther without the rest of the ranks, but maybe they were worried about two separate parties climbing the peak at different rates as opposed to one.

Regardless of any mental hyperventilation, we were all together as should be, and all appeared in relatively good health, but Dick seemed quite tired. After we talked over the communication confusion, all seemed well as Ned and I put up a tent for the newcomers to crawl into. We had had the most wonderful day of climbing with our synthetic sealskins adhered to the base of our skis to prevent back slide and then ripping them off for incredible descents in about five inches of powder. It had been snowing some in the nights, and the consistency of the snow was delicious. Woo hoo, this is what we came for, cranking turns as we looked down into brown desert and high peaks in three different countries. I took pleasure in skiing without a pack. This would be the only time, on this mountain, from now on.

Galen joined us for a run on the slope. Ned called Galen's style "the milk stool squat." Galen was stocky and strong and a latecomer to skiing. His technique was stout and stable, but he didn't have the pretty turns that Ned had. Ned had been skiing and competing since he was three years old. I've never seen anyone better on skis with a giant pack in the big mountains than Ned and would be surprised if I ever do. Galen on the other hand had a bulldog determination hard to beat. I watched him climbing in a cotton t-shirt, with his jacket open, getting wet and focused on getting where he wanted to go, regardless of the weather and wind. These two men climbed Mount McKinley, now called Denali, in Alaska in one day, up and down. It's remarkable the trust, determination, and skill of these two men. To date their speedy ascent has not been bettered.

July 16 was 25 degrees in the morning with a blue sky, a weather change. It's generally thought that the third day at a new altitude is the hardest; you're depleting yourself while adjusting, creating more red blood cells to carry more oxygen to your needy brain and muscles. The thinning high-altitude air has less oxygen in it, so more blood cells are needed to carry oxygen throughout the body. When your body reaches a modified homeostasis, you feel good, but it can take a few days. For me, consistently the third day is the toughest. I become progressively tired each day, but from the fourth day on things improve. I had come up on July 12, and now I was ready to rock.

The plan was to carry up heavy loads to establish camp two. From there we would attempt the summit in a long hard push round-trip in one day when we and the weather were at our best. Ned's temper flared as Galen took off with his camera gear while Cam, Ned, and I carried community gear. Okay, here we go again, miscommunication and then jumping to conclusions, again perhaps unwarranted. Now Ned is wondering if Galen is taking it easy staying below and carrying light so that he'll have more strength when the rest of us are worn out. I started to see this as nothing major, just something between Ned and Galen, both used to being leaders in their own right and now second-guessing each other.

The joy and the sorrow of it all was that I was close enough for Ned to say his very thoughts out loud to me. He wouldn't have expressed much of this to other men, but I would listen. I suppose I gave more cues that I was a good listener—nods and such—to Ned than the men did, and yes, believe it or not, sociolinguists find that women listen more than men and interrupt less. They have pinpointed this gender difference in speech.[3]

At first male researchers determined that women are less confident than men when they speak because they use more tag questions like "isn't it?" or "don't you think?" Women also nod more when others speak and hedge more, saying "sort of" or "maybe." To men, and male researchers, nodding while listening shows compliance, and tag questions and hedges show uncertainty, so women look less apt than men, but what these male researches couldn't do was think like a woman and understand her natural way of speaking.

As more female researchers looked at the data, which is sound, they realized the results are all in the interpretation. Men use language to improve or delineate status or create hierarchy.[4] Woman use language to support and bond. When a woman nods or uses a tag question or hedges, she's not unconfident; she's leaving room for discussion, input, and negotiation with the other party. A woman would typically say, "We're going to camp two, aren't we?" whereas a man might say, "We're going to camp two." He is creating a hierarchy with him in charge, and anyone thinking otherwise would have to challenge him, while the woman is leaving room for others to give their opinions without feeling challenged or feeling they have to challenge. The other can then safely say, "Well, I don't think it's such a good idea," and discussion ensues rather than a deadlock.

Women tend to work more democratically; men more autocratically. (It has been studied and noted that women in leadership roles are more democratic, males more autocratic.[5]) Women aren't necessarily uncertain, less confident, or less able to be decisive than men; they just work differently; they choose to connect in conversation and invite discussion. So the research was correct in terms of which gender was saying what more or less than the other, but what this correct data actually means depends on how it is interpreted.

Just as our moving up to camel camp earlier than the others had been innocuous, Galen heading out with a light pack of camera gear was as well. He wanted to get some shots of Dick skiing back down to camel camp as the rest of us unloaded our loads. Galen was feeling the photo responsibility for *National Geographic,* and Dick was to be our crack skier because of his speed-skiing experiences.

Galen blasted off a roll of film in no time with a motor drive that can take five frames per second, and Dick carried on his way, shushing back down to camel camp. The snow was good. Galen rejoined us, and we skinned only about one hundred yards up and made the decision to make this spot camp one. We had initially thought this would be the day to put in our high camp, which would eventually become camp two, at around 20,000 feet. But we all agreed, and this was truly a good omen, that this should be our starting point on the glaciated, snow-covered part of the mountain. It made sense that camel camp was just an unloading place, and where we stood now would be deemed camp one, our first on-snow camp for our ascent.

Camp one was situated at 18,000 feet, only 1,000 feet higher than camel camp. We skied down this distance in no time, although it was evident that Cam was having trouble with the deeper powder. I suspect most of his skiing had been on groomed slopes; big mountains demand more of you. Winds were variable. Clouds had come into the clear blue heavens. We busted into the tent, where Dick was brewing up some tea, with our good news that camp one had been determined, and we were going to pack it all up and head back up there for the night. Dick didn't seem excited, as a matter of fact he was quite disappointed.

He'd had problems with altitude before and had promised himself to take his time on this mountain, acclimatizing at his own rate. He calmly, rationally told us he needed to stay here, at the very least another night. Cam announced that he was whipped. The descent had taken more out of him than the rest of us, and although he had agreed on putting in camp one today and still did, he had just had enough. Cam and Dick nestled in their down bags, settling in for a good round of hydration, melting snow for water, and, I'm sure, some good conversation.

Climbing back up, carrying loads of maybe forty pounds of gear on our backs, we felt solid as we slid on our skis weighing several pounds. Ned, Galen, and I were now functioning as a team; all suspicions seemed to be put to rest, and communication between parties above and below seemed to be good. The ease and humor between Ned and Galen at camp one was more like what I had anticipated.

In the morning it was 20 degrees outside, and my pulse was 70 again; it had returned to 60 at camel camp. I elected to stay put on this gorgeously clear day. I had camera equipment to repair and would sort out our food for the days to come. Galen and Ned opted to take loads up in search for our high camp, camp two, establish it as our next home, and return—climb high, sleep low.

Midday I spied Dick coming over the lower rise. I called to him to warn him of crevasses. Ned had walked over one, marginally bridged. When Dick reached camp he put his arms up and threw his head back in a hallelujah! This was the highest he had been as well, a record for both of us. He had me take his pulse, after giving me warm hugs of welcome. For fun we unfurled the Harold's Club Casino banner in front of our two tents, and with the icefall behind camp as a dramatic backdrop, took some photos. It read "Harold's Club Casino or bust," with 11,444 miles and an arrow pointing one way and 13,456 miles and an arrow pointing the opposite way. I got behind the banner and stuck out a leg and a thumb as if to hitch. Stupid humor, but we got a kick out of it.

We were getting concerned about Cam. Yesterday Cam had fallen over a dozen times as we carried up loads. He was struggling a bit to get used to the skins under his skis, and it was complicated by the heavy weight on his back pushing him around and off balance. The rest of us had no falls, so Cam had put out a whole lot more effort to go the same distance. Today apparently Cam had trouble keeping the skins on the skis, so he left the skis, carried up his pack, and went back down to get his skis. When he finished his double effort, Cam was dog tired and feeling a bit frustrated, perhaps to the point of self-inflicted alienation.

Moisture had gotten between the skin's adhesive and Cam's ski; one can't let the tiniest bit of snow accumulate—one of those things I know about and take for granted. High-level mountaineering is so much about body maintenance, mental maintenance, equipment maintenance. Galen and Ned came whizzing down over the rise. Camp two had been located and established. Our mission was becoming clear in our minds. Ned and Galen could taste the summit from camp two and brought a taste of it with them in their stories. The only downer was that Galen had prereleased from his bindings four times on the way down, suffering the inevitable crashes. We all went into equipment repair mode.

Exhausted yet encouraged, we all went to sleep at 9 p.m., which, taking time zones into account, would have been about 5 p.m.; we were spent. Next morning, July 18, we had two inches of snow and it was gusting up to 20 mph. My pulse was a high 75, but I felt good after my second night at 18,000 feet. It was a whiteout outside; we weren't going anywhere today.

We brewed tea in the evening and tried to drink as much as a gallon of water each, to acclimatize, so the nights were punctuated with pee breaks. It was blowing and snowing outside, and I had to face into the wind or suffer everything being blown back into my dropped trou! This I like to avoid. If I can. During the night I heard Dick asking for the bottle as I was taking a leak in the pee bottle, kneeling in my bag inside our tent. He assumed it was Ned in the dark of night with the audacity to pee while in his bag into the water bottle, or at least the only one in our tent to have the ability. Apparently he didn't think it would be the woman. I just laughed when I passed the empty pee bottle from our tent to Dick's, and he figured it out.

Throughout the day we told stories, read, and talked books. This was a wonderfully literate crowd. We were a well-educated and well-read group, although backgrounds varied, adding spice to our reading choices: me, a farm girl, age twenty-four; Galen, initially a grease monkey and garage owner, age thirty-nine; Ned a blue-blood ski school director, age thirty-five; Dick, a beat-generation-type writer, age forty-one; and Cam, a full-fledged M.D. and our senior member, age forty-three. Ned and Galen earned their livings as bonafide writers and photographers. I still mixed teaching skiing and freelancing to get by.

Another stormy night, and the morning of July 19 was 20 degrees and still a whiteout. My pulse was down to 72, but Dick's had risen considerably. Toward the very early morning Dick crawled into the other tent, feeling quite sick, to be with Cam. He found it was time to retreat. I slipped into Cam's tent to comfort Dick as best I could by rubbing his hurting head. Just as Ned unzipped the tent to see how things were going, Dick leaped forward and threw up all over just outside the tent door, barely missing Ned. The silver lining was that the warm stomach acids melted through the snow to unveil our missing ice ax.

Cam had tried to quell Dick's monster headaches the previous evening with codeine, Tylenol, and Valium, but this end result was inevitable despite the drugs. Dick was succumbing to altitude sickness. Both Ned and Dick laughed despite the seriousness of the situation, and Ned dug out the ax. Dick said, "This is the second time I've thrown up in ten years. The first was when my waist-length pony tail was cut off." Galen had checked Dick's pulse the night before; it had gone from 64 to 88 this morning, with no activity.

Cam had lectured us on edema, pulmonary and cerebral. We were all going higher than we had ever been before, and we were all in our own adventure zone, entering our own personal unknown. Galen and Ned wouldn't be in new territory until over 20,000 feet, but for the rest of us, we were all in the wonder zone, wondering what the hell was going to happen. Lack of oxygen can cause fluid to leak into the lungs and around the brain as their tissues can no longer hold it.

In pulmonary edema, the lungs filling with fluid, there isn't enough room for oxygen, and one eventually dies. When the brain swells there are symptoms of losing consciousness, losing the ability to think leading to eventually coma and death. Cam felt Dick was suffering from acute altitude sickness; things hadn't progressed to any edema, and we didn't want to wait to see if it did. In Dick's own words, for several hours he had been, "Vacillating between passing out, vomiting, defecating, sweating, shivering, and losing self-control to pain."

We had deep concern for Dick right now, and his only cure was to descend, no other options. Dick needed more oxygen, simple as that.

Dick had had to retreat off Denali once, but it was hoped that, that was an isolated case. Apparently 18,000 feet was looking like Dick's ceiling. Ned and Cam slowly walked Dick back down to camel camp, starting arm in arm to support Dick, with head down and feet dragging as he stepped.

The next morning, July 20, was 5 degrees, the coldest yet but clear. We divided into two rope teams, Cam and Galen and Ned and I. After walking Dick down, Cam and Ned returned, and Dick was able to carry on from camel camp on his own, after resting there. Dick was probably retuning to base camp from camel camp this morning as we were heading up in teams to establish camp two. Galen had been open but brief about expressing his desire to put in this camp, high enough so that he and Ned could make a dash for the summit, weather permitting. He was feeling that either Cam or I could be problematic if we faltered during the summit attempt, and he wasn't keen on either of us going.

Skiing roped together is such a test of friendship or patience, whichever is the stronger of the two. Galen was easy on Cam, who had some difficulties with pace and kick turns as we traversed our way up the slope around crevasses. Cam fell numerous times on the way up under a good load of maybe thirty to forty pounds. It took so much more effort for Cam to skin up to camp two, with the crashing and burning, that he was just beat. Ned and I were somewhat used to having to match each other's pace; it was just annoying to have to whip the rope out from under the skis, as the one traveling in the back had to keep a small amount of rope coiled for a little give and take as we moved yet still have the rope taught enough between the two of us to arrest a fall into a crevasse by either partner.

The sun beat down with intensity; it was draining and piercing as it reflected off the snow. We covered our faces in zinc oxide to keep our skin from frying. We worked to stay well hydrated and paused to eat and drink periodically. From sun up to sun down we labored under loads and around crevasses and found a spot at 20,250 feet to put in camp two. Throughout the day we had glorious views out into the desert surrounding the Pamirs, with fading violets and browns like a watercolor painting as far out as one could see. Muztagata's glaciers cut into the moraine at the bottom, looking like white tongues licking the desert sands.

We all knew, despite our efforts, that we were in an incredible place in an incredible time. The day was passed mostly in silent meditation, punctuated by our regular, heavy, rhythmic breathing. Although we were together the ropes necessitated that we keep our distance from each other for safety, so we all worked quite independently, listening to our own individual thoughts. There is a cathartic feel to these long, arduous days spent in an almost constant, meditative state.

At our site Galen and Ned began digging a platform for the tents, while I began setting up the tents. Cam was having difficulties participating, so I pulled out the stove to give him a focus and asked if he would light it for us so we could all be rehydrating soon. We were working like a team. Snuggled in with tea, cradled in our down bags inside the tents, life was feeling much cozier. I wondered if there was anyone higher than we were right now in the world. Galen seemed to be expressing more confidence in me in small ways in his speech and as we accomplished small tasks together, sorting gear, that sort of thing. I felt he was letting go of my age and sex; I was becoming a person to him, as opposed to being seen as Ned's ward.

July 21 was again a perfectly clear day, an obvious summit day. I had slept very well, had no headache. I also hadn't used any Valium, which we had nicknamed vitamin V, to slow down my body to sleep. Hearts were working, pulses were up, and sometimes a sleeping aid was used to get some much-needed rest instead of thrashing all night and waking with sleep apnea. I had spent three nights at base camp, four nights at camel camp, and four nights at camp one, equaling eleven nights below 20,250 feet, the height of camp two. This amount of acclimatization seemed to be working for me.

Cam announced that he wasn't going anywhere. He felt he wouldn't be able to muster any energy to ascend; he was staying put. We looked at one another, trying to interpret what this meant. My fear was that Galen would ask that I stay with Cam while he and Ned became a team to ascend, but he didn't. Galen had come to accept me as another climber, in good shape, on a good summit day. Cam reassured us he had food and water. He was exhausted but not deteriorating in condition; he would be fine alone. He just couldn't get up now; all he could do was to rest.

The next big decision was what to pack up with us. The weather, as far as we could tell, was looking stable. We opted not to take bivouac gear. But this committed us to determining a turnaround time for retreating to camp two whether or not we reached the summit so that we would not be forced to spend a night out on the upper regions of the mountain unprotected—possibly losing limbs to frostbite or losing our lives. Because biting off close to 5,000 feet of vertical above 20,000 feet is a giant endurance effort, when the rule of thumb is 1,000 feet of vertical a day at altitude, we opted not to take much for weight on our backs in order to ski up as efficiently as possible.

Our protection would be that with skis on our feet we could descend rapidly and thus could climb this amount of vertical with more safety than the Russian and Chinese climbers. We could devote almost the entire day to going up, because the descent would probably be less than an hour. The Russians and Chinese had had to put in more camps to ascend and descend, because they climbed the entire peak on foot.

We set 8 p.m. as our turnaround time, because by 9:00, the sun would be dipping below the horizon. We would have an hour before complete darkness to ski down if we pointed our tips down, no matter where we were on the mountain, at 8 p.m. Moving up to camp two had been our most dangerous day with crevasses and potential for icefalls tumbling. Today was straightforward, and the wind hadn't blown the four to eight inches of new snow from the past days off the mountain. We couldn't believe these ideal conditions—powder, sunshine, and no wind. Skill is involved, of course, but I was learning that so much of high-level mountaineering could be chalked up to staying healthy and just plain luck.

We put on our plastic boots, which had been beside the camp stove in order to thaw enough to pry open as we made our tea and gruel, then headed out. We worked for hours, not saying much. Ned was the strong man breaking trail. Making a track in, up to eight inches of snow may not sound like much, but when you are approaching that kind of elevation any little thing is arduous. You have trouble thinking straight, and you have a very impaired ability to move the lactic acid out of your muscles, which translates into great muscle fatigue.

Galen, on the other hand, was not feeling well. I could hear him breathing heavily behind me. He reiterated, "I feel like I'm falling asleep." I was concerned. The angle on this mountain was relentless. It looked like the back of a white whale, barely rising, but continually rising, never ending. It was psychologically discouraging to keep working without a visual end in sight.

Fortunately Ned was as relentless as the mountain. I seemed to manage to carry on. At 2 p.m. we stopped to brew up, fill water bottles, and ditched our gear in an all-out effort to make the summit. It was now or never. A little while later I threw up the food I had ingested during our break. I felt better and surprisingly felt more energy. Ned was flagging, and I took a turn at breaking trail. Oh boy, did I ever appreciate what Ned had been doing all day long. Galen had told me as I took the lead, "I've never seen a woman perform like you at altitude." Nice words to hear at a time like this. We were all zombies, droning zombies at this point.

Meanwhile, behind us Galen had fallen to his knees a couple of times and picked himself back up again. He was determined. As we waited to collect together to decide who could or would now break trail, I gave Galen the last of my food, some granola and dried fruit. I didn't need it. I'd probably throw it up anyway. I also handed him the Dexedrine Dick had given me from the medical kit in case I was in any trouble on the descent. Most all mountaineering accidents occur on the way down, when you let your guard down and are often totally exhausted and prone to making foolish mistakes. Dick knew I was somewhat green and was probably looking after me by giving me legal speed. I'd never used it before and didn't think this was the time to try. Galen could have it.

I had taken to repeating the names of all my six siblings and the order of their ages. I selected something I knew so well that it was part of me. When I caught myself mixing up my brothers' and sisters' names or their birth order, I became aware that I was suffering from hypoxia more than I realized. It has been shown that chanting or singing can alter consciousness and calms the mind. The brain is also organized to recognize patterns, language, and numbers. Without really knowing why, I was naturally tapping in to a survivor's mode of mind control by continually running my mind through this mental exercise.

After seeing Galen brought to his knees, and as I was throwing up a second time, I knew lack of oxygen was taking its toll. Ned was incredible but was feeling the depletion of having made the way by breaking trail for Galen and me for hours. Galen and I chose to carry on. None of us had been this high before, and feeling altitude effects like this were new to me. I wasn't afraid; I just didn't know my time line for how much energy I would ultimately have.

If I went down, up here, it wasn't good for anyone, not just me alone. Ned assured me I was still in good shape. How the heck he could tell I'll never know, but I bought it. I wanted to carry on. I just needed confirmation. Ned led us on again after our short regrouping. Galen was falling back again but suddenly began divesting himself of any last additional clothing, streamlining himself. Maybe he just needed the food, but for the first time, 400 to 500 feet below the summit, Galen took off. We actually didn't know at the time we were this distance below the summit, but I feel somehow Galen sensed it.

As he passed by me, albeit slowly in reality but in relative terms to the altitude and our state of mind it seemed fast, he left me the last of his water. I'll never forget this for the rest of my life. He could not have given me a better gift, that alone at that moment in time was just what I needed. In our oxygen-deprived states, without much calculation, Galen and I in our own ways had looked after each other. He needed food, I needed water, and in that moment, without thinking about our future personal needs, we gave each other what we had for the greater good of us all. It seemed so simple and logical at the time, but as the years have gone by it has meant more to me. It was a symbol to me of a compassionate state of mind.

For actual survivors of tragedies—shipwrecks, plane wrecks, people

lost in the wilderness, and such—finding empathy seems to be an important quality for surviving these events.[6] Fatigue is not just lack of food and
water; it is also a spiritual collapse, a loss of hope. But when someone helps
someone else, these benevolent actions buoy up both involved; obviously
the one who is aided feels better, and the one taking the action is buoyed
by the response to their helpful action. Bonding, looking after each other,
will increase your odds of survival in more ways than one.

My ears began ringing, and Galen looked like he was floating in front
of me. I could see his yellow hat and his arms out like outriggers, planting
his poles. I knew we must be finally reaching a plateau because of the way
Galen floated in front of me instead of above me, I was looking ahead at
eye level, not looking up. "How far?" I shouted to Ned, who relayed it to
Galen. The answer was five to ten minutes. Ned began surging ahead. I
didn't know if it was after Galen or after the summit. What did it matter?

I was annoyed as I recalled all the conversations to convince me to
leave Colorado and come on this expedition. Ned assured me the summit
didn't matter; we should just do something fun together and see what
happened. Flashes of our New Zealand trip came back to me and the
ending of that trip when Ned had surged ahead then as well. Perhaps a
near goal becomes all too compelling, addicting. I shouted up, "Thanks
for waiting," as I chugged along. Ned paused and found it in him to wait
a couple of minutes, which enriched the whole experience, for me anyway.

As Ned and I carried on side by side, we met Galen 150 yards below
the summit. "There's the summit," he shouted, as he pointed to three
measly hillocks on the plateau. The wind was gusting between twenty to
forty miles per hour. "I'm going down. My feet and hands are like blocks
of wood." Then Galen looked at me and said, "Are you sure you want to
go?" I immediately threw up on his skis and smiled, "Yeah! I came this
far. I'm going to the top." Galen's question seemed like a silly statement to
me, but maybe I looked like I needed some concern. What's 150 yards of
flat sliding after all we'd been through already?

It was deeply satisfying to reach the summit with Ned, together. We
each had someone to share and savor this culmination of planning, dedi-
cation, hard work, and triumph of human spirit. From dream to reality,

we had gone through it all together. The beauty from the summit was overwhelming. The dark hues of violet and brown were enriched by the setting sun. It was 9 p.m. We had done what mountaineers should never do; we had ignored our turnaround time in favor of the summit.

I was plenty warm enough and felt okay with remaining on the summit to savor being, perhaps and most likely, the highest people on our incredible Earth at that moment. We took time to take photos and watch the sun begin to touch the edge of Earth below us, her rays still angling up and reaching the summit, causing an incredible mountain shadow stretching across the desert. A phenomenal light show was surrounding us. The opposite side of the mountain from our ascent was a shear drop-off. There was a feeling of being blown into oblivion looking down that face of the mountain. Ned and I checked each other's bindings as we locked them down to begin our descent. This was no time to make a mistake.

The soft powder, glowing golden in the last, rich rays of sun, was unbelievable to turn in, light and forgiving. My energy was low, but my spirits were high. In my excitement of gliding straight on to gain enough speed for some strong turns, I forgot myself. After about four or five turns I came to an abrupt halt and just leaned over onto my poles and sucked in air as hard as I possibly could. I felt as if I had been suffocating and didn't know it.

Slowly, rhythmically working my way up to the summit had been aerobic. Breathing may have been labored, but it was regular. Skiing down was anaerobic of sorts, as I worked to power my legs left and right, much more quickly than an uphill stride. I had been holding my breath somewhat as I pushed my skis with effort, and when I did breathe, I didn't take in nearly enough oxygen until I was so hypoxic I would have passed out if I hadn't stopped immediately. Wow, I wasn't going to make it down this way. I looked over at Ned, and he was a bit blue too. I hadn't even begun to imagine that I couldn't race down the hill, chasing the shadow of night that was creeping up toward us. I had to pick a slower, more regular rhythm, with wider swung turns, big arcs, and not quick parallel turns.

We easily caught up to Galen, and the three of us enjoyed the last bits of glorious snow, fading light, and unencumbered skiing together. All too soon we stopped to pick up our ditched packs and stove, which we had left when we brewed up at 2 p.m. that afternoon. This extra weight felt crushing to me. My fatigue was showing. Ned had an amazing day, but Galen and I had been fairly comparable in effort and timing, ebbing and flowing at different times. I soaked in as much of the beauty as I could before we all were swallowed into the darkness as we reached camp two. Any later and we could have been in peril.

Cam was very relieved to see us. He was well, feeling somewhat pert now. Galen had already slid into his bag, fully clothed, and Cam was pouring hot drinks for us all. I immediately threw up the cocoa and coughed so much I just kept gagging. I was glad I wasn't in my bag yet so I hadn't retched all over it. I managed to heave it up outside. Cam pulled some pill out of his med kit to stop my gagging so I could lie down and rest, hopefully to sleep. It worked, and I have no more memory of that night from this point.

I woke to the slowest morning I'd probably ever had. The feeling resembled a monster hangover. My system was devoid of food and fluid. I felt as though I'd been beaten around the head, which was fuzzy in its computations anyway. As the world came in to focus around me I was given hot tea to drink. I was sleeping so soundly no one thought there was any problem with my being so empty and didn't wake me. Now I needed to hydrate; there was work to do.

Cam was obviously disappointed that none of us felt we had it in us to make a second bid for the summit. He handled it like a gentleman. He thought more about what he'd gotten out of this trip, as opposed to what he was missing. What a guy. We'd just skied down close to 5,000 feet the day before at much higher elevation, after having first climbed up that same distance. Skiing down only to camp one should have been a breeze. It took us five and a half hours to ski from camp two to camp one, more time than it had taken to ascend between the two camps.

Cam had so many crashes under his heavy pack, taking time to right himself under all the effort, that we took it very easy. This kind of skiing was so far from groomed-slope skiing. The snow wasn't as good down here, not as smooth anymore, and the packs pushed you around on your skis. Balance was optimally important. I felt for Cam as he had to take off his goggles and empty them of snow again and again, as his face was pushed back into the slope by his pack on his back when he toppled.

The next morning Cam woke, rendered snow blind. Simply removing his goggles frequently to clean them, to wipe them devoid of snow, had allowed enough sunlight into his eyes that the typical rough, sandpaper lids of snow blindness had developed. Cam was in great pain every time he tried to blink or rub his eyes. He tried to lie still with his eyes closed as we packed up camp one.

Galen came up with the idea of lashing the skis together to make a sled and lowering the accumulating gear from all the camps down to base. We all walked, controlling the sled with ropes, so we could travel relatively unencumbered, and accompany Cam on foot to base camp, 3,000 feet below. He needed guidance but did very well considering. As we reached base three shots rang out from Chu's pistol. As soon as he knew we had made it, he grabbed his gun and blasted off the shots, just like he told me he would, if I made the summit. He did it out of true excitement for us, but it sure wouldn't hurt his status back in Beijing, the fact that the first group of climbers he had led, the first group of foreign climbers, was successful. And Chu had led the first ski descent of this gorgeous peak, Muztagata.

Then smells of real food hit my nostrils. I had been above base camp for two weeks, and, although I'd been drinking water and tea, I hadn't eaten since our summit day, two days ago. I just couldn't. Wang had started cooking while we hugged, debriefed with Chu, and took commemorative photos. Wang grinned as he offered me some dinner, knowing I was ready to kill for it by the look in my eye. Real sausage, cabbage, and peppers, and it was spiced; it had texture and flavor. Ah, the things we forget and take for granted in life until we no longer have them. Everyone should climb a peak now and then to realize just how good we have it in everyday life.

I was so looking forward to spending time with our Kirkiz friends at their yurts, but I wasn't looking forward to talking with them about their myth of the gardens on the summit. I had surmised, during those many hours of reflection on the mountain, that this story had perhaps encapsulated their culture in the form of a myth to be passed on, and I didn't want to kill the myth. I saw the story as a lynch pin, a keystone to their culture, and if removed by debunking the structure could fall.

To me the spirits in white robes tending the gardens were the actual glaciers themselves, which we had just skied on, covering Muztagata, Ice Mountain Father. The verdant gardens of fruit and walnuts that the spirits were tending were the very gardens of the Kirkiz and all the other cultures in the area, which were fed by the waters of these glaciers. If there were no mountains, this area would be desert, like all the surrounding deserts without the glorious snowmelt, allowing for the grassy meadows called the Pamirs and luscious gardens below.

And as the myths goes these white-robed spirits at the summit of the mountain, tending the gardens of fruit and nuts, lived in peace and harmony. The peace and harmony these spirits lived with is perhaps the very peace and harmony that these cultures, like the Kirkiz, share in their connection to the land and the animals and to each other, which creates a community able to survive in conjunction with the rhythms of our Earth. If the Kirkiz found out this myth wasn't true, would it undermine their culture on a deeper, unconscious level?

I obviously didn't want the responsibility of answering their question. Ned, on the other hand, felt I might be reading too much into this and felt he wouldn't elaborate but would answer: it had been so cold and so late that we didn't see much and hurried down, but in our haste we didn't see gardens, leaving them, he thought, to hold on to whatever they chose; either we didn't search far enough, and thus the gardens were still there, or we didn't see the gardens, so they never were there, ever. We never really did know which way they took the news. They merely seemed to listen.

We had too short time with the Kirkiz before our pickup came, and we were back in Kashgar and reunited with Dick. He had felt so poorly even at base camp; he had been taken to Kashgar and had been living with a frog in his bathroom for company. When Dick toasted me as being the "highest woman in skiing," I hadn't thought about this. I'd heard the guys discussing the fact that they thought this might be the highest ski descent yet done in the world. It was at least the highest descent from the top of a peak, because the fellow who had tried to ski Everest (which they loved to term as "the man who fell down Everest," as he tumbled and just kept going) had selected an elevation perhaps below ours to ski from, but it certainly wasn't from the summit. *National Geographic* would have to do the research to verify these facts for the article Ned was already working on.

As it turned out, I set a high-altitude skiing record for women by surprise. I didn't even know that it was a possibility when I signed up for the expedition. It was nothing I had set out to do. This had been a one-step-at-a-time adventure for me, and I had been lucky. I remained thankful. I recalled everything that had gone into that summit day, all my sewing of my special ski suit with a specific fabric, knitting of my sweater and hat just so, the years of training and careful planning in my training journals, ski racing, technique and speed training, my being number six of seven children, usually having to fight my way in to play with the older siblings, taking my physical and verbal knocks to be included.

Just about everything I could think of came into play on that summit day to get me to the top, along with the camaraderie of my two teammates, Ned and Galen, and all of those below at subsequent camps. Everyone had given me the gift of that day, and I owed them, big time. No one in this world ever does anything alone.

We returned to Beijing, I with my melon for Wang Fuchou, Chu's climbing partner on Everest, because he'd told me so much about their sweetness, and the others returned with stories to tell at all subsequent banquets. Wang laughed hard over the melon, and he hugged me, which is rare for the Chinese in public. All the old Chinese mountaineers were eager to savor the new tales of their beloved peak. Chu was proud. And, of course, Ned chose to strike while the iron was hot and asked amid toasts for permission to come back and climb and ski in Tibet. I would colead the expedition.

CHAPTER 3

FAILURE

I LAY ON MY BELLY, panting on the slope, with fifty pounds on my back pushing me into the fragile latticework of ice-encrusted snow. While descending on rappel, down an almost vertical slope, I had broken through a snow hole covered by a veneer of thin snow and ice, like a big cat into a Burmese tiger trap. I had fallen in above my waist and, without the ability to step up, had to claw my way out. Doing several minutes of pull-ups with extra weight at 20,000 feet might be likened to crawling on the ground using only your hands, while towing a vehicle attached by a chain around your waist. This sounds like a feat for the county fair, but I was in the Himalayas in the Everest Region in the harsh, winter season.

I really felt like I was groveling as I thought about the gorgeous summit and the beautiful weather above us. We had failed. I was flopping like a fish out of water on my way back down the mountain to base camp—retreating with the others just ahead of me when we should have been standing on the summit of this mountain, Pumori. Poor planning and equally poor acclimatization caused by naïveté and doing too much too soon had gotten the best of us. I had barely eaten in five days, hadn't been properly hydrated, and was probably suffering from a concussion. This was only the start of our big circle expedition. How was I going to get through the next two months? How would we all?

After Ned and I returned from the American Friendship Expedition we got jobs working for The North Face, whose gear and clothing we'd used in New Zealand and in China. We teamed up with their designers to create new or improved products. We were proof of the pudding that their gear worked in the most extreme conditions. It also didn't hurt that our *National Geographic* article had just come out about our climb of Muztagata and our record-setting ski descent. I had also done a story about the Kirkiz people living below the mountain for *Powder* magazine, and Dick Dorworth had done another article about our expedition for *Ski* magazine.

I realized people were paying attention to me with this type of media exposure. Me, the ski bum, was receiving notoriety? Consequently I was hired to rock climb for a film set in Yosemite. I fell in love with the place and the hard-core rock climbers living there. Now I was learning the ropes to become a climbing bum too.

The freedom of sleeping out every night, climbing hard every day, running miles on Yosemite's spectacular trails, and partying in the evening around a fire or a camp cookstove, laughing over our tales of near death like they were the latest joke was a dream life, ideal for me. The fact that there were no other women around didn't really even register. By this time, although I felt very female, I just considered myself one of the guys. Perhaps projecting this level of comfort within their ranks, sweating alongside them, swearing, and barking right back at them in good fun allowed the guys to forget I was female. Who knows?

At one point I led out climbing on a 5.10 pitch. I peeled and fell about twenty-five feet to the ground, whacking my head, which spouted blood. Heads are known for draining lots of blood, so I didn't think much of it while laughing at the idea of me having been gripped on the rock while the guys down below just shot the breeze. To them only a 5.13 was worth keeping the rope tight. They wouldn't even use a rope for 5.10. "What's frikkin' wrong with you?" the guys yelled.

I thought they were going to bark at me for missing the tiny flake of rock I should have clung to, which would have kept me from popping off. Instead they couldn't understand why I laughed while blood from my head pooled in the sand. As a kid my older siblings would never let me play with them unless I took their abuse without a whimper. Crying was unheard of. So I'd been groomed for blowing off crashes throughout life just to be where the action was. It was the price I had learned to pay for being allowed in on the fun.

My siblings had tucked me in a tractor tire, swearing they just wanted to see if I'd fit, then pushed me, sending me rolling furiously down a steep hill, circling like a spinning top at the bottom, flopping over to a stop in the center of a four-way intersection of road. They wrapped me in an army blanket and sent me rolling down our long flight of stairs. They sent me down, on all fours, blindfolded, into a maze of missing hay bales exiting out to a fifteen-foot drop-off.

This was life on the farm. Somehow it was transferring into my life of climbing. If I was a good sport I could go where the most fun was. Was this why, regardless of gender, I was so keen to do expeditions? Was it nurture, what I was exposed to in early life, or was it nature, what I had inherited, attitude and drive, which had steered me to expedition life? Are we the product of our environment or our biology?

Apparently laughing under duress, like falling off this climb, wasn't the response these guys were used to from the women in their lives. Although it had taken time for me to realize it, I had been assimilating a more male frame of mind. For the past couple of years I'd admired the likes of Galen Rowell, Dick Dorworth, John Fry, and the other men I had worked with, and of course I loved Ned. I suppose a certain amount of imprinting had been going on, and with the "quit whining and suck it up" kind of mentality in my formative years on the farm, I was being shaped to stifle my emotions and grow a virtual set of balls. I must admit on one ski trip I had earned the name "Jan the Man." The funny thing was I liked it. To me receiving this name was like a rite of passage. I felt accepted as one of the guys. But was I?

All other guys were my pals. Having Ned in my life eliminated complications and competition. I felt I could stay in Yosemite a long time as long as I could continue to evade the park rangers, whose job it was to kick out riffraff like me, staying beyond the allotted time limit for camping in the park. Although I was becoming somewhat of a high-profile mountaineer, sponsored on big expeditions, I felt I could easily forgo all that media exposure for a low-key, high-energy life, deep in the mountains, unknown to anyone.

The jury was out: Was I famous or was I just a climbing and skiing bum? Was I feminine in my outlook, projections, and portrayal, or was I as much a guy as the guys? But more importantly was I happy? I was having the time of my life. I didn't feel trapped by gender or success expectations set by society. Still, I was a female working with men, and it showed. We'd have the jokes about who would get to belay Jan when she led out, because on belay below me, the guys could look up my climbing shorts. Frankly I thought the jokes were funny and was glad they had noticed I was indeed female.

Upon my return to Vermont, Ned gave me a look that put me on the defensive. It's a sort of wild-eyed euphoria that I'm afraid to trust. "Jano, I've got it!" he announced. I knew he was ready to let me in on his fully matured expedition plan. Ned and I had received permission to ski in Tibet from the Chinese Mountaineering Association after our successful, record-setting ski descent of Muztagata. While I had been in Yosemite, Ned had been pondering how to turn this ski jaunt in mysterious, little-known Tibet into a viable, full-blown, commercial expedition that some sponsor would find worthy of funding. When planning an expedition Ned was like a dry sponge dropped in a puddle, soaking up water until completely saturated. Only when he had soaked up as much information and creative possibility as he could would he pronounce an expedition ready for funding.

"From everything I can research, more than one hundred people have stood on top of Everest, but no one has gone completely around. We'll ski in Tibet and get permission to ski in Nepal. We'll start here by skiing Pumori!"

Flummoxed, I thought this expedition was to be co-led. Where was the co part in the design of the deal? The contour lines of Pumori on the map, stacked tightly together, looked more like thousands of feet of in-run on consecutive fifty-meter ski jumps than a slope suitable for skiing. I knew I couldn't trust Ned alone with maps while I was in Yosemite, climbing. He traced the route around Everest with his finger, indicating five passes up to 22,000 feet to climb and ski, along with climbing to the summit of the nearly 24,000-foot Pumori, which means "daughter peak," sitting right beside Mother Everest herself. And to up the ante Ned was proposing to do the ascent of Pumori during the desperate winter season. It was the only time he could get permission for the ascent so that it would dovetail with the Tibetan portion of the expedition.

When I suggested that we do a wider more cultural circle around Everest, which would include meeting indigenous peoples, Ned gave me a look that said, "My plan is it. I can sell this, and this is a worthy, world-class adventure." So I made a deal with Ned: If he wanted his circle so bad, how about he make it happen. With permission and politics it's a full-time job putting the nuts and bolts together and shaping an expedition into a slick package to sell. Meanwhile I would go back to Yosemite to live in the high country of Tuolumne Meadows at about 9,000 feet for the next couple of months, climbing and training for this technically demanding, high-altitude expedition. He went for it, grudgingly.

This circle expedition would have way more technical climbing than we experienced in New Zealand, at almost as high an elevation as we had gone on Muztagata. This was more than adding all our previous expeditions together into one. I needed to be honed for this trip. I needed to get into killer shape. But I knew what was coming. I was given the logistics of organizing and planning food and equipment and the seemingly endless packing and recording of gear and supplies and communicating with companies we'd be working with on this project. I got the domestic, secretarial, and organizational projects, just like most women. Yet regardless of gender we needed to play to our strengths to pull this off, despite the cliché of our roles.

I held out in Yosemite as long as I could, swimming across Teneja Lake, running rough trails, and climbing the beautiful rock-walled domes daily. Working out at 9,000 to 10,000 feet doesn't make you fast; speed is difficult to develop in thin air. But elevation training does make you strong and enduring. My small, yellow dome tent was a nest of warmth, allowing me to curl up out of the elements in my otherwise totally exposed life. There is such peace in the simplicity of eat, sleep, climb, and train. For me this was living. Yes, I'm sure my parents were wondering why they bothered with my college education. When a guy became a bum it was disgraceful. But what did it mean when a female became one?

Ned eventually secured a sponsor, which freed up funds for our team to meet for planning. We chose the Grand Tetons of Jackson Hole, Wyoming, where Kim Schmitz, a prospective Everest Grand Circle Expedition member, was guiding clients on climbs. Kim, with high cheekbones, a stunning white smile, sandy hair, and the body of a god, was Ned's selection for climbing leader on Pumori. Kim was soft spoken and had a gentleness about him.

When I met Kim I could see why Ned had warmed to him. Kim was not overtly challenging, and in the arena of expeditions, where strong egos can get rubbed raw, Kim would be an easier blend in the mix of tough characters who would be inclined to accept a wild mission like ours. But Kim was cunning, I found. I arrived a day before Ned, so Kim suggested we go for a run. Before I realized it we were scrambling on rubble up the side of the Grand Teton. This is just the kind of thing I love, but I might have chosen something to wear other than the light nylon running shoes, thin nylon racing shorts, and tiny sports bra.

We'd been running for hours, and there was a tent set up at about 11,000 feet, apparently a campsite for clients taking a two-day guided climb to the summit. Kim said he just wanted to lie down for a bit. I waited and stretched in the sun. This was just like another day of training in Tuolome Meadows in Yosemite for me. Kim emerged eventually, refreshed, and said, "Let's keep going up." Well, it looked pretty steep, but I didn't want to spoil his fun. Before I knew it we were on the classic route blazed by Paul Petzholdt, who had to back off the crux 5.9 move on the first attempt. I didn't know anything about this route until Kim told me, as I looked at this exposed section of the climb. We had hit the 5.9 move, me in my flexible running shoes, tiny shorts, bra, and all.

"Kim, spot me on this, will you?" I asked. We had no ropes, harnesses, nothing. "What can I do? If you go, you go here," he said simply. We'd been climbing rock for some time, and the trip back, climbing down what we'd come up (which I reviewed in a flash of instant replay), would be overtly dangerous. Like closing the door on a roomful of gremlins, I shut out my mind's voice. I looked up, spanned the chasm below me with my legs, and made the move before fear had a chance to grease my hand reaching for the hold with sweat.

When I rock climbed I was used to supportive, flat, sticky-soled climbing shoes, chalk on my hands like a gymnast to avoid slippery sweat, and some clothing on my body that amounted to more than underwear. I made the move but would have died if I didn't. The rest of the climb was straightforward as Kim and I climbed quickly in sync. When we reached the top I was in wonder to see men coiling ropes with more ropes slung around their bodies, wearing big Gor-Tex jackets, helmets, and extensive climbing racks, while the wind buffeted them at the summit of the Grand Teton, elevation 13,770 feet.

The men stared at me, and I felt naked. I had no gear, ropes, helmet, not even clothes. I figured Kim was a guide here; I'd never been to Wyoming before. He was running, so I would too. I thought that was what you did here. Boy did I feel stupid. If I'd missed the crux move and fallen hundreds of feet down, people would smirk and say, "Well, she deserved to die. What was she doing there, on a big mountain in her running shoes and underwear, climbing with no rope?" About this time Kim yelled, "I'm freezing my ass off. Let's get out of here." My turn to stare. How would we get out of here I wondered? "There's an easy descent over here," Kim yelled again and took off.

I snapped to and took off with a wave to the well-clad climbers. Below the summit the wind was blocked, and we crashed and burned our way down, running and leaping. We eventually made our way to Kim's favorite local bar and began drinking while the day was ending. Kim, to my surprise, was having trouble holding his liquor. As he got sloshed he began almost babbling to me. This whole day had been a test, he admitted. He'd been afraid to trust me on our expedition, seeing me merely as a woman and on the team only because I was Ned's girlfriend.

I matched him beer for beer and ended up getting him home and shoving him into his own bed. He wasn't going to get there by himself. I left for my own cabin. But I heard several times that evening, although slurred, that he was impressed with my fortitude and endurance. I was okay. Kim felt he could trust me. I just had to solo the Grand Teton in my underwear and running shoes to earn his trust. I had to break trail for Galen Rowell at almost 25,000 feet and puke all over his skis while refusing to quit, just to earn his trust. What is it with these guys?

Renowned late psychologist Carl Jung, who fascinates me with his insights, nailed this idea with his term the *collective unconscious,* the storehouse of memory traces from all previous generations in our brains. This collective unconscious harbors universal tendencies to think and perceive in certain ways.[1] As men, perhaps Kim and all the other guys were still seeing me as something less? If this had any bearing on me, maybe unconsciously these guys just couldn't envision a woman in their male ranks. They literally had to see it to believe it. Perhaps it was a deeply embedded psychological thing, created over time, I concluded. If so, it was going to take a few generations to turn this Titanic of thought around. To them, unconsciously I may still have been Eve, just one of Adam's ribs, or Jan, one of Ned's.

The next day Ned and Steve McKinney showed up. Steve McKinney, who had held the world speed-skiing record for years, would be our super skier. He was equally as stellar looking as Kim, with piercing eyes and a laugh that was wild. His body—well, to hold a tuck at about 130 miles an hour when the wind is prying your body open with giant force, let's just say he was built. The four of us stuck to routes and maps by day and partied together by night. We were a stalwart crew in mind and body, with an aptitude for a good time.

Ned had put the route, team, and sponsor, together. He'd paid his dues, and mine were about to begin over the next couple of months in Vermont. I developed a high-altitude snack bar with our local health-food store for nutrition when you just don't want to eat at elevation, somewhat of a precursor to all the energy bars on the market today. I ordered clothing and tents from sponsors. I planned menus for on the mountain and off, called those in the know to find out what we could purchase at markets in the Himalayas for food, brought in the packing barrels, made lists locating everything, and so much more. Ned's house, which I shared with him, was strewn with food and gear throughout.

Crampons laced up over here, tents popped up over there. We were already living the expedition. I stayed in touch with Kim and Steve concerning food preferences and clothing sizes until we heard Kim had other expedition obligations and the timing wasn't going to work out. However, he would meet us at base camp following the Pumori climb to do the remaining portion of the circle with us. Devastated, Ned was in a quandary for a climbing leader on the quite technically demanding Pumori.

I suggested Jim Bridwell, the Jimi Hendrix of climbing, radical, edgy, and the best there is. He is legendary within the walls of Yosemite for the routes he's pioneered, but he'd just completed his first monumental alpine ascent in Alaska on the Moose's Tooth, making him a full-fledged mountaineer. I'd assisted Jim, who was working for a TV crew, while in Yosemite so I could earn some cash. I had been pretty broke. Jim and I had had some good laughs when I jumarred* up a tree

---

*A jumar is one type of mechanical ascending device that is placed around a rope. It grabs the rope when pulled in one direction (in this case down) and slides freely when pulled in the other (in this case up), thereby stopping the person attached to it if she moves (or falls) one direction, and allowing her to move freely (or climb) in the other. (Similar to the way a socket set on a ratchet "grabs" when twisted one direction and moves freely when twisted the opposite.) You ascend, or jumar, by scooting the mechanical device up the rope with your hands as you climb.

to hand him film, with no leg loops attached to my jumars. That's like climbing a tree by only doing pull-ups the whole way, with your legs dangling.

Ned thought I was nuts. Jim, he felt, wouldn't be okay with the likes of us. Ned was a solid climber, nothing flashy, but as strong as any you could find for going the distance. He was afraid Jim might be dominant, competitive, and ego driven and not give a rat's ass about Ned's leadership. Peculiar, I thought. I had no fear about working with Jim, but then again I was female. I didn't have the coronary-prone behavior of males, the aggressive, hostile, competitive, impatient nature that might shave a few years off the average man's life.[2] By the tender age of two, studies have shown that these masculine attributes already separate the boys from the girls.[3] Maybe for Ned his alpha-male behavior clashing with another alpha male stirred some primal male mentality. A male doesn't invite another strong male into his territory unless he is sure he can still be dominant. Too much aggressiveness and competition wouldn't allow for the survival of the species, let alone the survival of the expedition.

I won out this time. We called Jim, and he was easygoing and ready. Jim by nature was quick and fast and highly technical; Ned was long and strong and very practical. These two were a complementary match if there ever was one. Jim didn't want Ned's responsibilities, and Ned didn't want Jim's. This was obvious from the beginning, so we were spared a male pissing match. I realized that is what had, perhaps, been going on in the past between Allan and Ned in the New Zealand Alps and between Galen and Ned on Muztagata—the "who's in charge here" kind of friction. This is what I meant by strong egos getting rubbed raw. After two previous expeditions with men, I started to see patterns. I hoped my being involved in team selection would help change the existing pattern.

Before takeoff Ned and I had to do a press conference for our sponsor in New York City. I was wowed by the fact that our sponsor would pay us $300 per day for our work preparing for and giving the conference, even $150 for our travel days. To a climbing/ski bum this was unheard of sums of money. Between this and The North Face stipend, I guess you could say I was a professional athlete. In New York numerous national magazines and newspapers were to assemble, watch our preclimb presentation of just what we intended to accomplish on our Everest Grand Circle Expedition, and ask questions for their articles.

The potential drawback was the sponsor itself, R. J. Reynolds Tobacco Company. I didn't smoke and would never advocate it. When R. J. Reynolds offered to pay all costs for the expedition, I had to sit down and talk to my dad about whether this was ethical or not. He looked at me as if I were crazy to even question the idea. Of course I should accept their money. My dad had smoked a corncob pipe all his adult life and the occasional cigar. I saw smoking as evil. My father pragmatically pointed out that I needn't associate with their product, just their money. Rationalization was rearing its head.

Ned and I talked with the sponsor representatives, and they confirmed we never had to mention or advocate smoking. They were completely aware that we didn't smoke and wouldn't smoke. We knew at the time R. J. Reynolds was doing promotions and giving away cigarettes at bars across the country. Our rationale was that we would use their money to support athletics and take money away from programs as insidious as the bar promotions. Also, R. J. Reynolds was an umbrella company for many other companies, such as fruit producers and other benign businesses. In a sense aligning with us was a way for R. J. Reynolds to advocate adventure and to perhaps clean up its image.

Jim and Steve flew to Ned's home in Vermont from California. I had my hands full organizing the gear and the guys the last couple of days before our marathon flight to Nepal. One of our biggest laughs en route was over the small Pakistan fellow who tried to separate me from the boys during a flight change in Karachi. I was tracking our twenty-nine bags, and one bag was missing after my careful count. Out on the tarmac, during the dark of night, I was flinging bags around on an open-bedded truck looking for the one that had disappeared. You could never get away with this in the States, but this was Pakistan and years ago.

This local man, who had followed me, climbed over the bags and put one hand on each of my breasts, which have plenty of high relief. He threw his head back looking into the night and said, "Your breasts, this must be where you get all your strength." Personally I thought this was hilarious. But Ned, who had been looking for me, started stumbling across the bags on the moving truck when he saw this. Before Ned could reach me, he saw me shove the guy away with such quick force that the Pakistani dumped on his ass amid the sea of bags. In a single moment Ned's face turned from tight aggression into surprise followed by loud laughter.

No one was even supposed to be on this truck, but I felt responsible for all the bags and barrels. I'd simply jumped on the truck to find what was ours before it went to Timbuktu instead of Kathmandu. This fellow had followed us to the bus, which would transport us to the flight, and told the men to get on, trying to separate me from them in the throng of people. I had already planned to ditch out before the bus to sneak a look through the baggage anyway and recognized this Pakistani fellow massaging my breasts as the one who had tried to divide us. Ned had hopped off the bus stairs as soon as he realized I wasn't with them and ran to my rescue. I found the bag anyway, so that was good.

I guess these Pakistani men weren't used to seeing women in close-fitting athletic clothing throwing heavy weight around. I'd also been told they thought Western women, especially Americans, were looking for action wherever and whenever a man wanted to give it to them. Perhaps this was because we were not covered with a veil and of good Muslim persuasion like their women. I didn't feel threatened; I just felt sorry for the women of Pakistan. I had learned about the liberation of women in China under Mao for better or worse. I wondered when a liberation of sorts would ever happen for these Muslim women. The imbalance between male and female in this area of the world has created such a complex, negative life for both sexes by suppressing the female tendencies and expression in their culture. Women need a voice for a balanced society.

Kathmandu seemed vibrant, dusty, and ancient to my weary senses when we arrived. Unlike China, it was wild and free here, almost a frenzy of life. Yet already there were signs of the communist revolution, which are still occurring today. There were chants shouted in the streets and a strike going on, but today it has escalated to a confusing, bloody battle between the Nepalese police and a citizen group called the Maoists. The Communist Party was breaking up in China, and it was emerging among the citizens in Nepal to fight the monarchy. We are a strange species, we humans, trying to organize ourselves in different ways and killing each other in the process.

The next morning at breakfast as we listened to some soft, eerie Indian music while the guys were falling asleep in their plates of eggs from jet lag, we heard a shrill, piercing, staccato, electronic sound playing "The Yellow Rose of Texas," mysteriously and seemingly out of nowhere. Jim lifted his face off his plate and with a sheepish grin admitted, "I don't know how to turn the damned thing off." None of us could. From Kathmandu to the height of Pumori we heard "The Yellow Rose of Texas" at 8 a.m. sharp, a constant joke and reminder of home in a larger sense while hanging off cliffs in the Himalayas. This was the beginning of many quirky jokes on this expedition.

We drove through the cacophony to an old building housing our outfitter, Mountain Travel Nepal, and Bobby Chettri, our expedition facilitator, at the edge of town. Here we also met Anu, our Sherpa sirdar, or leader of our porters. He was shorter than I, but muscular and young, maybe my age. His face was very handsome and he was shy. He introduced himself and right away let us know that this was his first time as sirdar. Our mountain of gear had arrived, and he was checking on it for us. He and I connected and bonded over managing the gear, which had been, up until now, my responsibility.

With Anu, I now had someone to help me manage and pack into loads: double-plastic climbing boots with closed cell foam inners, double-leather cross-country skiing boots, ice axes, ice hammers, 9-mm rope, 7-mm rope, webbing, ice screws, deadman anchors, snow stakes, carabiners, crampons, jumars, cross-country skis, climbing skins, ski poles, gaiters, polypropylene long underwear, overboots, sleeping pads, high-altitude meals and snacks for forty days, cooking stoves, lighters, pots, fuel containers, water bottles, down booties, running shoes, snow shovels, repair kits, first-aid kits, headlamps, batteries, mitts, gloves, socks, hats, silk balaclavas, face masks, dark glasses, goggles, sun cream, toothbrushes, nail clippers, drinking mugs, spoons, backpacks, duffel bags, books, writing tablets, tape recorders, cassettes, eight 35-mm cameras, two hundred rolls of 35-mm film, 16-mm camera, 16-mm film, air tickets, visas, travelers' checks, and lots of cash.

Oh geez, and I forgot to mention sleeping bags, Gor-Tex pants and coats, down pants, coats, vests, and who knows what else I've forgotten. I had gathered this for our four climbers and several Sherpa porters and had gotten it all to Kathmandu. Now Anu would see that it all made it to Pumori base camp, with my help and my never-ending lists. Ned was still wrestling with obtaining permission, believe it or not. Here we were ready to climb, and we were only allowed to climb Pumori. Bobby Chettri informed us we didn't have authorization to go over the three passes up to 22,000 feet to skirt around Everest for our first half circle. In shock Ned took immediate action.

We all zoomed off to the Ministry of Tourism to speak with a Mr. Sharma after Ned briefed us, "Whatever you do, *don't* mention the circle. They might get suspicious that we're up to something, maybe illegal. They don't want us near *any* border. If they say no, the whole expedition goes down. We've committed to our sponsors, the press. Just don't say anything about the circle!" Upon arrival, when Ned had explained that we intended to "trek" the three passes after climbing Pumori, Sharma answered immediately: "I would not recommend such a trek. No, it is much better for you to stay in the Khumbu [the populated area on the approach to Everest]. The high passes are no place for a man in the winter. It is not sensible."

Steve McKinney stiffened and blurted out, "You must let us go! We have to go. We have to get around Everest." Ned kept it together, but I know his airway must have been constricting with tension. "Everest? I thought you were climbing Pumori?" Sharma queried. "What he means is that to climb over the high passes, we will have to detour around

Everest. The important thing is to see more of Nepal. It is our first visit," countered Ned.

When Ned had quietly investigated crossing the border between Nepal and Tibet to make a complete, uninterrupted circle around Everest, he'd received a resounding no from both countries. We determined to do two half circles instead, so the expedition wouldn't become an international embarrassment. If we were caught crossing these borders we could potentially be banned from both countries on future travels and expeditions, if we weren't shot for being spies. No sponsor would ever want any part of these illegalities. So it was certain our Everest Grand Circle Expedition would be in two halves.

Back in our taxi, headed for our hotel, we skillfully dodged bicycles, rickshaws, tractors, and other bruised autos. Our driver leaned on the horn rather than the brakes for control of our destiny. A little boy squatting over an open sewer gutter jumped up as we approached, pulling up his pants at a run. Steve hung out the window, ogling tiered pagodas and spiked temples sprinkled between open-stalled shops and small wooden buildings. People wandered the streets shopping and talking in the thick haze of car and motorcycle engine smoke. "What a place of contrasts," Steve remarked. "We're going to be continually walking off the edge of our assumptions." We had already heard rumors about yogis eating themselves piece by piece and the latest sighting of tigers in the Terai.

Jim jumped out of the car and headed down the alley where our driver had told us we might find some climbing gear, bartered and left behind by other climbers in exchange for gifts to bring home to lonely girlfriends around the world. When we resumed our drive to our hotel Steve queried Jim, "What did you get?" as Steve admired his own fake yak bone artifact. "I got a 600-footer so I can run it out if I want." This means he can climb for 600 feet on one rope and not stop to put in protection for himself, or belay anyone else up. He could cover a lot of vertical, fast, this way. I suppressed a motherly instinct to caution him. That's an awfully long fall if you blow it climbing.

"Yup, 600 feet, and it's polypropylene." Poly rope has an advantage.

It's light, like a waterskiing rope. The disadvantage is that one wouldn't want to take a lead fall on it because it would be weak. "And I got a great deal," Jim smiled, "I got it secondhand." We couldn't help it; we all burst out laughing. This long, thin, used rope would be strung right out, all 600 feet, by Jim, with little to no protection when he led our climb. He felt confident he wouldn't fall, which was good, because this rope, potentially already damaged by previous use, would just snap and let Jim fly through the air, in front of our eyes, thousands of feet up on a cold Himalayan peak. It was clear that Jim had taken many risks in his life, and we would be too by association.

In a couple of days we found ourselves in a De Havilland Twin Otter flying east along the southern escarpment of the Himalayas. Although the plane could seat nineteen people, we had it pretty much to ourselves. The ceiling, which was duct-taped together, was typical of the plane's interior and exterior appearance. The local airport that we had taken off from had lax, unorthodox procedures, pilots without uniforms, and shabby pit crews, which was unnerving to say the least. I surveyed the interior of our plane searching for light through the cracks and had tried to size up our pilots as I watched them—through the missing cockpit door—get ready for takeoff. I figured this would be as good as any ride I'd had at the county fair.

When it came time to land, as I peered down through the doorless opening into the cockpit, all that was visible through the gritty windshield was steep hillside. We seemed to be flying right into it. There had to be an airstrip under us—somewhere. We dove down, and I saw what looked like only two hundred yards of gravel strip that ended at the hillside. When we actually touched our wheels down, it was as if we were a can thrown onto the ground—thunk. The brakes were applied full force as we lurched and screeched to a halt, just yards before the looming hillside, barely apparent through the swirling dust and dirt we had kicked up. We were in Lukla, a small grouping of simple buildings surrounding the gravel airstrip, set at 9,000 feet.

As soon as we poked our heads out of the door to deplane we saw Anu, our sirdar, being the sharp, muscularly tight, fireplug of a guy that he is, with a grin that could calm anyone's fears. His face radiated excited charm. Anu had style; he dressed more Western with a t-shirt and jeans. The other Sherpas had more traditional clothing, dark padded pants and dark cloth coats. Miraculously within an hour our equipment, including our skis, had been distributed among the Sherpas Anu had hired, and we were off down the trail. We had six Sherpas in all, but Anu's main men were Angpura, a general handyman, and Phutashi the cook.

Angpura reminded me of the Cheshire cat in *Alice in Wonderland* with his round face and big, perpetual grin. Phutashi's skin had been pitted by chicken pox, and his lower jaw and teeth protruded beyond his upper teeth. Phutashi was proud of his Western-style pants and wore the same pair of blue-and-gold houndstooth check polyester pants for the whole expedition, only alternating the shirts he wore with them.

Because the Sherpas carried all our loads we climbers were free to hike, gaze, and converse along the trail, soaking up where in the world we were, without a care. None of us had ever been to these great mountains before. We were walking through an amphitheater of phenomenal snowy peaks. As we trekked I could hear the familiar creaky squeakings of my swaying pack and smell my salty sweat. I felt I had to carry a few personal things. I couldn't handle being totally taken care of!

We ducked into our first Sherpa teahouse, a simple stone hut, to warm ourselves and drink. I sat between Ned, a past New England, Ivy League Olympian, and Steve, the once long-haired, bearded hippie from California who dropped out of high school and left the U.S. Ski Team to push the limits of speed. They were different men now drawn to the same adventure. It was dark inside and wisps of smoke from the open fire hung in the air. Seating was rudimentary, but the Sherpani, wearing a dress that wrapped around her with a wool apron tied in front, served us while smiling and trying to teach us some simple Nepali words.

We started with tea, then realized we could have eggs, potatoes, and, most wonderfully, *chang,* a rice or barley beer served anytime, anywhere. I went for the chang. We had to hydrate, so I legitimized many chang stops throughout the day. When we reached our campsite for the night the Sherpas had already set up our tents and laid out our bags; they served us sweet, hot milk tea when we arrived. Dinner was on the way. All the Sherpas treated us like royalty, but it was Phutashi who would rouse us in the early morning with his soft voice by offering us sweet milk tea as we lay muffled and snug in our down bags. To me this luxury was unbelievable. I was quietly astounded to see that it seemed to please the Sherpas to serve us well.

Hundreds of years ago some Tibetans migrated into the Everest Region of Nepal, which they called the Khumbu. These Tibetans came to be known as the Sher Pas, meaning "east people" in Tibetan, who in turn created their own dialect and culture based on trade. The Khumbu is centered around the world's highest peak called Sagarmartha by the Sherpas, who told me it meant "Goddess of the Universe." When Sagarmartha was determined to be the world's highest peak by India's surveyor general Sir George Everest, who measured it as part of his Great Trigonometrical Survey of 1920, it was named after him by the Western world.

The kings of Nepal had kept their country closed to the outside world until about 1950. Until that time the Sherpas carried goods for barter over the crest of the Himalayas, allowing international trade from China to India to flourish on foot before the steamships brought goods from Asia to India. Then Nepal opened itself to the outside world, allowing the Sherpas to begin their work hauling loads for international expeditions and trekkers, just as China took over Tibet in 1950 and closed Tibet's borders to the outside world.

On our second day on the trail we were to enter the Sagarmartha Park, a project backed by Sir Edmund Hillary, one of the first two men to stand on the summit of Mount Everest, with Sherpa Tenzing Norgay being the other. When Hillary went up to Everest base camp his party cut hundreds of porter loads of juniper bushes to burn for cooking and such. Every subsequent expedition did the same until Hillary himself said, "Now the juniper has virtually been wiped out. The whole area up there is just a desert now, which is all eroding."

Soon the number of visitors swelled with the influx of groups of trekkers, along with more climbing expeditions. Sherpas chopped wood to cook for these visitors and to build lodges to house them. With the wood supply dwindling they began to burn yak dung, like the Native Americans who burned buffalo chips for cooking. This depleted the soil of nutrients as the dung had acted as a natural fertilizer, which further complicated the situation. The Sherpas were watching their land erode and literally wash into the rivers and out to the Bay of Bengal during the annual monsoon rains.

Hillary worked with the local Sherpas to understand the concept of a park, with designated rules of use to preserve the 480 square miles encompassing the south side of Everest. It was a strange concept for the locals at first, to be told what they could and couldn't do with their own land. They too needed money to feed their children, and cutting and burning wood and building wood shelters for the trekkers earned them money. Why shouldn't they cut their wood and have money like all the other people trekking through and visiting them from around the world?

Traditional education had been handled by the Buddhist lamas and monasteries and was being supplanted by schools introducing Western ways. Foods cooked for trekkers was changing the local diet; Western clothing and music was fast becoming popular. Heavy traffic and foreign values came so quickly that the Khumbu in particular resembled an adolescent child, struggling to keep up with its own growth spurt, tripping over its own feet and unable to control its changing voice. The Sherpa culture, which had developed facing East, was all too suddenly facing West. As I entered the park I was too aware that we were part of the problem.

Just after entering the Sagarmartha area, Angpura motioned for me to come into a Sherpa home. He couldn't tell me what was up, but it looked like he was trying to show me something dead by the looks of his hand and face gestures. I heard this collective, low, guttural, repetitive sound above me. It was a human sound, but unlike anything I'd heard before. The building was a barn at entry level, housing some yaks, and had a ladder in the center, which I groped in the dark to ascend.

Above, the room had tiny, square windows with no glass and was so dark I had to wait for my eyes to adjust. Eventually I saw smiling faces seated around low, rudimentary tables drinking tea and chang.

Men and women wore the usual dark, wool tunics, men with pants, women with striped aprons. The women wore silver, coral, and turquoise earrings and long necklaces. They were all dressed up for the occasion and were facing an altar with numerous flickering candles made of yak butter and gorgeous yak butter sculptures. There were rice mounds about eight inches high looking like little snowmen, and some Sherpas were drizzling red dye over the rice. The sound I'd heard was chanting from the monks dressed in red robes, sipping tea, rocking back and forth. I was in the midst of a funeral. Now there were drumbeats punctuated by horns made of bone. Angpura pointed to his leg; I'm assuming he meant human thighbone.

I whispered the only word I knew, *namaste,* while bowing my head with my hands pressed together against my chest. There were head nods all around, and the greeting returned to me. I leaned up against a wooden beam, steadied my camera against it, and took a timed exposure. Later, I would see that the photo came out beautifully. I blended into the background to observe, careful not to disturb for about twenty minutes.

Then Ned came in bumping and banging, cameras clanking around his neck, stuck his tripod into a rice snowman on the floor and was asked to move. You could see he was almost frantic to get a shot. The Sherpas in attendance simply watched him, and then a monk rubbed his forefinger and thumb together indicating money, which Ned handed over. Oddly enough my photo was the one used; it was better than the several Ned took with the tripod.

I slunk out of the room and descended before Ned even noticed I was there, feeling guilty and a bit ashamed. This scene represented all the changes in the economy and culture in the Khumbu to me. Outside, an English-speaking Sherpa named Sange, a sirdar who had learned our language through his work, cheerfully told Steve and Jim this was his father's funeral. The head lama, the highest-ranking monk, had just slept a couple of days with his father's cadaver, and the body had been burned on a rock above, on the hillside.

This ceremony and celebration inside would go on for ten days in total, but in a week this high lama would inspect his father's ashes to learn how his father would be reborn. Then there would be a big party. Sange's father had become a lama himself, after Sange's mother died, and he had cloistered himself in his own monastery. Simplistically, if one has been bad in this life, one is reborn as a suitable animal for your indiscretions, or if one is good, one is reborn in a favorable human life. If one has been enlightened, learned all human lessons of kindness and compassion, shall we say, while alive, then he or she will cease to be reborn and will have reached the ultimate state of nirvana, being one with all being.

I knew that there had been a system of rebirth taught as part of the Catholic religion, but it was stricken out of practice and the belief system hundreds of years ago. Fueled with thoughts concerning religious and cultural definitions of proper human behavior, I sped my way up a 3,000-foot uphill stretch to the major trade village of Namche Bazaar, set at just about 12,000 feet. Whether it was Taoism in China, Buddhism in the Himalayas, or Catholicism, people structured their culture around ways to be "good" and to be at peace, such as being at one with the Tao or reaching nirvana or heaven. Were these states all in the mind? Were they the same state of mind? To me the idea of Buddhism and compassion are feminine traits; they involve caring and nurture at their core. I found this very compelling.

I eventually made my way through the maze of tiered pathways to Anu's house, Everyone in town knew where Anu lived. Inside I had to climb the lower barn ladder to rise into the upper living space. There was an open fire on the hearth and a huge copper pot holding water and, of course, sweet milk tea waiting for me. But there were no men waiting for me? I expected everyone to be sitting around wondering where I was, while I had looked at vendors' wares in town. Given time the men came trudging in, looking whipped. After a wonderful dinner of yak stew Ned threw up.

Apparently the altitude gain was affecting the fellas. We'd climbed a total of 4,000 feet today and had risen more than that the day before coming up from Kathmandu. My pulse was sixty beats per minute. Life was good. Anu led us into a room adjacent to the families' living quarters, which was a well-kept Buddhist monastery. We had to step up over the doorway stoop, built up to trip the evil spirits, Anu told us. The temple walls were a frescoed panorama of brightly colored creatures. Ned wondered about one figure in particular, a four-armed wild thing holding a tiny, helpless human in its grip and squeezing the life out of it like toothpaste from a tube.

As we unrolled our sleeping bags, Steve began to recite Coleridge's poem "Kubla Khan," with lines such as "A savage place! as holy and enchanted / As e'er beneath a waning moon." But I was too tired to look or speculate anymore and fell asleep as soon as I lay down. The next morning we were awakened by Mama Anu, as we affectionately called her. She went to a chest-high altar on which sat a large Buddha and other small figures. In front of them were seven large silver cups and fourteen smaller ones.

Chanting softly Mama Anu wiped the cups and filled them with water for the good spirits to drink. Then she rotated a three-foot-high prayer wheel set into the altar, and a bell rang delicately each time the wheel made a complete turn. Anu came behind his mother with a ladle of burning incense to "cleanse our souls." It reminded me of the Catholic priests when they walked through the church during ceremonies with burning incense for a similar reason. Anu's family, like those of the other Sherpas I met, were neither proud nor embarrassed about their firm beliefs. Their only concern was to share the benefits with us. I noticed Mama Anu was the keeper of tradition: she led the way, Anu followed. Women are the holiday and celebration machinery of the world, the keepers of the family culture.

Anu announced apologetically that he'd need the next day to rustle up some high-altitude porters; carrying any loads higher than Namche was considered a bigger job, and some of his Sherpas were finished here. We were all relieved to have a day to rest and get our physical and mental bearings. I was still feeling like I'd slipped through the looking glass, even though Steve and Jim were reveling in experiencing the things they'd read about for years, and we all certainly needed to acclimatize. Ned remained focused on the circle goal and was perhaps less influenced by the culture around us.

Throughout the day we meandered around town, read, ate at tea shops, and simply enjoyed where in the world we were. Steve, of course, went shopping. This time he surprised us all when he returned in the evening. Instead of plastic "yak bone" carvings or fake antique trinkets, he had what we all thought was an authentic meteorite. It looked like a clover leaf the size of my palm and was extremely dense and heavy, very black and smoothed from spinning. The vendor had asked so little for it that Steve wasn't sure the man knew what he had for sale. We dozed off that night imagining how this meteorite came to be on the edge of the Himalayas. Was it through trade, or did it land near?

In order to trek to our next site, Thyangboche, we needed to descend to the Dudh Kosi River again and then back up even higher in elevation than Namche to the Thyangboche Monastery, where the highest lama lived, the lama who had performed the rites to the funeral we had experienced. Although we stuck together most of the day, when we hit the uphill, I took off. I had energy to burn. Apparently Ned had turned to Jim and said, "I never heard the starting gun go off!" To which Jim replied as he saw me banking around a switchback above him, "She's just bending over backward to show us she's not holding us back."

Maybe I was. I hadn't analyzed it. It felt good to stretch out. I had spent long months honing my fitness, and it felt good to go with it. However, I may have unconsciously felt the need to prove myself. In several studies noted by Janet Shibley-Hyde in her book *Half the Human Experience,* men and women were given an exam with the potential of earning up to one hundred points.[4] After completing the exam these women and men were asked to give their estimated score before they actually received their true score. The men automatically guessed their scores would be higher than what they actually earned, while the women estimated their scores would be lower than what they actually earned. This is a problem because men will aggressively take a position based on false notions, and women will pass up opportunities based on false notions.

This difference has been found consistent in many studies from pre-school age on up.[5] Psychologists interpret this as indicating that females have lower self-confidence than males do.[6] This gender difference in self-confidence is an important one. There is evidence that people with lower expectations for success avoid challenging tasks. Consequently this gender difference may have important negative effects on women's careers and accomplishments; without confidence challenges are not tackled and overcome, potentially creating a lack of success or not reaching potential.

But perhaps, most importantly, it was discovered that if the females were given clear, direct feedback about how well they were doing or how good their abilities were, then their estimates of themselves were not lower than the males.[7] In retrospect, although I hung tough, I felt Allan and Tom, on my first expedition to the New Zealand Alps, wouldn't give me a compliment to save their lives. Perhaps it was because we were all young, and praise and support comes with maturity. But on Muztagata in China, when Ned, Galen, and I worked together toward the summit, the confidence the men had in me fed me, fueled me on. This direct, positive feedback allowed me to gain more confidence in my abilities.

Already on this Everest Grand Circle Expedition, Jim and Steve had given me great positive feedback for my efforts of collecting, packing, and tracking gear and for my pure physical output. Without realizing it at the time these guys were scientifically backing my confidence. In hindsight I could track my progress of my own expectations for myself, based on teammate feedback throughout the various expeditions. The more confidence and maturity a teammate had, the easier it was for him to dish out compliments or remark positively about others' exceptional abilities. This in turn positively affected my estimate of my own abilities as a woman among them. Somehow I think Jim knew this all along, and he just kept priming me. The more he complimented me, the more he got out of me.

By the time we all reached Thyangboche the skies had cleared enough and we saw Everest for the first time in our lives. The mountain showed itself during a dramatic sunset. The pink alpenglow added to the enchantment, wonder, and awe as we grappled with the idea that we would be climbing entirely around this incredible massif. In no way did any of the terrain from this vantage point look skiable. None of us had ever skied anything of this magnitude or steepness, and only two of us, Ned and I, had ever skied at these altitudes. This overwhelming scene of beauty and magnificence gave me a moment of pause, one of those moments where you can't quite believe you've gotten yourself into this.

On the last night on the trail before reaching base camp it was my turn to have the pounding altitude headache and a bit of a queasy stomach. Ned thrashed all night as well, and I could hear Steve and Jim rustling in their tent through the night too. But the Sherpas and Sherpanis sang and danced and stomped their feet into the wee hours of the morning. I'm sure there was plenty of chang and *rakshi,* a distilled form of chang, drunk throughout the festivities. I thrived on the thought that they didn't find any need for a band or a building to party in. The party was within themselves, waiting to bust out.

In the morning after drinking my warm tea, while swaddled in down in my tent, I realized I'd missed good fun when I noticed how slowly the Sherpas were packing up and how disheveled the loads were. My altitude hangover probably felt about the same as their rakshi hangover. At least they had a good time earning theirs. No one was moving very deftly on this last day on the trail.

Through gestures and a smattering of English, the Sherpas asked why I didn't join the party through the night. Decidedly, I strode over and lifted up a sorted load of gear, elbowed a Sherpani I had watched and admired over the past three days, and set the load onto a yak's back. She got the idea immediately, laughed, grabbed some rope, and together we fell to work, silently. Like many of the shy Sherpanis with us, she had a handsome full face, beautiful honey-colored skin, and big white teeth that filled her wide smile. She wore the typical long, black wrap dress with a woven square of material pinned at the waist with a silver clasp, like an apron. I was intrigued that these locals would wear the same clothes, day in and day out, regardless of temperature and weather. We sahibs were constantly adjusting our layers.

As the caravan began to move out this Sherpani, named Saile, waved to me to come along. I gladly put my cameras away for the day and again became a yak herder myself. She and I belted out our yak and cow calls, causing her to laugh, doubled over. Then after a bit she pulled a harmonica out of the folds of her dress and played me a couple of tunes as we walked. Her face rose in surprise when I took the instrument from her hands and played "The Swanee River," "Oh! Suzanna," and some other American classics. She laughed again, like a child.

I was reminded of my time with the Kirkiz in western China and their deep sense of humor and childlike sense of fun. Could a simple life of herding animals, trade and barter, cooking over open fires, and living in basic shelters with no running water develop this attitude of making your life as playful as possible? When life is hard, does the human spirit drive us to lighten our load with a mental disregard for our toils to balance our days? Could this be why the Sherpas could party at the drop of a hat, with nothing but themselves to create the festive atmosphere? I wondered if our modern society had lost its way, slipping into anxiety and depression as we became softer in a life of ease, disconnected from our natural world and from each other.

My lungs wheezed, but my legs held strong as I pushed and shoved yaks over the uneven moraine at about 17,000 feet as we neared base camp. One of Saile's yaks became stuck, but I had to keep mine moving or be stuck as well, so I reached base ahead of her. I pulled out a green print silk scarf that I had purchased in India. When Saile came trotting in I offered it to her, and she snatched it to her chest, glowing with pleasure. We set about unloading yaks, again in comfortable silence. Kinship was felt through the understanding of hard work and anticipating the other's efforts to work seamlessly together. As a farm girl I had common roots with Saile, and halfway around the world this allowed cultural barriers to disappear.

As Saile waved her arms to me from the top of the moraine on her way out, I felt a sinking in my chest. Not only was she the last woman's company I would keep for a couple of months, but she also represented my strong, initial desire to swing wider around Everest and live with the indigenous people. I was committed to our hard endeavor now, bowing my head in a last namaste to Saile, honoring the spirit in a people I ached to know. The Buddhist culture enthralled me.

"This is the sandbox of the Himalayas," Ned let out in a hoarse voice. He was lying prone in his bag with his head outside our tent looking up at Pumori the next morning. The glacial silt had pocketed here in this flat area among the boulders and swirled around like light, volcanic ash. It was in our hair, our teeth, our eyes, everywhere. Maybe this silt would provide the bulk and fiber our diets would soon be lacking, I thought with a laugh. Ned wasn't laughing. He'd really succumbed to altitude and had oatmeal head, as we called it, and it throbbed any time he went vertical, thus the horizontal position.

Pumori rose above us like the perfect triangle a small child would draw to represent a mountain peak. This mountain had gorgeous symmetry. The funny thing was, after all that map reading and speculating, the skis were unloaded from the yaks and put aside. After the guys got one real good close-up look at the peak, they realized we'd never slide an inch on Pumori. Now it was clear to all of us that Pumori wasn't skiable.

Was it purely chemicals that made my approach and the guys' approaches so different before our approaches merged in the reality of the event? Did testosterone cause an aggressive "can do" approach, and did estrogen cause a softer "I'm not sure" approach? What I did find was that when the objective was actually under way, our attitudes, or shall I say chemical responses, merged; we agreed on what indeed was skiable or possible.

So we weren't going around Everest with the locals as I had encouraged, and we weren't going to ski Pumori either, or ski the passes for that matter as Ned had encouraged. The great thing is, in the end, with men and women working together we did not overestimate or underestimate our abilities when we reached our objective. The reality was we were going to climb and climb and climb. And that was going to be a lot of hard, physical work. This was not going to be smooth or quick like skiing Muztagata, or straightforward like our ski in the New Zealand Alps.

The next day Jim asked if I would head up the mountain with him to begin designing our climbing route. I noticed Jim asked me, not one of the guys. Jim was sensitive to our various personalities, and he was probably still successfully priming my youthful enthusiasm and willingness to please. I was like a puppy barking and nipping at his big-dog heels. He knew I'd be pleased as punch to partake in route finding and certainly wouldn't be contrary to his particulars and preferences of style. We wouldn't be two alpha dogs competing for the opportunity and credit; we were yin and yang, male and female, master and apprentice, a more balanced pair.

After a two-hour hike over the moraine, Jim and I decided on a glacier-striated peninsula of rock at about 18,000 feet as the site for our advanced base camp. There we sat looking up at Pumori. I hazarded a guess at the route. Jim listened to me work my way up the mountain, then patiently pointed out my mistakes and explained why he would vary the route at critical points. Jim described his route as "the line splitting between disasters," because the avalanche danger was tremendous on either side of it. In fact our route might be impossible any other time of year, because new snow could make it lethal and the winter storms had yet to come.

Jim decided to name his route "Sapphire Bullets of Pure Love," after a song by the band They Might Be Giants. Rock-climbing routes in Yosemite often had names evocative of a feeling or an attitude instead of classic mountaineering route names like the Northwest Buttress. We made our way back to base to let the others, who were fitting crampons, testing tents, and breaking out the stoves, know what we had in mind for ascending this gorgeous peak. At the end of his route description Jim paused, lipped his cigarette, then continued, "The quality of excitement in a new route is so much higher. It's all the unknowns. The engineering of a new line is art." All were amenable.

We began ferrying loads of about forty pounds to advanced base; in a couple days, on December 15, we were in place to begin our ascent. As we all left base for our last time to make advanced base our home, we regretfully left behind Phutashi and his food. Under his makeshift tarps tied to boulders we would eat buffalo and yak meat, potatoes, pancakes, cabbage, carrots, eggs, and cartons of ketchup. Steaming cauldrons of tea were always on the gas burners, which kept the tarp tent slightly warm and moist in this dry, cold place.

We were also leaving behind what we'd affectionately named the great American Buddha, our kerosene stove. In our small, community tent where we ate, sitting with legs crossed meditation style so we could all fit in, we'd huddle around this warming device as if to pay homage to the heat. In the evenings we'd loll around the stove with bellies too full to allow our lungs to hold enough oxygen, dozing in our gluttonous, hypoxic state. Who needs drugs when you have heat and altitude?

The good thing about moving to advanced base would be melding as a team, caring for ourselves and planning our every move to dovetail with each other. No room for ease or sloppy timing or partial effort. Ned's sense of urgency had taken hold upon arrival, and he was impatient with Steve's relaxed attitude. Ned was irked that Steve would sleep in or lie in his bag listening to music or smoking when things could be done to help out the group. I jumped in to diffuse the situation, "Ned, remember, this is Steve's first expedition, and perhaps he isn't quite aware of all the little things that need doing. Just give him time. Let's cook dinner for everyone in our tent tonight."

I also wanted us all together in the tent for dinner for another reason. I finally piped up when we started eating: "I don't think I'm going to be able to climb, you guys." Ned stared at me, dumbfounded, "What

. . . ?" "It's my boots. I didn't realize it until today. I've noticed that up here over eighteen thousand feet I swell so badly that my feet fall asleep within minutes." I hadn't said anything earlier, but I watched Jim hack away at his inner boots with his ice ax to release pressure points on his foot, so I knew he had had similar problems. But my condition was so extreme that I would have to shave away most or all of the insulation of the entire vapor-barrier inner, rendering it useless.

I had used ski mountaineering boots on Muztagata no problem. Perhaps it was the cut of these climbing boots that shut off my circulation. "Who knows, maybe I retain more fluid, maybe that's why I get so swollen. But how can I climb without my boots? It's winter out there you know," I said, trying to lighten up the announcement with a little humor even though I was devastated that I might not be able to climb high. But I hadn't been able to come up with a solution.

Jim spoke up, "Phutashi has a pair of climbing boots the American Medical Expedition left for him. I'll bet he'd lend them to you." "Yes, I thought of that but they're big on him. They're probably larger than a size 10, and I wear a 6. Just think, each step would be a brand-new surprise. Are my crampons in contact with the ice and snow or not? It sounds a bit chancy to me. Balance would be difficult at best." We licked the mushy, freeze-dried beef stroganoff from our plastic spoons in silence for a while.

"Why not try your cross-country ski boot inners in your climbing boots?" Jim suggested as he stirred the glop in his plastic cup. "That just might do it!" I exclaimed in wonder. "My cross-country inners are much thinner than these vapor-barrier inners, so they'd give my feet room to swell. I could double up on overboots to make up for the thinner inner boots, and maybe my toes will stay intact. Why didn't I think of that? Jim, you're a genius," I teased.

I realized that I'd still need to go back to base camp to retrieve my cross-country inners or Phutashi's boots. "Just as well," Ned said, "I've got a list of things we've forgotten. Jim, Steve, and I will start the route, and you get the gear and the boots straightened out." I was pleased that there might be a relatively simple solution but disappointed that I would miss the first day of real climbing. The others would set the first couple of pitches while I returned to base camp.

Among the gear that Ned wanted me to get was some additional rope, but when I got to base I found there still wasn't enough and reported the shortage when I caught up with the rest of the group later. "I saw a bunch of rope at the medical station in Pheriche. I think it was left over from the medical expedition on Everest. I'm willing to go back and retrieve it," Steve suggested excitedly. We figured Ned, Jim, and I could haul our gear to advanced base the next day without Steve, going up the newly fixed lines, and decided it probably was best if he fetched the additional rope. I wondered why, after his first day of real climbing, Steve was anxious to be away from the mountain rather than on it.

On December 17 I began to "climb" Pumori. I had volunteered to lead the first pitch, which was a long, sloping traverse of ice ending in a *bergschrund*—a crevasse that forms when moving ice separates from the firn, or stagnant ice, above. Jim and Ned laughed, explaining that it wasn't worth roping up for; they hadn't bothered the day before. If someone fell on the traverse, he'd probably pull the others with him over the cliff at the edge of the slope. Also rocks, as well as little snow sloughs, had been washing over the traverse periodically. It was best to go across solo and fast.

I paid close attention to foot placement on the traverse. One slip here and a climber could plummet off the high cliff above the moraine floor. It took a few arduous moves to get over the bergschrund and then up a clean snow slope of 55 degrees to a rock outcropping we called the perch. When the three of us were safely across and up we sat on the perch eating frozen gorp and gazing over at Everest and the Khumbu icefall curling around the peak. As I listened to Ned and Jim exchanging facts and rumors about the many Everest expeditions before us, I was delighted to be right where I was in the world at that moment.

Jim had an idea: he would set up a pulley system at the top of the next pitch above the perch to haul up the loads. Ned wanted to climb the following pitch along with Jim, so I waited on the perch until the system was rigged and rappelled down. The pulley system hauled our heavy load of food, fuel, stoves, and tent stuffed in a duffel up to Jim and Ned, who secured it to our high point with a couple of ice screws. I continued on down to advanced camp alone. Although I dreaded the final solo traverse just as a student would a final exam, I didn't have any problems.

The next day, the eighteenth, Jim and Ned wanted to string the route higher; carrying more loads and climbing with three would be too slow. It was decided that I should stay below and clean our finicky camp stoves, clogged with the dirty fuel we purchased in Nepal. Statistically, women are better with fine motor skills and men better with gross motor skills, so the decision was appropriate. My mind seemed to wrap itself around the subtle engineering of these things anyway, and it was looking like I had a knack for keeping these stoves functioning well. I was happy to look after them. No stoves, no water. No water, no hydration. No hydration, no expedition. These stoves were key for success.

I listened to the men's voices filtering down and heard them from inside the tent throughout the day. At one point I went out to photograph them on the route, when an avalanche started below them and cascaded down beside our route, across our icy traverse, and over the cliff. This mountain was alive. I was alone at advanced base until Ned and Jim returned. The following day, the nineteenth, Steve returned, and all three men wanted a rest day before committing to climbing to camp one from advanced base. Much of the rope Steve returned with was useless, meaning we didn't have enough rope to fix or leave our route permanently placed on the mountain. This worried me. There would be no line of escape! I reminded myself again that worry is a wasted emotion.

On December 20 we left advanced base to commit to our climb of Pumori. We began on the unloved traverse. Ned had determined this four hundred feet of slanted rock and ice to be the most treacherous and dangerous place on our route. To add to the difficulty factor, we would cross it at the beginning and the end of the day, when we were morning stiff or evening tired. I watched Jim and Ned crossing ahead of me when suddenly Jim's legs veed up in the air as he stabbed his ax sharply down and pulled his legs, like a gymnast, underneath himself

into a squat. Jim carried on as if nothing had happened until I heard
Ned yell like a judge at a gymnast competition, "Clever, a ten!"

Although there was some distance between us, I could see Jim turn
and yell back to Ned, "Still the nerves of a diamond cutter, eh," with
a wide grin spreading across a very cocky-looking face. Meanwhile I
thought of myself as Grandma with my ice ax as my cane while I carefully picked my way over the ice, using my ax for stability. Once across
I looked back, worried about Steve. He'd been messing with personal
gear back at camp and had just begun to cross. Now I could tell he was
fussing with a noncompliant crampon, adjusting it while placing an ax
and standing on one foot. Steve had this air of always trying to catch
the day while it ran away without him.

I felt good and wanted to give something extra. So I offered to go
up last, climbing behind the haul bag as it was pulled up in order to
push and shove the bag when it lodged itself in the mountain's irreg-
ularities. I'd had plenty of haul bag experience when I climbed Half
Dome in Yosemite and knew of the extra mental and physical energy
that went into engineering the ascension of a huge duffel up a mountainside. Besides, Ned and I worked together most of the time, and I
thought it would be good to work alone and let Ned and Steve climb
together.

As I waited, crowded on the stance by the bulky duffel bag, I looked
up at the pitch the others had continued on above me. It was steep, fairly
solid, blue ice, angled at a steep 65 degrees, and pockmarked by fallen
rocks that had heated in the sun and then melted unevenly into the ice.
With plenty of imagination the formation could be termed a staircase.
It took Ned, Jim, and Steve more time than they anticipated to negotiate the staircase and fashion a pulley to haul the bag. Meanwhile the
wind had kicked up and the sun had disappeared.

I was dressed only in my thinnest polypropylene underwear beneath
my specially designed, insulated climbing suit. I had actually been hot
while active and warm while waiting, until the weather changed so suddenly. The temperature probably dropped 30 degrees almost instantly,
and it was well below zero. Now I was cold. The belay stance by the

bag was tiny and awkward for wrestling my pack off and securing it well enough to dig for more clothing. I kept rationalizing that Ned and Steve would have the pulley working soon and that if I dressed for resting I'd be sweating too much when I climbed.

If I got too cold I'd run the risk of becoming hypothermic. If I got too hot I'd sweat away precious fluids and become dehydrated—and again run the risk of becoming hypothermic from the damp chill that would set in when the sweaty work was finished. So I waited, pressed against the snowy slope for more than an hour. Where I stood at over 20,000 feet the atmospheric pressure was only half that at sea level, creating a drastically reduced air mass that is never thoroughly heated by the sun. The warmth that I had felt as I climbed had been solar radiation piercing through the thin air. Consequently when the sun went down, or behind the clouds, the temperature dropped dramatically because the thin air mass had little capacity for heat retention.

A wave of relief flooded through my frozen limbs when I got the signal to cut the bag loose and climb up behind it. The staircase pitch was difficult, because the increased angle demanded more strength. The effort was compounded by the fact that my energy had already been drained by the cold. Regardless of my work output, lugging my own pack and pushing the bag, my body remained cold. I consoled myself that one advantage of frozen muscles is that they feel little pain or strain.

Still, I tried to drive my sluggish body faster in hopes of rekindling my internal heat. Some of the "steps" in the staircase were giant for me, and I had to puff with all my strength to pull myself and both loads up and over. My competitive spirit egged me on to prove this pitch could be climbed faster than Ned and Steve had done it, and my sense of urgency in the cold increased my speed.

Meanwhile in the icy heavens above, Ned was worried as he had watched me stamping my feet and flinging my arms around myself to stay warm. He'd hacked out a tiny platform too small for the three men. Jim had climbed up a few feet while tied off to the haul line for some security. Ned and Steve were entwined in a mass of spaghetti rope trying to haul the bag. It was 2 p.m., and the sun had already slipped behind our mountain. The cold, wind, and late hour were pushing the men to use the minimum of safety to maximize our speed. At this point speed was safety and maybe our only hope. Somehow, until now, our lack of speed had gone unnoticed. I had no idea it was this late in the day.

As Jim had put it to the guys on his way up when the slack in the haul line went taut against his body, "Gotta move, gotta move, can't park your RV here." When I heard this from Steve and Ned, I cracked up despite our uncertain circumstances. I knew just what Jim meant. As renegade climbers in Yosemite, we tried to stay as long as desired in the park while the rangers worked tirelessly to catch us and kick us out.

Obviously Ned's tiny ice platform on the vertical ice wall, which could only accommodate two sitting, would demand that all four of us would have to stand, anchored in to the ice, chest to chest, all night without protection of a tent or a sleeping bag. Most probably we'd lose fingers and toes, maybe limbs, and possibly our lives by morning light. So we had to move; we couldn't park here. Jim took rope with him to fix the upper route while using up the last of our rope, doubling as the haul line. We were going to need it all in hopes of fixing all the way to this mysterious "hole" that we hoped would allow us to open a tent at the end of this ridge of ice and rock.

Jim was moving out of sight with swiftness and stealth as I arrived kneeing and punching the big, black duffel bag into submission. Ice shattered down on us like broken glass as Jim struck with his ax and thunked the front points of his crampons into the ice. He did a pull-up on a bare rock, lifted his leg to shoulder level, and leveraged himself up in a move called mantling. Jim could have been a pro ballplayer— his father was a pro baseball player—but Jim was an individual and rebelliously creative. Climbing seemed to be the extreme expression he needed to feel challenged and alive. During an easy stretch of travel Jim had told us, "On rare occasions you feel totally connected to inner motivation and power, and there are no limitations to what you can do."

This moment was looking like one of those rare moments Jim lived for. And if he pulled it off—leading this intricate, complicated route of rock and ice at high speed in the failing light of day in the Himalayan winter at high altitude—we would all live. Because we would be out of each other's line of sight and out of hearing distance and in the oncoming darkness, Jim had instructed Ned to wait for three tugs on the rope before allowing anyone to clip on their jumar to ascend. This would mean Jim would be safely off the rope, and it would be anchored to the slope so that the next climber couldn't pull Jim off the ice and fling him out into the air when the jumar yanked the rope with every step of the following climber.

I made a couple of moves and slid onto Ned's tiny belay stance, shaped like a frozen hand with the palm up. Steve, Ned, and I had to synchronize our moves to keep from pushing each other off. Ned tied onto the tail end of the haul line just to swing off the stance to give Steve room to take over the belay for Jim. I sensed the tension in the air. It was closing in on 4 p.m., and I had been alone in my own world, not realizing the difficulty we were slipping into. I was still under the impression this was climbing as usual. Shivering uncontrollably I opened my pack and realized I was fumbling. I had to take great care to make sure I didn't drop my precious gear off the side of the mountain.

I knew enough to recognize my lack of coordination as a sign of hypothermia creeping up on me. I clothed myself and said nothing. The water in my bottle was frozen when I went to take a drink. Hmmm, I thought, dehydration coming on too. I'd soon be like our dinners, freeze dried. That's one way to last forever. Ned strained to look up while standing with only the front points of his crampons sliced into the ice to keep him secured to the mountain while one hand clutched the anchored end of Jim's rope and the other gripped an ice ax, with the adz hammered into the ice. Knowing Ned as I do, I could hear his anxiety manifesting in sharp tones and choppy commands. I was easy enough with this, knowing it was Ned's emotional ownership of responsibility for us all, but it was causing friction between him and Steve.

Time seemed frozen too, and it felt like forever before Steve felt the three tugs on the rope, and Ned just about pushed Steve's butt up and over his head on the way by as Steve jumarred up the rope after Jim.

Ned wrestled with the hardware, removing his mitt for a moment to clip in, and started to swear, shaking his fingers. "You'd never know we're at the same latitude as Miami and Cairo," he said, trying to lift the mood. "One of the anchoring carabiners was found half open when we were sorting ourselves out, just before Jim went up and we began hauling the bag. Jim reminded me, 'Gotta stay scared. No shaking hands 'til it's over.'" I clipped my jumar on to the rope, without having had much of a rest, when Steve was past the first piece of protection, which anchored the rope to the slope. This spread out the stress of each climber on the rope. Ned came after me. It was a race against darkness up to the hole. There was no place to stop in between. After 400 feet of a wild climb, zigzagging back and forth across this wrinkle of rock and ice straight up the slope, we saw what Jim had selflessly, heroically, and, if it had been anyone else but Jim, foolishly done. Using his long 600-foot, secondhand Kathmandu rope, Jim tied it off to the slope at 400 feet so we could all start up before it was completely dark, and then used the remaining 200 feet to climb, without putting protection in to speed his ascent, as the darkness drew around all of us. This would mean that if Jim took a lead fall on this tiny poly rope, the force of falling 200 feet would snap it right off, sending Jim flying down to base camp thousands of feet below.

Jim didn't fall and had anchored the remaining 200 feet of the rope for us. At this point there was no more rope; the rope ended. When I got there it was bare, wide-open slope, no Jim, no Steve. It was totally dark; the wind was whipping my face. I was alone and climbing free in the dark with no rope. The train had run out of track. No time to dwell on it; I felt like Helen Keller with one hand on the slope and one on my ax, feeling for the kicked steps of the guys ahead of me. I had been lulled into following a route, sliding my jumar along the rope, not bothering to think sharply. Now I was faced with the Hansel-and-Gretel syndrome, no more crumbs to follow and the situation demanded that I snap to, despite a state of oncoming exhaustion.

I climbed up to and along a ridge, listening intently in the wind. About fifty feet down the other side of the ridge I could make out two black figures and hear them swearing viciously. I was peering into the hole; I'd arrived. Although I had felt barely able to put one foot in front of the other, it's strange how strength returns when you know someone else needs you. Instead of collapsing at the guys' feet when I reached them, I fell to my knees, digging like a maniac to increase a plot to put up our one two-man tent.

Then Ned arrived, and we relieved Jim and Steve from the frustration of setting up the tent. This was what had driven the guys to such foul language. As a honed team Ned and I had put these tents up in fifty-mile-an-hour winds, pouring rain, and complete darkness; we could do it in our sleep. At the time I didn't realize that by building the platform and relieving the other guys of tent duty, I was actually helping myself come back to life. Helping someone else is a sure way to survival. By looking after someone else you are taken out of yourself and away from your own fears. When you support someone else you become the rescuer, not the victim. This change in mental outlook brings with it newfound focus and energy. What you give to another person returns to you as support: you are buoyed by their deep appreciation of your aid, and your own mind-set shifts.

We had only two packs between us; Ned had pressured me to tie my pack off halfway up the last pitch, hoping to increase our speed of ascent, and Jim had done the lead without a pack. Between Ned's and Steve's loads we had one two-person tent, two sleeping bags, two headlamps, a stove, and almost no food—all the essentials for a wonderful evening in the winter-ridden Himalayas. Quite unexpectedly Ned's and Steve's headlamps burned out almost simultaneously. I had a feeling Murphy wasn't going to sleep a wink all night: everything that could possibly go wrong had.

Jim threw the two packs into the tent and ordered me in behind them to spread out the sleeping pads. I did as I was told, hiding my indignation. First Ned had ordered me to drop my pack, and now Jim was bossing me around. We needed organization, not a hog pile in the tent. I thought the packs should remain outside, but I said nothing. I was afraid making waves at this point might cause tempers to flare.

Then Jim changed his mind. "Pull Ned's backpack out and dump everything out to get the stove." I was dismayed. I knew that in the dark the pieces of our intricate mountain stove were likely to get lost in the snow. That would never do—a functioning stove was necessary for melting snow, and we were all terribly dehydrated, almost disastrously dehydrated. Abruptly Jim jumped into the tent mumbling something about freezing. Ned and Steve dove in after him. The tent was a disheveled, crowded, lumpy, jumble—and completely dark. Crammed miserably together, literally on top of each other, we vied with each other for resting and breathing space. Jim and Steve had strewn the contents of Ned's pack all over the tent as they crawled in and had pushed me into the back corner. I saw a bad situation getting worse.

At this point I lost it—or rather regained it. "Look, Steve, why don't you and I change places, then you and Jim can stretch out in the back." The wind blew viciously making it hard to hear, and spindrift was blowing in all over us. "Ned, you and I can sit close to the door, and give me that stove before you drop all the pieces." Steve and Jim relaxed, relieved of duty, and used the contents of Ned's pack for necessary padding over the cold, hard spots in the tent. They also located our only two sleeping bags and draped them over themselves.

I rescued the stove that Ned had been abusing, but as usual he instructed me how to assemble the stove and light it, despite his own failure. Regardless of the fact that it was completely dark, I'd assembled the stove so many times that I did it by instinct and promptly got the thing going, then placed it outside. We all settled back into whatever niches we could find, congratulating ourselves for finding the only possible space to level out and erect a tent for thousands of vertical feet. When the snow had melted I handed the pot back to Jim. He took a sip from the cold, gray rim, and to my amazement shot forward and spat it out. Somehow kerosene had gotten into the pot, and our water tasted contaminated. Considering we'd had a hard day and were at 21,000 feet, it was imperative that we drink, so we took our chances with this batch of water and drank gingerly. Hopefully the kerosene taste was stronger than the actual kerosene content.

We lay down head to foot and covered our fully clad bodies with the two sleeping bags. Beneath me were plastic boots, fuel containers, and other hard lumpy objects. Everything had to be either in packs secured to the slope by ice axes or, since we blew that option long ago, inside the tent with us so it wouldn't be blown away. We twisted and turned, trying to settle ourselves into some comfortable position between all the shrapnel of equipment. Out of the darkness a voice boomed, "Steve, will you stop wiggling?"

"I have to; that way I know I'm alive," was the serious or silly reply, I couldn't tell.

My space was tiny and decreasing minute by minute. Every time I turned over in search of comfort, Jim filled in my space a little tighter. I was miserable. Midway through the endless night I asked Ned if he thought his space was any better and would he mind trading. He succumbed.

"I don't see how you fit here, Jano." "I didn't," I answered as I settled into relative space. "Thanks, g'night." Still I couldn't sleep. I felt absolutely envious when I heard Ned begin to snore.

As the light hit our tent "The Yellow Rose of Texas" blared out of Jim's watch and stirred us to consciousness. Damn that frickin' watch. We crawled out of the tent and away from the foul smells of moist vapor barriers, farts, wet wool socks, kerosene, and other fetid, unidentifiable odors and squinted in the surrounding, white, sparkling, odorless snow. We felt awful, as if we'd been on a weeklong binge, suffering headaches, lethargy, fatigue, exhaustion, confusion, and incoherence. "A person is an adventurer in direct proportion to shortness of memory" was a favorite saying of Ned's, and it applied now. How long would it take us all to forget this night?

We needed to retrieve our gear dangling on the side of the mountain if we were to continue. Jim, our hero of the night, would remain, brewing up water for our bottles, while Steve and Ned went all the way down to the frozen hand belay to retrieve our gear left there. I rappelled halfway down to retrieve my pack. As I descended I could see in the light of day what I couldn't in the dark of last night. This ridge was not a simple structure but flawed, broken and uneven. As I reclimbed the pitch with my pack, every time I pulled up over a headwall, turned a corner, or crossed a crest, a new technique was called for to climb a gully, sidle across a traverse, balance on an edge, scrape over rock, spread eagle over a dihedral, or heave up pure steepness.

Close to the top of this long, 600-foot-plus pitch, I encountered a great mushroom of lacey ice. The formation was vertical, and the entire structure seemed so delicately balanced that an overly enthusiastic whack with an ice ax might fracture and topple it. Needless to say Jim kept it upright. The artistry of Jim's lead on this entire pitch was instinctive and beautiful. Maybe his was the only line that could have actually worked. How did he do it in the dark? I wondered what it must be like for Jim to have such an extreme talent with so few people in the world who could truly appreciate it. Those who did appreciate his talent thanked Jim with their lives.

I felt whipped and bone-achingly tired as I crawled into the tent to drink tea with Jim. I felt safe under the giant ice serac, which protected our tent from avalanche, provided this serac weighing several tons didn't fall down on us. Jim started talking about his wife, Peggy, and his little boy Layton, three years old. Layton was doing some of his first skiing now at home in California, without Jim. Throughout the conversation Jim's voice softened, and then he was quiet. Then he looked me in the eye and said, "You know I think it's good to have a woman on a trip, because I think she monitors things."

Without another word he started rustling around and collecting climbing gear, and the next thing I knew he was asking me to belay him on a tricky traverse that would lead us to our next pitch. Later Jim confirmed what I had suspected: he was homesick for his family and wanted to do something to distract himself, even though this pitch was to be left for tomorrow. For most people hanging off ice unroped at 21,000 feet would have been a drastic measure, but to Jim it seemed just what he needed. Jim's is a dual nature: his leathery skin and chipped teeth give him a tough exterior, but that hides a heart as warm as any I've encountered. His sense of adventure raises havoc with his home life:

when he's with his wife and child he pines for adventure; in the midst of adventure he longs for his family.

Ned and I had raised the newly retrieved second tent and had begun cooking up some food by the time Jim eventually returned. We were nauseated at the thought of eating and even just the efforts to cook exhausted us, but we needed to eat, to refuel. Ned described our life here at camp one as being no better than a shanty existence and likened us to high-altitude hoboes crouched over peel-top food packets, crammed into a tent, and sitting on mounds of uncomfortably hard climbing gear. Our dinner was hot Tang, mushroom soup, or tea and powdered mashed potatoes with powdered cheese and bouillon cubes sprinkled on top. We ate as much as we could get down without it coming back up.

Jim announced that the weather looked stable and the route clear for a summit attempt the next day, December 23. We were hardly ready physically; we were worn from coming to altitude too quickly and pushing up the route in order to beat the winter storms said to descend by Christmas. We felt we needed to take any opportunity we had to rush to the summit before the jet-stream winds, blowing hundreds of miles an hour, swept the tops of the peaks and potentially took us with them. With the shortest days of the year, the coldest temperatures, and the highest winds, it was painfully clear why no one had climbed here in winter before.

That night our hearts pounded at such a rate that we couldn't sleep. Yes, insomnia is a common problem at altitude along with the headaches, lethargy, and nausea during acclimatization. Because we can never fully acclimatize above about 18,000 feet, a human being cannot live this high. Basically a human would be constantly degenerating, continually dying at this elevation and above. You could say we were dying to reach the top. To complicate this sleep issue in our tent, Ned decided to sleep with his clothes on, climbing harness and all. Or should I say he wrestled with them all night and kept me awake?

He complained that his one-piece suit rolled up tightly in his crotch. I knew it would annoy him, but I couldn't suppress a laugh at the thought that being dressed for action in the morning would be worth a sleepless night. I dressed quickly in the morning as Ned tried to fire up the stove. I heard the harsh hissing of the stove's flame and low voices in the other tent. I knew Steve and Jim too were up and performing the ritual of coaxing their stove and watching the water boil.

Our light stoves had an ever-so-tiny hole to permit the gas to escape, keeping the cooking flame alive. Because we hadn't been able to bring our own white gas to these foreign parts, we had to purchase some obscure, dirty fuel that clogged this hole. This combined with the low oxygen meant that the stoves needed to be humored. With a little tender loving care they would come around to your point of view, but they balked at any kind of brute force.

Ned was muttering under his breath because the stove had choked itself out. Ned slammed it down and rustled out of the tent, tugging at his twisted suit, still struggling to settle his body comfortably inside it. The tension seemed to blow out of the tent behind him. Relieved, I coaxed the stove to life. We were late on our summit start; Ned had slept in his suit for nothing, and he was distraught we were burning daylight. Jim, at his own insistence, was supposed to have woken us while it was still dark. It hadn't happened. A pee bottle extended from the other tent in Steve's hand and dumped out in the snow. Jim's head peeked out from behind the tent flap.

"'Ello Ducko, noyce die foor a cloimb!" I said in my best fake, low-brow English accent. Jim smiled his hand-in-the-cookie-jar smile at me. We talked to each other in this fake accent for grins to lighten things up. He had a good dose of foolishness in him that I could relate to. Laughter doesn't take conscious thought; it's automatic. Laughter stimulates the portion of the brain that helps us feel good and to be motivated. This stimulation alleviates frustration and anxiety. I suppose this silliness helped Jim and I to deal. Things were getting tense, and we were getting funny. It's been found that humor is a trait of a true survivor.[8]

Soon I looked out of my tent and saw Jim way up there with his belay rope just dangling. I shot out of the tent to see Steve backed up to a crevasse, squatting, with his suit down, to relieve himself. He had plenty of confidence in Jim's ability I thought, as I grabbed the belay rope and secured it around my waist. Our camp area was so tiny we were living in a white toilet bowl of sorts. You couldn't go any distance without flying off the mountain. So everything happened within the near vicinity. We never melted the colored snow though.

Ned followed Jim out. I went as soon as Ned clipped off the 250-foot traverse, which swung under a huge ice bulge. My first step out of the hole gave me 3,500 feet of exposure, a straight shot directly down to base camp in one fell swoop. It was exhilarating. To compound the danger, the anchored rope was horizontal, necessary for any traverse, and a fall would put a sharp, right-angled pull down on my jumar, making the mechanism more likely to fail, popping off the rope with the force of the twist. I clipped a carabiner on the rope, which was attached to a sling around my waist to counteract this possibility.

There was no one below me. There were no other climbing parties in our vicinity in the arms of Everest in this winter weather. This exclusivity was stimulating. We had panoramic views of Everest from this upper slope of Pumori. We could see her beautiful face in Tibet, as well as her face in Nepal. She was a gorgeous, commanding chunk of rock, with the Khumbu icefall curling its gaping crevasses around her like a flowing white stole. I slipped into my imagination in this extreme moment, surrounded by outrageous scenery and wild, committing exposure.

I often live in my imagination when I attempt a physical endeavor. I had studied a bit of ballet as a child, and as I began the traverse I imagined that the front points of my crampons were the wooden blocks at the tips of my toe shoes. I forgot about the pack on my back and the layers of bulky clothing and dreamed I was dancing ever so delicately across the stage for a terribly discriminating audience. Then I remembered I had put on toe shoes before I really deserved them. I hoped I had paid my dues for my front points.

Ned and I had one of those fleeting moments truly alone on a high Himalayan expedition when we met on the belay stance, with Jim above us and Steve behind us. Romance in this thin-air environment was described as decidedly platonic by Ned. While bundled up in layers of clothing, with spikes of axes and hammers sticking out all around us, we might as well have been a couple of porcupines trying to hug each other. Regardless, the comfort was encouraging. Ned kissed my cheek and then we moved on, fleet and dexterous, just like any other athletes on a ball field or in a gymnasium.

I bent over and cupped my hands to yell to Steve. "Come on up, nice views." When he arrived on the belay stance, I gave him a hearty welcome, wishing I could see his eyes underneath his glasses. Of the three men Steve's moods were the most difficult to read. He always pushed an eager expression at you, leaving you guessing at his intimate thoughts. "Feels good to be off the dread traverse, doesn't it?" I asked in a tone that admitted I thought it was dicey too. "Mmm-hmm, we need to make some time today. I better get going." I patted his back, clipped on, and began my steady step up. Both Steve and I are dreamers, for better or worse. The ramp was about one hundred feet of 45-degree angled slope. I moved along in a rhythmical fashion, letting the low hum of the rope through my jumar lull me. I was very relaxed. Quite suddenly I heard a loud whizzing and felt a sharp pain.

My teeth slammed together so hard that their impact sounded like a big bang inside my head. Black spots blotting my sight began to rapidly knit together into a black curtain. I made myself concentrate on trying to keep my foot in sight as I focused on lifting it up. I was deliberately forcing myself to move in my oncoming blindness, fearing I would otherwise black out completely and just dangle off the fixed line like a dead fish out of water. I blinked hard several times, struggling to see, and pulled my foot up to finally make a step. My tunnel vision began to expand slowly, as the black began to recede. I continued to move up.

I felt steady enough to stop and reached for the top of my head. My hand was wet from the blood that had soaked through my hat and two silk balaclavas. My immediate thought was that heads bleed a lot, so this didn't mean much. I remembered that Steve was below me. I glanced down to see if he'd been hit, but he was moving along fine, minding his own business. I just kept moving up, my head throbbing with every step. I kept all my headgear on, hoping it would help slow the bleeding. My hair already had a few weeks of grease on it. I was less concerned about the bleeding than I was about infection.

I ignored Ned's calls to me and just focused on getting up. It was too difficult for me to shout. I told myself to be diplomatic as I climbed up, but I couldn't help myself. The first thing I said when I reached the stance was, "Neddy, why didn't you tell me that was coming?" "Well, it didn't look like it was going to cross your path and I didn't want to disturb you. Then it hit something and changed course. If I yelled to you then, you might have looked up and gotten it smack in the face." I began to feel lucky that I didn't have a broken nose, black eyes, and maybe cracked cheekbones.

"Boy, that was the closest I've ever come to blacking out," I said under my breath. "That dinner plate of ice fell about two hundred feet before it honed in on you," Ned said suppressing a laugh. "Dinner plate! It felt like a turkey platter with the whole bird on it!" I exclaimed.

Jim had previously given us a sermon about how he feels helmets attracted rocks, legitimizing why he never climbed with a helmet on. Both Jim and I felt that under the containment of a helmet you were too closed off from your immediate environment for keen reactions; your vision, hearing, and just plain innate senses were dulled under that brain bucket. Jim felt there was safety in complete awareness. However, this ice incident gave me pause.

When Steve reached us and took a look at me and my blood encrusted head and face, heard my story, and then looked up at Jim on the nearly vertical ice above, he had an expression that I identified as wishing he were just about any place other than here. We could hear Jim above us breathing hard when he stopped to place ice screws. Although he looked so smooth and controlled as he climbed, we knew he was delivering everything he had to put up this thrilling pitch at 22,000 feet.

Following Ned, I felt like a pack animal for this pitch: my function was to get the load up however possible. I used style when I needed it, but front pointing at this elevation, especially with a load, made my calves feel like hot potatoes. If you've ever done toe raises in a gym, try doing it with forty or fifty pounds on your back with lactic acid flooding and fatiguing your oxygen-deprived muscles; then you'd have our experience.

As I approached the relief in the slope I spied Ned heading out on the next pitch and Jim at the stance. I slogged up to him. "My hands are freezing in these gloves," Jim said very matter-of-fact. "Here." I swung around and put my back to him, almost knocking him off balance with my pack. "Back left pocket." He asked how I was feeling as he slipped my mitts on, which came from the pocket. Because I felt pretty good Jim said, "Why don't you go on up?" I was thrilled. I thought Jim was being quite gracious to allow Ned and me to be the first to reach the Breadloaf, look into Tibet, and check out the route to the summit. I humped on up, looking back at Jim once. I smiled to myself to see Jim, the big hulking guy, standing there with my little red mittens on that had Jan written over them in huge black letters. I'd grown quite fond of him.

What I think Jim meant when he said that a woman monitors things on an expedition was that with a woman around the ambience shifted a bit, the conversations were perhaps more varied, and the egos more likely stroked than rubbed raw. I did none of this intentionally, but I've learned men and women do speak differently.[9] Perhaps the way I spoke encouraged a different way of relating to each other. He didn't say I was supervising things or controlling things; I think he meant that my feminine influence defused situations, and attitudes were diffused.

I reflected on the other night with the four of us crammed in the one tiny tent. I had no problem with others taking the lead, but when I see things really going wrong, I am confident enough to make sure I am heard. But the way I am heard may make a difference. I do remember saying, "Steve, why don't you and I trade places," indicating that the switch would allow him and Jim to stretch out in the back. This comment wasn't premeditated; I wasn't trying to talk like a "woman," but the "why don't" in the sentence invited discussion, unlike the demands

Ned and Jim had been giving me earlier. I had had to comply with their demands or risk conflict.

I sensed Jim liked being able to talk about warm and fuzzy things, like his family, to me. I noticed when any of the guys were with me alone, they were more likely to talk about how they felt, which they didn't do when they were with the other guys. I suppose this also helped with monitoring things. I knew from conversations with Ned that I was much more aware of how things were going for the others than he was. Knowing this always came into play on a daily basis when deciding to push hard, move slowly, or stay put. I didn't think this awareness was exceptional, but I did think I was just naturally different enough from the guys and may have smoothed things out a bit; at least I thought that was what Jim was trying to say to me. When I pressed him to explain what he meant he just said, "You know, I think a woman, (pause) she just (pause) monitors things." It was said as a simple compliment.

I had one moment with Ned, after hauling my load up the pitch ending on the ridge atop the Breadloaf, before Jim arrived behind me. Jim had been shouting up to Ned, asking if the route would "go." Ned had been staring up toward the clearly visible summit as if in a dream. I didn't know if it was because of blurred thinking at altitude or if he was taking great care to assess the situation in minute detail. Either way he wasn't responding to Jim. Jim slowly walked toward us and immediately understood why Ned hadn't responded. Still breathing hard Jim lit a cigarette and blurted, "Yuh, I was thinking the same thing. This thing is bigger than any of us thought."

It was two o'clock in the afternoon, and little more than three hours of daylight remained. We were now in shadow, and the temperature was plummeting. Lenticular clouds capped Everest, and Pumori's plume had lengthened since we had arrived; the winds were really kicking up. Continuing on would entail an all-night bivouac without food, water, sleeping bags, or shelter—insanity in the killer cold of winter. We would certainly lose limbs if not our lives if we continued to ascend the peak and were forced to spend a night out, unprotected, unfed, and dehydrated, wherever we found ourselves when darkness fell on our way down. We could not possibly reach the summit and return to camp in the daylight remaining, certainly not at the rate we were traveling at 22,000 feet and up.

Above us the summit slope stood as a beautiful, snowy pyramid. At its base, near us, was a jumble of ice blocks and crevasses. The top had a massive cornice like a jaunty hat, tipped to the side, indicating that a nasty prevailing west wind had designed it. Looking over the side of the ridge, Tibet spread out below us. The Pumori Glacier flowed into the West Rongbuk Glacier, with countless crevasses looking rumpled and creased, like an aged face.

Steve finally appeared, coming off the last pitch. He was crawling toward us. A rope he had hauled up had tangled and wrapped itself around his legs. Our strong man was barely dragging himself along. This sight made it ultraclear that our only option was to descend, and quickly, before the jet-stream winds lowered farther and caught us in their grasp. Although it was strange, a feeling of elation rose in me. From this vantage point our imaginative approach to Everest was unfolding before my eyes. I could see far out to both sides of Everest North and South while standing on this borderline ridge and view the lion's share of our circle lying dormant below me. This was one of the joys of circumnavigating Everest instead of climbing her: there was always a new adventure around the corner. By touching the border between Nepal and Tibet on this ridgeline, we could now officially start our circle. We hadn't failed; we had just begun.

These thoughts warmed and cheered me as I turned my thoughts to the others to see how they were adjusting. Steve gave off a slight indication of relief and seemed anxious to descend. I had heard him say earlier in a joking manner that Ned was Captain Ahab and Pumori was his great white whale. I didn't think the disappointment cut him too deeply. Ned and Jim, on the other hand, were drowning in dissatisfaction. They hadn't fulfilled their own expectations of themselves. They were trying to cover their moods, but the deep disappointment was working inside both of them.

Rappelling back to camp went along routinely even if our technique was a little unorthodox. Without much gear for anchoring our rope to the slope, Jim chose to hack some bollards* about two feet in diameter to lay our rope around so we could rappel down and then be able to pull the rope back down to us. Jim would take his ax and hack another bollard, double the rope around it, and move down again. In this manner we could use the same ropes over and over again, as we had no fixed line left on the slope until we got back to the dread traverse.

Ned made me dangle around a bit while on the last rappel before the dread traverse to take some photos. I noticed how much this annoyed me; I felt irritated and interrupted. Maybe my disappointment was cutting deeper than I realized? I wondered. I looked across the traverse into the hole of camp one while I was literally hanging around, and it appeared as if I would be tiptoeing across steep ice into an open blue mouth with large white teeth. As I began this traverse home, thoughts of hot tea and a warm sleeping bag at the end coaxed me across. My legs were soft with fatigue, and my mind somewhat vacant from the hard work at altitude without proper acclimatization, food, or much water, but I forced myself to concentrate on my foot placements. On an expedition it is seldom possible to choose an activity to suit one's mood—the key is responding to the situation at hand.

We all rustled into our respective tents, anxious to get the stoves going. The din of voices in the other tent began rising in decibels. We heard "hey watch it" and roaring curses. Then suddenly a burst of flame catapulted out of the front of the tent, burning delicate nylon in its course as the stove landed in the snow with a metallic clank, still sizzling. Jim had handled the stove with the old theory: if you can't deal with it, destroy it. We had replacement stoves below, and that was where we were ultimately heading, so I saw humor in the event. Laughter, however, wasn't appropriate.

---

*A bollard is a large knob of ice or snow carved out on a slope as an anchor for a rope; a rope can be wrapped around it unobstructed so it can be pulled off easily and used again lower on the slope, when another bollard is carved.

Ned had been hovering and fussing over our stove for some time now, and I could see the pressure gauge rising on his face. I knew we all needed to get this stove to light properly so we could melt some snow for drinking water. I asked Ned to let me try, as it had worked for me that morning. No response. "Ned, you're making it worse, give it to me." My concern for water overwhelmed my more diplomatic self in my exhausted, dehydrated state. Ned turned his black tangle of hair and beard toward me. His eyes had that look of rapidly eroding self-control, and he lashed out, "Someday someone is going to smash your nose in." He didn't say he was going to smash my nose in, so I ignored him and lit the stove anyway.

It is common for people to react negatively to females using male autocratic style. I think this was just what was happening between Ned and me concerning the finicky stove. I simply made my demand, and he felt affronted, whereas receiving a demand from him was more of a norm for me: I took it in stride, knowing and carrying the bigger picture in my head. I would know, for the most part, where Ned was going with his demand and could live with his style, keeping the ultimate or group goal in mind, knowing he had everyone's best interest at heart. It was strange that this didn't work in reverse when I demanded something of Ned. Does testosterone create or increase ego?

In the middle of the long night I was semi-awake and very confused, wondering where I was and even who Ned was for a brief time. I chalked it up to dehydration and exhaustion and whatever disorder was going on in my digestive system. I had diarrhea and a raging stomach, necessitating my explosion from the tent and bold, naked exposure of my skin to the Himalayan winter weather in the dark of night to relieve myself. Pleased that I never slid off the mountain, I didn't think to question my mixed-up mind as possibly being a result of the whack on the head I had had from the ice block.

When I asked Ned who he was that night, he looked at me quizzically as if I were attempting some joke and told me to "cut it out." I probably did suffer some kind of concussion that day, but I was confused enough to wonder if I was faking—of course I know this guy.

Why did I just ask him that? I just blew it off. Once my face had been cleaned of encrusted blood with snow, we were all too exhausted to look under my balaclavas and hat to see what was going on. I could barely light the stove so we could melt snow to drink. After that we all just lay our heads down for the night, unable to do another thing. I had eased Ned into the morning of our summit attempt after his restless, sleepless night wrestling in the clothes he slept in, and now Ned was easing me into the night of this failed summit attempt by soothing me, as I wrestled in and out of the tent over and over, sometimes with my words not making sense. Soon we both slept.

The next morning was a bit ugly. There was no joy in packing our goods for the long descent back to base camp. We worked quietly and monotonously. I was trudging up and out, toward our fixed rope at the top of the ridge, when an awkward step caused my knee to buckle. I fell and caught myself. I had already known that I was physically weak from our hard work at high altitude with little food, but now I was aware that I wasn't mentally acute either. A lapse in concentration caused my slip. I could see myself falling prey to one of the most familiar truisms of climbing: because the descent is anticlimactic, attention drifts and climbers are more vulnerable. Most climbing accidents occur on the way down.

I rappelled last. The descent was painfully tedious and wearing under our heaviest loads yet, evacuating everything off the mountain at one time, especially when I broke through the crust of a snow hole on the ridge. Because the hole was deeper than the length of my legs and because I had extra weight on my back, I had to claw with my hands to drag myself out, crawling on my belly as I floundered around. I swore like my father did when his milking machinery would break down in the barn. When I had successfully extricated myself I had to laugh at the things children learn from their parents and then keep with them forever.

After negotiating the latticework of ice on the ridge, Jim decided to use a bollard to anchor our rappel ropes to descend the steep pitch over the lower traverse. Before we descended we had a discussion to determine the pecking order. Should the heaviest go first to test the bollard for our maximum load? Or should the lightest go first, followed by the rest in graduated succession? We all agreed it probably didn't matter either way with Ned, Jim, and Steve, because they and their loads were of similar weight. But it was decided that I should have the dubious distinction of rappelling last. The others rationalized that the lightest should be last because that person would be the least likely to tip the rope over the top of the bollard.

After Jim and Steve had descended I held the rope down on the bollard for Ned. "Whatever happened to ladies first?" I said in mock indignation as Ned carefully slid down the rope. He laughed back and told me to be careful. I suppose this was the ultimate compliment, to have the others feel confident I wouldn't peel off down the mountain when I slung my weight below the bollard. I truly was an equal, one among them, damn it. As I clipped myself in to rappel, checking my equipment twice and then again to make sure I had made no mistake, I anxiously climbed out to the side. I used my climbing axes to keep my weight off the rope and eyed the bollard constantly to see if the rope was staying around the top of the knob.

Once below, where I could no longer see the rope over the bollard, I carefully put my full weight onto the rope. Any fall or slip here could pop the rope off, and I'd have a fast trip to the lower traverse and over the cliff, landing next to base camp. That would be good, but the shape I'd be in if I were alive wouldn't be. I moved carefully and consistently, with no jerky motions, and I was down, whew. However, the lower I descended, the lower my heart sank. Leaving the mountain unclimbed was like opening a gorgeously wrapped package only to find nothing inside.

Yet, I felt warmed to see Anu's eager face waiting for us at advanced base camp. "Good, you make top!" Oh no, I thought, the upper portion of the route wasn't visible from base camp. Because we made our push from our high camp in the hole, our Sherpas had assumed that with all the good weather we'd surely reached the summit. I replied simply and softly, "No, Anu, we just weren't prepared." It hadn't dawned on me until now how deeply disappointed and almost embarrassed I was to admit to someone else that we had failed. Anu just shrugged and hugged me again.

We had to make the long walk over the moraine before we could indulge in the comforts of base camp. The moon was rising and cast a gray glow on the rocky glacier's tongue. Ned kept looking back at me, calling for me to join him, but I wanted to be alone. It was Christmas Eve, and the night was beautiful. I wanted to wrap myself in the stars and saw absolutely no need for hurry. We had all been together on our umbilical cord, up the mountain for several days. I had forgotten the delicious feel of independent decision and freedom to move, and I was savoring it now.

A couple of hours later, when we all gathered together in our big dining tent at base, the mood had shifted 180 degrees from the morning. The Sherpas served us hot french fries with ketchup, along with gallons of sweet tea. We had eaten meagerly for the past five days because of lack of appetite and ability to keep food down at higher altitudes, so the fries were not only palatable, they were a feast. We laughed at each other. We laughed at ourselves. In retrospect, the first night in the hole with all four of us in one two-person tent, Ned's threat to punch my nose in, and Jim's daring dash out onto the traverse had all become very humorous. I went to sleep that Christmas Eve, naively satisfied we'd shaken our failure from our minds.

CHAPTER 4

WHAT GOES AROUND . . .

WE HADN'T EATEN IN FIVE DAYS, and we were holed up in a small cave. We were okay with that for the most part. We were still moving on with our loads on our backs, although we typically felt pretty low by sunset, while sipping our daily brew of hot water. At least we had water by following this river, knowing, as it flowed out and down from the Himalayas, that we'd surely reach a remote village at some point. But this was the rub: How long would it be before we reached that point? How long before we would eat? We'd each lost about twenty pounds already by a conservative estimate.

We didn't hold it against Ned that he had forgotten. We truthfully found it very funny and made jokes about it regularly. With the enormous amounts of gear packed in numerous barrels, flown overseas for high-profile expeditions to the Himalayas, it's beyond easy to let something slip. Actually it's normal to forget something. With almost every expedition you wait with amusement or trepidation to find out what it will be and where you'll be when you suddenly have a need for the forgotten item.

Craig Calonica, Ned, and I had descended our last 20,000-foot col in the Everest Region on our Everest Grand Circle Expedition when we went to check the map to see what our exit from the Arun Valley would be. We wanted to mentally project what our next few days would be like while thrashing out to meet our Sherpas. We were tired, low on food, but thrilled to have completed our first half circle around Everest, arriving near the base of Makalu, the world's fifth-highest peak, on the border between Nepal and Tibet. Ned went to pull out the map. Up to this point all climbing and objectives had been obvious, standing right in front of us; no map consultations had been necessary.

"No map" was Ned's quiet response. What do you mean no map? We have miles to go, down a remote valley, with plenty of side routes open. There were too many ways to go wrong. These were the thoughts running through our minds, which were only articulated by the dumbfounded look on our faces and the disbelief in our eyes. Ned had been in charge of all maps by his own determination. Ned and I were coleaders of this trip and allowed each other to self-determine responsibilities. So here we were, five days later, post map search, looking into our cups of boiled water for breakfast. We were inside a small cave that we had ducked into for the night, wondering where the hell we were and how long before we'd eat.

I remembered Brenda, who always wore the trendiest shirts from the head shop boutique in my old hometown, as I reflected into my cup of lukewarm water. Long ago, when I was twelve, she had told me, in our junior high school hallway by her locker, that I was existentialist. Apparently when I told her I had decided during my previous night's homework session that "your life is what you make it, and the world is what it means to you," she was ready to categorize me. I looked up *existentialist* in the dictionary pronto. I wanted to know if there was something really twisted in my thinking. Did this mean I was going to hell when I died?

The first definition was: "Philosophic doctrine of beliefs that people have absolute freedom of choice, and that the universe is absurd." Well there was no hell in that one. By culling I came across "conscious choice" and "responsibility for one's choices" as the mainstay for the language of existentialism. I also ran across "self-view, and view of the world" as two things that could always be changed by a person if so desired. I took it to mean we humans were always free to reassess our own lives and can take measures to alter our lives and our concept of the world as we see fit.

I was only slightly wondering if my life, as my own creation at this point in time, was a mess, while my stomach rumbled as I sat shivering in the cave. The tepid water was helping to fill the void in my belly, but my empty mind was rapidly filling with doubts. Yes, I'd made all the conscious choices to put myself right here, with Ned and Craig, scrambling in the Himalayas, and only I was responsible for that choice. Was it the right one? Is there such a thing as a right choice? Perhaps there are only choices, which lead to other choices. In that case the selected path made the difference, more than any individual choice. Was my chosen path as a professional climber and skier a good one for me?

As I began to pry open my frozen gloves to dress for our day's march to nowhere, Craig burst into my thoughts. "We go this way! I know this. I've been like this since I was a kid. I just get this feeling and I know where to go. I could always find the way!" Was this hunger talking, delirium maybe, or was Craig on to something? Craig hadn't even been part of the original team. He'd come in place of Kim Schmitz, who was to be our original climbing leader on Pumori. Kim had assured us he would be with us after the Pumori climb for the rest of the expedition, but it was Craig who had showed up in Pumori base camp instead of Kim.

On Christmas Day, our first day in base following our failed attempt on Pumori, we got a message from a Sherpa runner sent by our expedition outfitter in Kathmandu. It told us someone named Craig Calonica would be trekking in to meet us in base camp in place of Kim Schmitz. "If Calonica is coming in," Steve McKinney blurted out, "you guys don't need me." Steve and Craig were great, longtime friends. Steve knew that we would be in good hands with Craig around and thus opted to return to his girlfriend and his skiing conquests.

This was such unorthodox expedition procedure in Ned's mind, to trade climbers like pieces in a board game. I was afraid this was setting up Ned to automatically dislike Craig. I, on the other hand, was tremendously curious to meet this fellow Craig, willing to risk his life with people he'd never met before.

That Christmas evening I laid out presents I had brought for everyone from Kathmandu and lit candles in the dining tent. Anu surprised us with little rugs of Tibetan wool, handmade in his village, with the word *pumori* woven into them, one for each of us. Phutashi brought in a big bowl of yak stew in a creamy sauce, his version of turkey and cranberries. To the guys, Christmas was a place not a feeling, and the place was home, and we were here, so there was nothing to celebrate. Steve was still leaving; Craig was still coming; Ned and Jim were still stewing over our failure. It wasn't merry. Maybe there was a Buddhist cure for this Christmas failure, I thought.

Mysterious Craig arrived by dinnertime the next day. My first impression was of a heavy, barrel-chested man with a cherubic face. His hair, wound in tight frizzy ringlets, framed glowing cheeks. He wore several wild scarves knotted around his neck, and his fleece mountaineering clothing was creatively embroidered with deep colors. His speech was slow and filled with the latest slang. He was a good-time California boy, footloose and sniffing for adventure. Craig was also strong and experienced: he had climbed with Jim in Yosemite and raced the speed-skiing circuit with Steve. Craig could hold his own and more.

I swear Ned and Jim must have smelled fresh testosterone when Craig walked into camp, which amped up their own supply. That night Ned woke me in the middle of the night to ask if I would attempt Pumori again instead of heading out over the passes around Everest as planned. The next morning Jim was already packing for Pumori; he didn't even question if anyone wanted to accompany him. Although Craig had just left San Francisco eight days ago, he was game for anything, regardless of acclimatization. He had never been to altitude before; base camp was the highest he'd been, but he'd go anywhere we were going. I'm not for watching the nest while others fly, so I packed up too.

I was hoping it wasn't an inauspicious sign for Craig when his climbing harness, not fastened properly, fell down around his legs just as a rock came whizzing by his head on the low traverse past advanced base. He had no chance of dodging, moving right or left, as his legs were "tied" by the harness around his ankles. He curled into a ball and held his head and was barely missed. If he'd tried to move and slipped he'd have fallen over the cliff at the edge of the ice. Grinning, as we all met at the other side of the traverse, Craig simply said, "Oops."

Jim, Craig, and Steve all came from the Lake Tahoe area in California. Their skills were the best. But their cavalier attitudes and senses of humor belied the level of danger they constantly kept in their lives through their extreme climbing and skiing. These lighter attitudes kept these guys from becoming mind blind, a term for overarousal that paralyzes a person's actions. In a state of emergency it can become too difficult for most people to dial 911 or press send on their phones. Their heart rates go beyond the athlete's zone of arousal and high performance of about 115 to 145 beats per minute to more than 175. With this higher heart rate, bodies begin shutting down to many sources of information and people become useless or mind blind.

Whether Jim, Steve, and Craig knew this intellectually or just instinctually I don't know, but I would guess the latter. Their light-hearted jokes and their tendency to disregard impending danger were perhaps what had kept them alive all this time. By making light of just about everything, their levity mentally controlled their heart rates and thus deterred the panic zone of mind blindness. Top-flight fighter pilots are known to have similar attitudes of levity and twisted jokes. This perspective may be a prerequisite for survival in all extreme endeavors.

The following two days, December 31 and January 1, ended up rest days. We'd mutually decided to rest and pack loads and spend New Year's Eve at advanced base, but New Year's Day found Jim unwell, necessitating another day of rest. One never knows in the Himalayas if low-grade sickness is altitude, a strange virus, or some weird intestinal bug. Time would tell. So we took the time. We spent much of our time discussing our subsequent climb over three 20,000-foot passes that would complete our half circle in Nepal.

Thinking of more strenuous work before we'd even washed our hands of Pumori oppressed me. High-altitude mountaineering is, in fact, just a grueling long-distance event—one that deals with time in terms of months not hours. It's an event where mental fatigue may play a more debilitating role than physical stress. The real high points on an expedition are about as rare as natural pearls found in a bed of oysters. But with the perseverance of a strong mind and the willing ability to continue, these high points can be strung together like pearls on a necklace, creating a life of unparalleled moments.

On January 2 we completely committed to our climb for the second time. We worked our loads up to the gear we had clipped in at the top two days earlier and moved up most everything over the porous, intricate ridge to the hole. Again, as I climbed over this 600-foot pitch, I marveled at Jim's earlier expertise in the dark, crocheting this route over this increasingly thin, fragile, lacy ice and loose rock. These unstable rocks rolled out from under my crampons, and the brittle ice broke away, making foot placements precarious at best.

This time we brought a two-person dome tent for the hole, much larger than our lighter, smaller assault tents we had used for the first attempt. I was delighted to have the warmth of the middle slot between Ned and Jim in the bigger tent, while Craig slept solo in an assault tent. He chuckled when I asked if he was cold or lonely on his own, as he confessed he was feeling relieved to have the space to stretch out his big body. That night Craig told us he was feeling "funny."

When Craig unzipped our tent and crawled in the next morning, we could see the whiteout outside. We were engulfed in a thick cloud. "I don't want to be caught out if this storm takes hold," Jim deliberated. He was anxious to get the climb over with, and I could feel our morale sinking. I had never stopped to think that we might not make it this second time around. Craig had never slept this high before, at 21,000 feet, and was feeling worse, with the pounding pain in his head increasing. The kerosene fumes from the stove were making him sicker in our tent. He didn't know if it was the fumes or the altitude, but he felt he was deteriorating.

The course of action Craig chose left a lasting impression on me. He was strong enough to carry on but chose to use his strength to rappel down on his own so as not to jeopardize our chances of success on the peak. If his condition worsened our expedition would turn from a summit bid into a rescue mission. No question about that. Without previous altitude experience, Craig just didn't know what his body would do next. Craig's decision to descend had nothing to do with fear; he was unselfishly thinking of the rest of us.

The next day when things cleared, Jim, Ned, and I took only four hours to lug all our gear up over the remaining pitches to the Breadloaf, including the exhausting 70-degree Swiss cheese pitch, named for its holey ice. Our persistent coughs, which we dubbed the Himalayan hack, laid us low in the tent we shared, but warm friendship and positive energy surrounded the three of us, who had persevered to this point, our previous high point. We had nestled our camp two in tight to an icefall, protecting ourselves to the south and west and exposing ourselves to a gaping crevasse on the other side at about 22,000 feet.

The next day, January 6, dawned clear. We foolishly calculated the next 1,500 feet would take us about three hours to the summit. The route steepened up a gulley that looked as if a giant ice-cream scoop had dredged down the mountain and peeled it out. Jim graciously let me lead here, on what I considered the prettiest pitch. It was a thrill I will always savor as I recall looking down on the men and into the belly of the Khumbu icefall below. It was frightening to think this Khumbu icefall curling around Everest could surge forward, like the frozen river it is, as much as four feet in a day, toppling ice blocks weighing tons and crushing anything in its path, including whole expedition parties.

At one point the rope went taut between Jim and me, and when I looked back at him I saw him lighting up. "Bridwell, I don't see how you can climb and smoke," I yelled down in my raspy voice. To which he yelled back in return, "I don't see how I can climb and not smoke." Jim was a gnarly, wild character to be sure, I thought, as I shook my head and breathed deeply in air so thin it had about half the oxygen content of sea-level air. Maybe this is why he let me lead, so he could smoke! This says a lot about Jim's ability and not much about mine: Where I felt challenged, Jim felt like he could relax with a cigarette!

I was relieved that my thin cross-country inner boots left enough room in my boots for proper circulation. I had two overboots on as well. Jim had only one. Because our thermometers didn't go below minus 20 degrees Fahrenheit, we didn't know exactly how cold it was; the thermometer had bottomed out awhile ago. The wind was gusting up to about forty miles an hour, creating a great wind chill factor. The relaxed day had drawn a sense of urgency around itself. Although tied in, I had felt largely alone to this point with only my rhythmic breathing for company, as we needed to keep space between us for safety.

Jim was leading now, and he began to push himself with an intensity that I hadn't seen. I was tied in behind him, hoofing it as fast as I could manage. The rope became taut between Ned and me, and Ned assured me later that he wouldn't have wished for any faster pace. The last five hundred feet were dotted with sastrugi snow cones two to three feet high created by the continuous high winds. Jim was madly winding in and out of these horns of snow, so I had to keep stopping to unwind the rope from the horns. By the time I got the rope straightened out, I had to scramble straight up the steepest portions of the slope to avoid having the rope snap taut between us. It was exhausting. My breathing was coarse and uneven as I sucked in the air that was so cold and dry my throat felt like it was burning.

The wind was howling so fiercely we had no audible communication. Jim finally realized what he'd been putting his second through when he dashed up a ramp to the north side and continued across the summit plateau. The rope tightened between us, and I faced an overhanging climb to reach the summit. When I stood my ground, Jim came to an abrupt halt. He retraced his steps over the elliptical plateau, realizing he'd have to leave me some slack to reach the ramp. I walked up slowly, still puffing, and stood, at last, on the summit.

As Ned moved up, Jim began jumping and stomping around. I wondered if Jim had gone crazy, then I remembered his feet. Meanwhile Ned began circling us, snapping, what seemed at the time, hundreds of photographs. It was probably at least thirty below and blowing about sixty miles an hour. It was a slicing, noisy cold. The roar of the wind killed all other sound, and I felt as though I were observing Ned and Jim in a silent movie. My level of hypoxia had me feeling separate, removed from the scene that I was actually part of. Then I was pulled back into the scene as Jim began to howl like an animal. He wanted off. He looked at me and I threw my arm in the direction of the ramp, indicating as best I could, "Let's get the hell out of here."

Ned, oblivious, was pulling on the rope in the opposite direction, furiously recording the event. While Jim and Ned had been moving about the summit I had been stationary, gazing at the 360-degree view. Situated between the two of them I was subject to the Maypole effect: they had wrapped the rope around me, and I began working frantically to untangle the mess. I tugged on the rope to Ned, urging him to come along as I tumbled after Jim down the ramp. Once under the overhang we could hear each other as we shouted. Jim was frantic about his feet. I told him to untie if he felt comfortable alone, and he was off like a desperate rabbit.

Ned looked up from the tangled mess of rope he was trying to unravel and glared at me as he saw Jim bound off. I grabbed the rope from Ned and coiled it, tying us in closer together. Ned wasn't angry because he thought my decision to let Jim he go solo was bad but because I'd made the decision without consulting him. Although most of the rope was coiled between Ned and me, it still caught on sastrugi continually and threw us off balance as we tossed the rope up and over each time. Ned lost his temper while catching a crampon in a rope coil and tripped, sprawling to the ground. He arrested any slide, but we knew too well this part of our expedition, on descent while exhausted, left us the most vulnerable to making mistakes.

I was quiet on descent, leery of Ned's mood as we made our way down the last steep couloir, through the tilted seracs, and over the gaping crevasses to the ridge where we walked with one foot in Nepal and one foot in Tibet. The descent was complicated and exacerbated by being so tightly roped. Both Ned and I were more comfortable attached throughout the dangers before us, but our low energy and oxygen-starved muscles and brain made working together a hard exercise in patience. Ned assured me afterward his foul temper was aimed at the rope not at me, but at the time I wasn't so sure.

Jim had his toes protected and tea ready by the time we arrived. Ned and I crashed down onto the snow outside the tent and still with full climbing regalia on—boots, crampons, and all—sat there outside the tent, drinking the warm, soothing liquid as if there could be nothing better in this world. When we finally pulled off gear and wrestled into the tent, the disruption to the calm sent me into another coughing spasm, which I'd become quite prone to now. Jim kept badgering me, affectionately calling me a pinhead for not eating the chocolate he had out for me. I knew I would just throw it up when coughing wracked my system again, but he persisted. So I shoved the chocolate down my throat and promptly began to cough; I leaned forward, putting my head out of the tent, and threw it up. This time I could safely say, "I told you so." When I laughed Jim just looked at me quizzically, unsure why I found any humor in the situation.

This was just like banging my head on the rock and laughing as my head bled when I fell climbing with the guys in Yosemite. Sure, banging my head or throwing up wasn't pleasant, but each time I was so unable to control my body that it appeared ridiculous to me. My mind, quite separate from my body, thinks, "Okay, here we go," and in my mind's eye I just watch my physical self do what it's doing, completely without the control of my mind. I find it funny because I feel like this helpless bystander, watching the mishap happen to myself.

Ned was content now, encouraged by the fact that we were some of the first to be successful in the winter season in the Himalayas, and he told me I was the first woman to climb in the winter and to summit Pumori. When things settled down in the tent, Jim said, "I've never seen a face as determined as yours was today." To which I shot back in good humor, "I didn't think you turned around long enough to focus on anything. You were wild. I had to dredge up any grit I had to stay on your tail." The three of us sank into sleep in minutes.

The following day the completion of the descent off the mountain was quick and so were our tempers. Jim took off dragging our 600-foot rope behind him. The rope looped and caught and snagged as Ned let it out while Jim descended. Jim cursed, waiting for Ned to descend, when

Ned's descent got hung up by this auxiliary rope. No one wanted to carry the rope as it would be a heavy load on top of our packs of about forty-five pounds each. Then Ned cursed as he tried to untangle the mess when he reached Jim. We were all just worn thin. In the end I tripped on the bergschrund, fell flat on the ice, and wound up cursing myself for getting cut.

The next day, January 8, I was sitting on a box in the cook tent at base camp, situated just under 18,000 feet, swinging my legs absentmindedly, surrounded by warming steam, bubbling pots, and good smells. I could eat again. After several days of little to no food, this was heavenly. The heat felt wonderful, and the level ground gave me such a feeling of freedom. I didn't have to be superconscious of every foot and hand placement to stay alive, as I had been on steeper territory. Down here I could walk where I wished, when I wished. This expedition had taught me to appreciate things as basic as walking and eating.

I peered out of the tent and saw Saile floating into camp carrying a load of wood. Even when encumbered she moved with a shy grace. When I stepped out of the tent to greet her, she flashed a big grin, pointed up at Pumori, and nodded her head up and down vigorously. I reflected her smile and slowly nodded yes. At that moment the initial emotion of relief was replaced by a growing, deep, smooth satisfaction. For me successfully climbing a peak doesn't bring about elation, just a strong, satisfied feeling that I accomplished what I set out to do. I was pleased to tell Saile that I had made it.

Later that evening, under the moonlight, we watched a wondrous sight after an incredible roar drew us from the warm cocoon of our tent. Ice cliffs on the East Face had collapsed, toppling ice blocks and towers on its way. An entire quarter of the mountain in our view was exploding. The avalanche swept over the lower part of our climbing route where we had been a little more than twenty-four hours before, taking everything in its path. As climbers we really are only as good as our luck.

Starting out on the next leg of our expedition I was probably ten to fifteen pounds less than when I arrived in Nepal, and I was pretty honed when I arrived. Our packs would be the heaviest yet, as we needed to carry everything with us from start to finish. I felt like an unambitious kid being sent to summer camp by her parents against her will as we set out on this portion of our circle. I was wrestling with the change in attitude since Jim had left us for his home in the United States. His good humor had balanced Ned's frequent gloominess and had added snap and color to our conversations. He had also shown a certain respect for my attitude and suggestions.

Suddenly I felt like I had been demoted to the class of draft horses and yaks. It irked me when Ned and Craig ignored my comments as they discussed our route over the open map and folded it up while I was still pointing something out. I was disturbed that Ned had not heeded my calculations concerning money and the number of porters we needed to get from Namche to the base of the Mingbo La. We ended up just as I suspected, short of cash and asking our Sherpas to carry more than they should have. I decided to bide my time and wait to see how things unfolded in the field. I tried to cool down and relax as the Sherpas trekked back to their homes, leaving Ned, Craig, and I to fend for ourselves.

January 17 we headed up to the Mingbo La, *la* meaning "mountain pass" in the local language. Craig led a steep 65-degree pitch to get up to the base of the fluted wall of the Mingbo. The flutes were a series of perfectly matched runnels of hard snow, running parallel from top to bottom on the pass. This wall was a gorgeous, natural sculpture with such elegance and symmetry. The design looked like white ruffles on ice. We chose the centermost runnel and climbed for five hundred feet, straight up. My pulse was one hundred beats per minute, consistently, as I hoisted the sixty pounds on my back with every step up, while slamming my crampons into the ice for support and balance.

We climbed as three together tied into one rope, not simultaneously, but belaying one another up after we each had finished a one-third portion of a rope length. Craig and Ned then decided to tie in closer and do the last pitch climbing simultaneously with me belaying them below to gain some time. As I watched them above I came to the easy conclusion that this was not smart. If they peeled—and one would surely take the other with them—I would never be able to hold them both, especially considering they hadn't put a single ice screw in between them and me to defray the pull. They had basically set it up for all three of us to pop off if any one of us blew it. Considering I was anchored into the slope and not moving, most likely one of them would take us all down.

Craig hit the cornice, the frozen wave of blown snow, at the top of the slope. He had to stand on front points and hack through it with his ice ax to haul his big body and heavy pack through it to the top. Without one single piece of protection holding our rope to the slope between Craig and me, it was looking quite precarious. I wondered for a flicker of a moment what Jim would have done and realized that was a distraction. He wasn't here. My thoughts turned to having confidence in Craig. He pulled it off, but not without a lot of grunting, which I could hear from more than one hundred feet below.

Ned and Craig were being buffeted in the wind while I was belayed up, so we all skedaddled down just as soon as I arrived. After jumping a couple of crevasses we were on an easier slope and stood to marvel at our surroundings. There was a special magic to this portion of the circle because of its remote isolation and tranquil stillness. At this point of our expedition we were committed, as we had no radio and no Sherpa support back in a base camp. We were alone going from point A to B, carrying everything we would need on our backs. In some ways this part of our endeavor was more dangerous than our technical climb of Pumori: if we suffered an accident here, a rescue wasn't possible.

We walked two miles on glacial snow as smooth as carpet after coming off the Mingbo La. It was getting dark. To avoid the crevasses dead ahead where the glacier ended, we moved to our right onto a frozen stream, climbing down little frozen waterfalls like giant stairs until we reached our campsite for the night. Ned continued to appear tuned in to Craig, racing along down the waterfalls with or against him; I couldn't tell exactly which. But what I could tell was that I was growing impatient with my demotion to load-bearing chattel and serfdom.

Teammate Tom Carter cranking telemark turns on cross-country skis down the New Zealand Alps during the Southern Cross Expedition.

Jan Reynolds climbing up the New Zealand Alps on cross-country skis.

Ned Gillette running the gauntlet during Southern Cross Expedition.

Jan Reynolds crossing an estimated 33-degree glacial stream au naturel to keep clothes dry for the other side.

Camels for bearing loads up to 17,000 feet, with the peak of Muztagata
in the background during the American Friendship Expedition.

Kirkiz women and their babies surrounding one of
their traditional yurts near the base of Muztagata.

Galen Rowell and Ned Gillette breaking trail and avoiding crevasses
while skiing up the peak of Muztagata at almost 25,000 feet.

Jan Reynolds skiing on Muztagata, where she set
the women's world high-altitude skiing record.

Jan Reynolds trading earrings with Tursunhai, a Kirkiz woman, near Muztagata while sharing a meal of yogurt and tea, and lots of laughs.

A Tibetan/Sherpa funeral puja, a blessing ritual as part of a funeral for a loved one, complete with yak butter sculpture and yak butter candles on the altar, that Jan Reynolds attended while on the Everest Grand Circle Expedition.

Pumori under the moonlight in the Himalayas at the start of the Everest Grand Circle Expedition.

Ned Gillette at high camp on Pumori with Everest in the background.

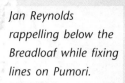

Jan Reynolds rappelling below the Breadloaf while fixing lines on Pumori.

Jan Reynolds leading Ned Gillette on Pumori.

Jan Reynolds rappelling down West Col, one of three 20,000-foot passes on the Nepal side of the Everest Grand Circle Expedition.

Fearless leader Ned Gillette forgets the map as they make their way out, down river to civilization at the end of the first half the Everest Grand Circle Expedition.

Jan Reynolds with Anu—the Sherpa sirdar, leader of the porters—who managed to find Jan Reynolds, Craig Calonica, and Ned Gillette after five days with no food at the end of the first half of their Everest Grand Circle Expedition.

The truly amazing truck that got the team into Tibet, high in the Himalayas, with their Chinese translator, driver, and liaison officer to start the second half of their Everest Grand Circle Expedition.

Ned Gillette jumps for joy to be able to finally ski on this supposed circum-skision of Everest during the second half of the Everest Grand Circle Expedition.

Jim Bridwell smoking a butt at high altitude while trying to help Ned Gillette figure out where in the world they are in the gray area on the map, not drawn to scale.

Jan Reynolds with her rifle, Sweetie, training for the U.S. Biathlon team.

Test flight of the balloons over the sacred stupa Boudhanath in Kathmandu.

Phil Kavanagh navigating the balloon, checking the chart to make sure they are on course for Everest.

Chris Dewhirst inside the huge balloon as it is loaded with hot air for a test flight in Kathmandu.

A friend beckons Jan Reynolds in for a meal of potatoes and a place to lay her head on the Nangpa La salt trade route from Namche, Nepal, to Tingri, Tibet.

One of the last great yak caravans with Tibetan herders just finishing their crossing of the 20,000-foot Nangpa La, the ancient salt trade route, the highest trade pass in the world.

The moraine leading to the Nangpa La glaciated pass.

Traditional trader who has just traveled the glaciated
pass from Tingri, Tibet, into the high country of Nepal
feeding his yaks and naks tsampa, or ground barley.

Tibetan trader negotiating a good trade while asking for tea as he uses his calculator to figure the worth of his rug.

Yanomami beauties in the Amazon Territory of Venezuela use red onoto seeds mixed with ashes to make black makeup by hand during Jan Reynolds's travels for her Vanishing Culture series.

Inside an igloo large enough to sport windows of lake ice, Akak prepares caribou skin to make clothing for her family during Jan Reynolds's travels for her Vanishing Culture series.

Jan Reynolds playing her recorder for the Tuareg man, one of the last camel caravan drivers, and his child in the center of the Sahara Desert in southern Algeria the heart of the Hoggar Mountains during her travels for her Vanishing Culture series

Women are shown to lose motivation in competitive situations, and males tend to thrive. Studies show females are better students in school, achieving higher grades than their male counterparts, yet females don't fare better than males in the workforce.[1] I realized as Ned and Craig bonded through competing and racing against each other—which also resulted in their private conferences to make decisions—I, on the other hand, was put off by the competition. Although I hated to I knew I needed to confide in Ned how I felt so I wouldn't blow up about it at the wrong time.

I realized I could be seen as easily influenced, just as women in studies were seen,[2] on this portion of the expedition, but I didn't feel unconfident. Just as the female researchers uncovered, I wasn't unconfident; I just think and operate differently than Ned and Craig.[3] Women appear more easily influenced because of their choices to conform for the sake of harmony. Women just want a harmonious setting and are more willing to sacrifice for it by going along. Women aren't necessarily influenced to conform; they *choose* to keep things harmoniously going along with decisions so as not to rock the boat.

Even in the toddler stages males show increased aggression and self-confidence compared to females; females show connectedness, bonding, and an emphasis on the importance of interrelatedness and relationships.[4] There is no better or worse here, just a different point of view and different ways of thinking and interacting in the world. I was living it right here on the expedition, a little microcosm of the big world. I had been holding on to my thoughts for the sake of harmony, going with the flow of Ned and Craig's decisions, but because I wasn't unconfident the time had come to speak up. I could go with the flow if we had been safe, but I questioned that.

I called ahead to Ned, and we had our little tête-à-tête. He took it well; we ended in a hug with arms too short to wrap around our backpacks, which added a little levity to the scene. An ounce of prevention is truly worth a pound of cure, especially in the microcosm of an expedition.

Ned and I heard Craig's whistle. He'd found a likely camp spot for the night and was drawing us in as the darkness wrapped around us in the belly of this wild, desolate valley, deep in the frozen Himalayan landscape. I had found the day draining, both physically and mentally, and looked forward to totally decompressing in the comfort of our little two-man tent, housing the three of us. First, my inflatable Therm-a-Rest went flat. I had carried this heavier mat instead of a lighter closed-cell foam pad because I thought the comfort and extra insulation from the cold ground would be worth it. I had compensated for this extra weight by taking my lightest down bag. Now my deflated pad was close to useless for anything, and my bag had minimal warmth.

Next, the pot was put on for tea and Craig tipped it over. My skimpy sleeping bag was now even skimpier because it got soaked. I thought nothing else could happen to make my night more cold and miserable, but I was wrong. The tent zipper broke on my side and the wind came surging over me. As miserable as I was, cold and wet, lying on lumpy ground, I couldn't handle it anymore—I broke out laughing. Craig and Ned joined me. After I put on all the dry clothing I could find, we all drifted into a long night's sleep.

We slept for twelve hours that night, in our nylon bubble affectionately dubbed the "beach bungalow" out of wishful thinking; it was set up on the edge of a frozen lake. I was encouraged that things had relaxed a little. Maybe the discussion between Ned and me had been worthwhile. The next day we shuffled over the lake until an ice tower collapsed off the edge of the Mingbo Glacier, at the head of the lake, causing a tremendous crashing sound followed by eerie undulations and cracking under our feet. We flew off the lake onto the disheveled moraine. We thought it preferable to slog over rough terrain than to sink like a stone into the depths of freezing water.

We groveled through bare boulder fields until we reached a milky blue lake, not frozen, called Hongu Pokhari. Although it was only two o'clock we set up camp on this "beach" and called it a day, after just three hours of working. Ice chunks had been pushed up on shore and frozen upright, looking like solid waves from our tent and adding to the beach effect. Anu was due to meet us on the other side of the passes in four days, and we had made great progress on our route already. Tomorrow we would be halfway when we reached West Col, so everyone had now come to the conclusion that there was no hurry.

Hongu Pokhari was cupped at the lowest point of our journey. We could see Everest and neighboring Lhotse Mountain peeking over the ridge. I marveled at the idea of Everest growing a quarter of an inch each year as India slides under Asia, squeezing this giant hunk of rock up. I was from the Green Mountains in Vermont, much older and rounded by ancient glaciers than these young, Himalayan punks, still flexing their tectonic muscles. We could glimpse some of the formidable East Face of Everest, another personality of this three-faced beauty. We were honoring her moods and character from every angle, over months through different seasons. My respect for her was deepening daily.

Our day was straightforward, humping loads of almost sixty pounds over glacial rubble and old lake beds. Craig entertained us with tales of his speed-skiing misadventures. "I once had the world's record fall! In 1978 in Kilometro Lanciato, I stalled in the compression and hit the snow face first at 193 kilometers an hour. It didn't hurt 'cause I got knocked unconscious. I don't remember a thing. They say the helicopter crew that flew me to the hospital flipped out when they stripped off my vinyl stretch suit—I didn't have a thing on underneath. My hair was in a long braid, and I was naked except for my sunglasses when they wheeled me in to the hospital. They slapped me in the mental ward! When I woke up it was impossible to be released. So I snuck out. Steve McKinney found me wandering around Cervinia in slippers and a bathrobe!"

I'd probably lost fifteen pounds or so by now. And I noticed Craig's belly receding almost daily. Ned seemed to be maintaining, although his legs were thinning. Those power thighs of his were losing girth. We three constantly craved food. That night I noticed my dreams had shifted from being about gorgeous, chocolaty desserts, probably as a result of my constant low blood-sugar level, to dreams of roast beef, because of burning my own muscle mass as fuel. When Craig kicked over the stove and pot again, pouring out all the melted snow that had just reached boiling to cook our next freeze-dried meal, we could have eaten him! Craig earned his name, Boy Blunder, after performing this pot-tipping ritual for the second time in a row.

We were climbing the equivalent of three Denali Peaks in Alaska by crossing over Mingbo La, West Col, and Sherpani Col, all set at over 20,000 feet. We had no base camp to retreat to or yaks and Sherpas for load carrying. It would be another few days of laboring under our loads with sparse food before we would meet Anu and his merry men at the end of this exhausting, endurance leg of our journey. We had 1,500 feet to climb first thing in the morning to cross West Col. We zigzagged through crevasses, post-holing as we went, punching through the weak crust with our legs and submerging up to our knees and thighs.

Craig led over a thin snow bridge across the bergschrund and front-pointed to a rock belay. Things were looking good until we hit another gaping fracture, which we had to straddle sideways, launching one leg over and slamming the side points of our crampons into the upper side of this giant crack in the slope while thrusting our ice axes in as well to keep the rising wind from blowing us over. We were struggling to balance the cumbersome, unwieldy weight on our backs as we leaped.

My heart sank when we reached the rock crest of the pass, sharp as a knife's edge, in the heavy, gusty winds. We had to traverse this nasty, pointed ridge, with double the possibilities of falling, as we could tumble down on either side. We were forced to crab along on all fours with our weighty packs crushing our knees and hands into the rock on this razor edge. We were unroped so as not to pull off rocks, or each other, if the wind blew us away. Twice we had to stand and awkwardly balance as we stepped out to the west to inch our wobbly way around a couple of big rocks. This traverse was entirely too nerve wracking, I thought, as the protective rope lay in a bundle at the top of my unwieldy pack.

After descending from our peril I was feeling good; the guys were dragging. This was the beginning of a physical shift I would notice through the rest of the expedition. We all had our swings of energy, both up and down, but I seemed to exhibit a bit of slow-burning energy that the men lacked. I was wondering if, as a woman, perhaps because of the additional subcutaneous fat layer men don't have, I was, over time, better able to maintain than the men.

We don't have sporting events as long and grueling as an expedition, but maybe this is what was needed, multiday events to give women a chance to show that our enduring strength can meet or beat that of a man's. We eventually camped at 20,300 feet, closer to Sherpani Col and our goal for the next day. We had two days of food with us, and I was keen to set ourselves up to cross this last col to meet Anu sooner rather than later. I was afraid the men would have a rougher time than I without food.

The wind had not abated, so we began building a snow wall around the tent for protection. As I felt strong, I worked diligently, unaware of how long my hands had been uncovered while I slid the tent poles into the tent sleeves. It came sharply to my attention, after handling the metal poles in the high wind, just how painful my hands were. I shook them to get the blood moving, cursing the fact that I was so tired of frozen fingers. A feeling of dread descended on me like a heavy cloud as I realized I never wanted to feel fingers this cold again yet I knew I would. The guys had already dived into the tent and were hunkered down in their bags, depleted of energy. I took over the cooking, safely away from Boy Blunder. I eyed the sky overhead with concern as I scooped snow for the stove, remembering our days holed up for a week during storms in New Zealand without food. I didn't fancy being trapped again, especially this high without sustenance for any length of time.

Sherpani Col looked deceptively simple from our viewpoint the following morning. The wind was pushing up the glacier on the opposite side, hitting the col furiously and tumbling over the top to where we stood. Ned, our passionate scout, had moved ahead, fighting the vicious, wintry blasts looking for the line of least resistance down the other side of Sherpani Col to the Barun Glacier and ultimately off the passes. I thought to myself that Ned's intensity might well affect his moods, but it also drives him to unhesitatingly risk his comfort for the rest of us.

Ned was nearly lifted into the air before he scuttled like a crab under a big rock, beckoning us to join him. After surveying our task of getting down the col, Craig led out from behind the giant rock, on my belay. He worked his way along a buttress of rocky teeth that littered the pass for the next one hundred feet. He crawled on all fours with his wind pants flapping and whizzing like a ripped sail in a gale-force wind. Twice he had to slither out on his stomach to peer over the ridge to scout a potential descent route. The wind howled in our ears as we waited, unable to speak in the wild noise.

After we made our way down to where Craig had stopped and tied in, as he feared hidden crevasses lurking below, I relaxed. I still felt I had good energy for continuing, but when Craig pointed out where he thought we could camp for the night on the edge of the map, I paused. I had naturally monitored our progress throughout the passes and had a feel for our rate of travel. Given the time we had before night fell upon us, if we shot for Craig's intended site we would probably end up in the crevasse field ahead, instead of beyond it, by the time it became too dark to see.

This area would be a treacherous minefield to travel through without good sight and an impossible place to camp. We simply weren't traveling fast enough to make Craig's goal. Continuing was foolish and inviting disaster. But when I explained my thoughts to Craig, I simply asked him if he knew the time of day or our rate of travel thus far. He didn't know either, and when I informed him of both, asking him if he thought maybe camping near where we stood might be a better idea, he discussed it with me.

It all ended in agreement to camp nearby because "Jan had had enough for the day." I could take the hit, the "blame" so to speak, if it meant doing the right thing. Given time I realized this was how I was able to make myself heard and to hash out decisions. I spoke much differently than the men at times and found it productive. If I had demanded to camp nearby or had tried to make my teammate look foolish for his suggestion or if I simply hadn't said "maybe," I could have threatened someone else's judgment. Instead I invited discussion. I felt the men often were more threatening with their direct statements, as opposed to my open-ended questions, and perhaps this male directness might have been what put the men at odds, by pitting opinions against each other instead of inviting discussion.

We camped that evening below the col on an expanse of glacier surrounded by sharp, peaked seracs that looked like giant sharks fins cutting through an icy sea. It was January 21. I lay back in the tent satisfied that we had made the passes in the time we had calculated. Craig was now a part of the team like a well-worn shoe, fitting comfortably without chafing and binding. As a tiny team of three, we had been far more mobile, traveling what is called alpine style, with no backup camps and everything we had with us on our backs. We were much more fleet than a large expedition would have been. And considering our self-sufficient circumstances, additional members would have only increased the possibility and probability of error or injury, without increasing our odds of success. Moving in alpine style, over the course of the entire expedition from Pumori to Sherpani Col, was proving safe and effective as well as fast, compared to an unwieldy, classic expedition style of climbing employing large numbers under singular authority, with camps spread out on the mountain for support.

The next morning we took a look at what was left for food: one freeze-dried dinner and assorted lunch leftovers. We searched the area for two hours for any signs of Anu and decided we would have the best luck finding him near Makalu's base camp. Using ski poles to balance ourselves, we headed down the valley, picking our way along the moraine that ran next to the Barun Glacier. The boulders varied from the size of my fist to that of a small car. The rock felt cold and hard, and much of it was unstable, sliding or rolling as I stepped or hopped from place to place. The unwieldy pack threatened to throw me off balance with the slightest wrong move. I thought about how easy it would be to slip between a couple of rocks and break a bone and the incredible ordeal it would be to get someone with a broken leg out of here. I became extremely aware of just how insignificant we were and imagined the three of us as little sand fleas crawling among pebbles and sand on a beach.

After having been on the move for seven hours and not seeing a trace of base camp or a sign of our Sherpas anywhere, we decided to pitch our tent on a pebbly outwash just beyond the terminus of the Barun Glacier. Ned inventoried the last of our rations while our final freeze-dried dinner was cooking: three small bags of tropical fruit mix, one plastic bag of chocolate drink mix, one bag of dried milk, six tea bags, and a handful of bouillon cubes. One fuel canister remained. Ned complimented me on my precise planning, and rationing: "Perfect if Anu had been here."

I went on hesitatingly, "You know, Anu didn't really want to come into here. His mother was afraid of bandits down in the Arun. She made him leave his necklace at home, so it wouldn't be stolen." Our half circle was completed. We'd done it on our own, but now we counted on the keen attention and the camaraderie of the Sherpas to get us back to civilization, physically and psychologically whole.

"Tomorrow, if we continue out, we walk off our map. I don't have the next one . . . no map," Ned admitted with painful timing. The tent was very quiet for several moments. I was glad it was dark. Then Craig lurched to his knees, snapped on his headlamp, which shone directly into Ned's eyes, and shouted, "Guilty!" He then bellowed a laugh, rolled back, and grazed the pot with his elbow, tipping all the water out, flooding the tent for the third time. Boy Blunder at his best.

It had begun to snow outside; the dread winter storms were moving in as the winds kicked up around us and we shook the cooking water out of our clothes and sleeping bags. We went to sleep cold, wet, and hungry, wondering what would happen next. This wasn't the way I had envisioned the end of our expedition; I imagined happily traveling with our Sherpas and reconnecting with the luxuries of civilized life. January 23, the next morning, we chugged on for three hours after breakfasting on chocolate drink with dried milk, only.

We had dropped below 16,000 feet, and the air felt thick and sluggish, like my dull mind and starving body. Then we spotted three tents behind a mound in the terrain, hidden for protection. Anu? Out burst a Frenchman wildly gesturing and waving us in. "I am Ivano Giardini, Chamonix guide." Inside the tent he told us his story. He was soloing

Makalu in winter on the hardest route. He was a vegetarian with no books, no radio, only the mountains for his company. "I am crazy, *un peu* . . . a little," he laughed as he looked at us through his thumb and forefinger in front of his eye, about an inch apart. He had literally been blown off his route. The wind was so strong it blew his rappel lines up in the air past him as he descended to escape with his life. He was waiting to make a second attempt.

He offered us tea and sugar, some cookies, and a bowl of peanuts, which Ned, Craig, and I fell upon, struggling to maintain a polite veneer over our urges to grab and hoard. As hungry as we were, we knew this man certainly needed his own supplies to survive. But Ivano, being the good soul he was, assessed our predicament and handed us what looked like a bag of sawdust. It was oatmeal. We gave Ivan our map of the Everest Region in return, which he was visibly grateful for. It was another way for the mountains to keep him company, up here, all alone.

He made us a map of our exit from the Makalu region, "There! Trail makes sharp turn, frozen river, very bad, very steep, need crampons." Anu and his guys certainly didn't have crampons. We and our Sherpas of the Khumbu region had underestimated this Arun Valley in winter when we planned to have Anu trek in to meet us at Makalu after we climbed our last pass, Sherpani Col.

Ivano walked down the trail a bit with us after tea and hugged us all tightly when we departed. He was an emotional, flamboyant man with a grin of a child. I noticed he held on to me a little longer than the men and cried, *"Mon Dieu!"* when he finally let go. I didn't think the mountains were really keeping him good enough company after all. Minutes later, any signs of the trail vanished. We looked down at the torn paper, which Ivan had drawn his map on, as snowflakes blowing in the wind caught in its folds.

Ned figured it was on a scale of about 1:250,000. "I wouldn't trust that thing," Craig concluded. "I trust my instincts, and my instincts say follow the river down." Then he grinned, admitting, "Even though we can't see it or hear it." Craig was as wild as the curls on his head, but somehow he made sense. His boyish charm and his childish sense of humor were a release in our growing concern. The going was precarious; we kept sliding down steep, muddy, unfrozen ground under the snow. Our ski poles helped us control our descent, but they still weren't enough to keep us upright.

"No need to ration anymore; that's it on lunches," Craig concluded. Well at least we had Ivan's oatmeal for dinner tonight, then that was it, I thought. Our hiking boots had gotten so soaked that they were collecting the damp snow at such a rate we seemed to be clumping along in oversized cotton balls. Our feet became increasingly cold and painful. We stopped to put old plastic lunch bags on our feet as protective vapor barriers, but they soon tore. We continued walking to diffuse the pain in our frigid toes—as long as we could feel the pain, we weren't worried about permanent frostbite.

Here at 14,000 feet the air had more oxygen, but I just felt heavy, tired, low on energy, and foggy brained with more air and no food, laboring under at least fifty pounds of weight on my back. I wasn't getting enough calories to maintain my body heat. Even in my bag at night I felt too cold to sleep. During the day, regardless of how hard I was working, lifting my load on my back up and down slopes with every step, I never seemed to warm up. I was getting stressed, having to pay attention to every step I made or suffer great peril. In training I could always push myself hard, but then I could lie on the couch and have a beer afterward. There were no couches here! The constant attention was wearing on me. I could see it wearing on Ned as well.

We'd been under cloud cover since entering this Arun Valley, which is a 20,000-foot chasm, the deepest in the world. We had been only able to see about 100 feet ahead of us at most in the swirling snow and low cloud. We spied a log bridge over the Barun River we'd been following and took our chances crossing to reach a rudimentary shack on the other side. This must be Na, which Ivan had told us about. In the spring and fall, when the trail would be evident without this blanketing snow cover, climbers and Sherpas would rest here en route to Makalu.

The rough boards had been hacked by hand and brought up to make a shelter from the rain and wind. Tonight it kept the snow off us and allowed us to build a blazing fire within its walls, protecting us from the weather. We polished off Ivan's oatmeal, a meal made up of mostly water with a little dried milk in it and some oats floating around. It sustained me nonetheless by filling the space between my belly button and spine, which had felt like it had been pressed together, flat. We had barely eaten in the past couple of days.

In the dark and cold of night we heard the swishing of footsteps in snow. Life was an adventure to be sure in this valley. Namaste was the greeting when two Sherpas poked their heads inside as they banged their feet on the door to disengage the clumped snow from their feet. They had seen our fire glowing. I got out the pot and made them hot tea with the last of our powdered milk, anxious to know what had brought them here, especially at this hour. "I mail runner. Message to Makalu," was the introduction by the first Sherpa. The second Sherpa said nothing. After snoring all night long the Sherpas departed for Ivan's camp.

We were down to bullion and tea for sustenance, so breakfast was quick, by the fire, before we went on. We had the Sherpa's footsteps from the night before to follow down the river, which was a good thing. I began to perk up, as Ned began to lag behind. We had been alternating in swings of energy and depletion for the past two days. Craig, who had spent less time at altitude and had brought some of his own energy reserves wrapped around his belly as fat, was more consistent and strong. Craig was in his element now, with route finding or intuiting. "My friends always say my way is faster than following a direct line but not always easier!" Craig confessed with a proud grin as we struggled to kick-start our hungry bodies.

We began our day with boulder hopping—one misstep and you would be washed away by the no longer frozen but now raging river. We then waded through thigh-deep snow over undulating terrain higher on the bank after we lost the tracks of the Sherpas. I noticed Ned lagging behind again and worried he was going down. It had begun snowing in earnest again. "There is no way the terrain we just came over is a major route. I'll bet there was a bridge across the river, a mile or two back, that we missed," Craig announced. He was right. But before we knew for sure, we decided we wouldn't retrace our steps but carry on this "wrong" side of the river until we found a way to cross back over farther downriver.

I was beginning to find it hard to stay alert. I was gradually letting myself lose the sharpness our travel demanded. When I would suffer low periods like Ned, it sometimes felt difficult to even stay awake on my feet. On a very steep section of the bank, covered with deceptive snow, my foot broke through and I began to slide uncontrollably down toward the river sixty feet below. Fortunately my reactions were still intact, and I grabbed an unsuspecting rhododendron bush, jerking myself to a halt. I still don't know how I gripped the thing with my hand bundled up in a slippery nylon mitten, but when adrenaline is flowing, your limits are extended.

When we looked down upon the river, once past this treacherous slope, we saw a bridge made of two logs spanning the rushing water. It was now evident we should have been on the riverbank on the other side of the river, as Craig suspected, and now the trail was crossing back over to the side we were on. We moved lower to the bridge and carried on down the real trail. I was still carrying the same amount of weight as the men yet had less muscle mass than they had to transport it with. I realized I would fall asleep if I sat down, so I kept moving despite the weight on my back, not daring to rest for fear of nodding off and falling way behind.

It has been noted that women are better suited for the "death zone" of high altitude than men, because they have better endurance and ability than men to adapt to thin air. Women suffer less high-altitude pulmonary edema, they maintain base body weight better, and their more efficient circulatory systems lead them to suffer less frostbite. Now, at maybe 12,000 feet, my advantages as a woman were moot, making my efforts more strenuous than that of my male colleagues, and I was feeling it. My womanly subcutaneous fat layer may have been used up by this time on account of my extra output compared to the men.

As we gathered near the log crossing Craig announced, "I saw some Sherpa footprints heading up, almost missed 'em under the new snow. I wouldn't have thought the trail would climb off the river." We marched up again and into a fairyland forest with huge rhododendron and other large plants. By dusk we found a large cave. The floor was covered with dry leaves, and the roof was blackened by past fires. Small birch trees curled out from the rim of the cave at the opening, causing the cave to look like an eye with lashes. Both Ned and I were enticed by the mysterious cave in this fairyland forest. We were both just whipped and plopped down, unable to move. Ned said he felt like "a marathon runner who just raced without ever having trained for the event."

Craig wanted to walk until dark, but we'd already had hard going for seven hours, so he went route hunting alone. Ned had found large icicles to break off near the cave so we wouldn't have to keep going to the river for water. He carried them in like cordwood in his arms and laid them down while I readied the fire. We both laughed to feel like Neanderthals in our cozy cave. This was a far cry from the Ritz in New York City where we had stayed during our press conferences before the expedition, when we were treated like rock stars. That had felt strange to me; this cave felt more natural. Craig returned, excitedly informing us he'd found Ivan's "ice river at a right angle up," and it would be strenuous going tomorrow.

The men both started picking up every stick I lay on the burning woodpile and repositioning it. After a couple of times I said, "This is a one-man—ah woman—job." They backed off, laughing, but it was still evident that they continued to lapse into taking control when it wasn't necessary. I probably started more fires in the rain than both of them put together, in all my canoe-guiding days. Coaxing wet wood into flame was one of my old specialties. Ned and Craig then occupied themselves with creating a drying line for our clothes over the fire.

It was laughable how content I felt in the cave, with bare feet lifted next to the roaring fire and fetid socks toasting above alongside myriad clothing. We had two cups of flavorful, although nonnutritional bullion for dinner, followed by two cups of boiled water for dessert. I was full, and life was good, for the moment. Tomorrow would be day four of this long march that Ivan had said would take us two. After dozing off I woke to see my boot's insoles in flames. I snuffed them out and dragged all of our boots farther from the fire as they were all twisting and warping into strange shapes when the synthetic components of the fabric and soles changed chemical form with the addition of heat.

We rekindled the fire as Craig served us breakfast; a tea bag apiece. "Help yourself to as many cups per bag as you like," he said graciously. While packing up for the day, feeling hungover with fatigue, I mumbled, "I hope there are no perils today." To which Craig responded, "Voilá, eet ees time to go up the ice river, non?" in a fake French accent. Digging the sides of our hiking boots into the ground under the snow and using the roots of trees as steps, we gained elevation through heavy vegetation. We climbed up and up for four hours, seemingly forever. As we struggled upward, slipping and falling, we again contemplated our heavy boots and crampons but didn't put them on, as we kept thinking the ice would end any minute.

We could barely make out the Sherpas' tracks climbing again, over another pass to the east, covered in deep snow. When I realized it was back up, wading through heavy snow cover, I wilted in spirit. "If another storm moves in with a whiteout we could get pinned down up here. I'll break trail; we need to move," Craig urged. "You're right Craig, but I'm out of gas, running on empty. I'd be dangerous on the next pass. I've spent the past two months looking at my feet, putting one in front of the other, and one more day won't matter."

Craig and I both had a point. We were all dangerously tired and hadn't eaten a square meal in five days, but we could get stuck here for a day or two if bad weather closed us in. Then Craig did the unbelievable; he unzipped his pack and pulled forth an unaccounted-for bag of dried, tropical fruit mix. He had been hoarding this for just such an occasion to ward off an emergency. I gingerly dipped my hand in, feeling as if I was the problem; I was the needy one. But we all ate from the bag, marveling at how, within minutes, we felt as if we had more warmth in our bodies. Were we hallucinating, or were we so low on fuel we could feel the energy infusion in such a pronounced manner?

Our feet were still freezing, however, so we finally did put on our double, plastic climbing boots and began our rhythmical, mechanical march up, yet again. I was so doggedly determined that I didn't dare fall off the pace for fear of straying behind. Apparently I was so emphatic that jolly, easygoing Craig turned around sharply at one point and snapped at me for "breathing down his neck." He felt I was pushing him harder than he wanted to go, meanwhile it was my attempt to just hang on. We didn't rest for the next hour and a half as we moved in relative silence.

A rock shrine was built at the height of the pass and a few tattered prayer flags flew from it. We descended steeply on the south side and could see the footprints crossing a stony ridge four hundred feet below in deep snow. The snow was thigh deep when we reached it, and we literally wallowed our way across, like worms through dirt. Exhausted, we congratulated ourselves for finally leaving snow behind us as we gazed on hazy blue foothills that dropped lower in regular tiers down to the lowlands of Nepal. We felt pretty sure we would come upon a village somewhere soon. We thought we could see some smoke rising far below, probably from some cooking fire.

We pitched the tent as the sky turned a gorgeous deep pink. We'd had enough after hiking a hard eleven hours that day on nothing but tea and bullion with a handful of dried fruit thrown in. We'd been accomplishing, perhaps, the equivalent of running a marathon or more for five days in a row with next to nothing to eat while carrying at least fifty pounds on our backs. We had all lost at least twenty pounds by now, including Craig, who hadn't gone on the Pumori instant altitude weight loss plan. Dragging our sorry butts over this rough terrain through deep snow for days without sustenance, following our traverse of the passes, had been enough to transform our cherubic, boyish-looking Craig, under his mass of dark curls, into a strapping, muscular man.

Early the next morning Ned found a mashed bouillon cube in his coat pocket. We used the last bit of gas to melt snow into lukewarm water, and then divided the cube among the three of us. As we toasted Craig's capable bushwhacking with our anemic drinks, I heard a sharp, quick *hey!* outside. I unzipped our tent enough to poke my head out—

and there was Anu with his troops behind him. I flew out of the tent and wrapped my arms around Anu and Angpura so tightly that I nearly choked them. The Sherpas began crashing through the bushes, snapping off dry branches and twigs. I'd never seen such a large fire built so quickly.

Anu had brought up fresh eggs from a settlement below and began cooking them and explained what had happened at the same time. Apparently none of the locals had been willing to hire out as porters because of the nasty weather and the tough traveling it had created. They also thought it was bad luck to go beyond the snow line, and they weren't prepared or equipped for the mountains in winter. Alas, Anu had known we were out of food for days and was so worried he finally persuaded some locals to show him the way into Makalu at least as far as the snow line, which was where we had spent the night.

The eggs were an incredible delight. After two months of eating mostly freeze-dried food, then no food at all, real sustenance was overwhelming. We poured ketchup on top of the eggs, and the spicy sauce went off like fireworks in my mouth. After our meal we continued our trek downhill for miles and miles. My knees hurt and so did Craig's toes—I had to laugh when he cut the ends of his shoes off to relieve the pressure on them. We reached Tashigan, a small settlement of thatched bamboo houses on a stream high in the jungle, in the late afternoon. The villagers were curious about us, to say the least. Because we hadn't trekked through their village on the way to the mountains they had trouble figuring out where we had come from.

The people belonged to hill tribes that had originally come from Tibet and were often the poorest of six or seven major ethnic strains in the Arun Valley. Most were barefoot—only the rich wear shoes. Most of these hill settlements are isolated, being up to two weeks' walk away from any bazaar town, and are self-sufficient: the wildlife and the barley, wheat, and potatoes they grow sustain them. Some people never leave their villages their entire lives. The outside world supplies only a few essentials—salt, jewelry, and metal for knives. Even without words it was obvious the women wanted to connect with me, albeit they were hesitantly curious in their approach, and the men, well, they looked askance and kept their distance from each other.

I was anxious to clean up a bit and wandered down to their glacial stream for a bath. Despite the temperature it felt wonderful. When I returned, sleek as an otter, the locals looked at my wet hair in amazement because they very seldom bathe and never in these temperatures. I stood by the open fire our Sherpas had built and were cooking dinner on. I was content.

It took us a few days to trek down to Tumlingtar where we could catch a small plane to Kathmandu. Although the Arun Valley was lush, beautiful, and mysterious, it showed signs of going the route of the depleted Khumbu. I had come to look at all of Nepal as an incredible land with an uncertain future as I peered out from the tiny plane window at the greenness below. I looked over at Craig, then squeezed Ned's hand as we flew away from Tumlingtar. It was January 29, 1982. All the pain, cold, and hunger as well as the deep satisfaction, achievement, and supporting camaraderie that we'd shared seemed like a dream, as if it had all happened to someone else.

CHAPTER 5

... COMES AROUND

WE WERE LOST, REALLY LOST AGAIN. This time, at the end of our second half circle around Everest on the north side in Tibet, we had a map. But the map hadn't been updated since 1921. This historic British reconnaissance for mapping the Everest area was led by the famous, mysterious George Leigh Mallory. Mallory and gang had a note at the bottom of our map: "The grey area may not be drawn to scale." Of course we were wandering in this proverbial gray area of life, this limbo of the map, trying to complete our Everest Grand Circle Expedition not knowing what represented what for physical features, with no scale to put the land forms in eyesight into perspective. And all the while we were wondering, "Are we there yet?"

This time being truly lost was a gift. Today we have GPS and cell phones; one can never be truly lost. But at this time in Tibet we savored the gift of being almost hopelessly lost on our big planet. It was a joy, because this time it was warm, we had food, and there was plenty of running water to drink and bathe in. This was unlike our epic of being lost on the south side of Everest during the past winter in Nepal, where everything was frozen, including us, and we had no food and were reduced to being walking bags of bones. Now in Tibet, we could weave ourselves in the sights and smells of this wild landscape, thick with flowering rhododendron plants twenty feet or more high. This jungle we crawled through was unlocking our animal instincts, demanding us to draw on internal senses for directional guidance.

Like birds and bears, we have instincts to direct us, but these instincts have been overlaid by numbers, letters, and abstract thinking. Civilization has left its mark on our species, which still has all the instincts, undeveloped and unutilized, remaining at our core. But in rare moments like this, to genuinely experience the animal self is truly a gift. It allows for the deep understanding that all of life is one, to permeate body and mind. This paradigm shift lasts a lifetime and is only honestly shared with those who have had the same experience. To describe it accurately can never be done because it is felt, not understood.

In Nepal we had a Frenchman draw us a map and Sherpa footprints to follow when we were lost. Here we had nothing but ourselves to rely on. Perhaps it was fitting that it was Jim who, without warning, took off without so much as a "I'll scout here and be back in a couple of hours, or before the sun is at high noon." We wondered, Was he mad, stark raving, or just mad at us? We were puzzled. He didn't really have that much for supplies for himself. Why would he disappear without warning? I think he just felt the call of the wild, truly, and bolted in answer. But where the hell was he going? This we did not know, nor did we know if we should try to track him and follow. Was he leaving us behind or showing us the way?

This second half of our Everest Grand Circle had begun again in Beijing, China, as it had when we were given this initial permission over a year earlier to "ski in Tibet." The Chinese officials were still unaware we had a grand plan of encircling Everest and that we'd already completed half the circle to the south in Nepal. Although we had general expedition permission in hand, the Chinese officials held out until we'd flown halfway around the world and arrived in person before giving permission for our specific route, just like Mr. Sharma of the Ministry of Tourism had in Nepal. If the Chinese officials refused to let us near the border, the circle would never be completed.

The Chinese officials couldn't understand why we wanted to ski in Tibet. They had even sent us a telex to the States, before we'd even begun the circle, which read, "According to material we get, the ice-skating or skiing cannot be conducted at the Rongbuk Glacier. Please consider your itinerary." But Ned handled negotiations beautifully. It took only an hour and a half, and in the end the Chinese officials gave us carte blanche for roaming the area around Everest on skis, calling us "pioneers of skiing in Tibet." Ned quickly responded by complimenting the Chinese Mountaineering Association officials for being "pioneers of free enterprise." A couple of days later our expedition, along with our interpreter, Chang Chong Min, were on the plane flying to Lhasa, Tibet, en route to doing our second half of our circle around Everest.

Rick Barker, a sometimes California surfer living in Sun Valley, Idaho, and one of the best backcountry skiers in America, was with us for his first international expedition. The big question was, Would he be okay living like a primitive and risking his neck daily, for months, just for a few, sometimes miserable, ski runs? The expedition mentality was much more arduous and austere than that of a fun-loving surfer. Jim Bridwell decided to rejoin us for the second half of the circle. Of course Ned and I were team members, and because Jim had missed a section of the circle in Nepal, we would be the only two to complete the entire expedition if we managed go the distance in Tibet.

As we were unloading and organizing our thirty-nine bags in the dry, dusty air at the Lhasa Airport, I heard Chang coughing hard behind me. "Not quite like Beijing here in Lhasa, huh, Chang!" I said over my shoulder. When I wheeled around to look at him, he appeared so disheveled and miserable that I began to laugh, although I tried not to. Luckily the humor was infectious, and Chang began to giggle. When he grinned his chubby face became all teeth and no eyes. "The Chinese have a saying," he told me, "'Laughter makes you ten years younger.' This expedition will make me many years older, so I must keep laughing."

Now that's what I call a good attitude, especially at altitude. We were at 12,000 feet now in Lhasa, and coming up from Beijing at sea level was a giant leap up, which created a demand for our bodies to adjust. Until physiological adjustments were made in the next couple

of weeks, we'd all be somewhat uncomfortable, with headaches, interrupted sleep, shortness of breath, lethargy, lack of motivation—basically
feeling like we had one hell of a hangover after a crazy drinking bout,
day after day. We knew from experience we would eventually feel better,
but Chang was unconvinced and a little scared. Chang was supposed to
accompany us to base camp at 17,000 feet. He was beside himself with
apprehension. Right now life was a bitter pill for Chang, and he was
trying his damnedest to swallow it.

When we reached our accommodations Rick was the only expedition member not feeling well. "Ned's smart," Rick said. "He sold
Bridwell the expedition as a climbing trip, he sold Jan the expedition
as a vacation, and he sold me the expedition as a ski trip." With percep-
tions as keen as that, I thought he'd do just fine; he was seeing clearly.
But regardless, I hoped he wasn't having second thoughts, feeling awful
starting out. We all knew we were in for a lot of miles and climbing.

Chang knocked on our suite door and exclaimed, "Time for shu
shi." We knew this phrase too well. We didn't travel across China to
this mysterious land of Tibet to take a nap. While Rick messed with the
complementary oxygen tank in the military guesthouse we were holed
up in, Ned persisted with Chang. This was our third time in China,
and Ned had learned tactics of his own. Ned won, and we were given
a quick lunch and then headed out to explore old Lhasa, the capital of
ancient Tibet.

China invaded Tibet in 1950, claiming, "Tibet is an inalienable part
of China," since the time of Kubla Khan and the Yuan Dynasty of the
thirteenth century. Tibetans see it differently, maintaining they won
their independence when they began self-government in 1911 after the
collapse of the Ch'ing Dynasty. The Tibetans also claim they are culturally and ethnically distinct from the Chinese. By 1959 the religious
and political leader of Tibet, the Dalai Lama, fled his own country in
disguise on horseback over the Himalayas into India. The Tibetan people feared the Chinese would imprison him or take his life, and because
the Dalai Lama was so revered and loved, the Tibetan people begged
him to leave.

When the Chinese Red Guard arrived in Tibet by 1960, the deep destruction began. Out of the 2,500 monasteries built as part of the feudal system controlled by Buddhist monks, only 10 were spared. Most Tibetan religious, medical, and scientific texts were destroyed, the monkhood was dismantled, and all religious worship was banned. Mao seemed determined to erase the Tibetan identity, thus crushing any rebellion against Chinese authority. Mao called this "democratic reform," yet the Tibetan people preferred their ancient system of government and mourned the loss of their peaceful Buddhist heritage.

As we neared the old city of Lhasa, leaving the perfectly aligned, cinderblock, tin-roofed sprawl of factories and housing built by the Chinese, we felt we had walked into a fascinating medieval city. Nothing was symmetrical. Whitewashed houses of stone and mud brick were crowded shoulder to shoulder with colorful doorways and flower boxes at the sills. Within minutes we were surrounded by hordes of Tibetans who tugged at us and pressed against us insistently. Women wore black shifts with colorful shirts and plenty of silver, coral, and turquoise jewelry. Men wore similar robes and often wore turquoise earrings. Some of the most noticeable wore sheepskin robes with one shoulder bare and fur-lined hats with one flap down jauntily to one side and had knives tucked into their belts. I noticed the houses, the clothes, the roads were all made by hand. The human touch was palpable here.

They began to whisper to us, "Dalai Lama, Dalai Lama, photo, photo," as if anything foreign might produce word from their beloved leader. We had been warned that images of the Dalai Lama could possibly land local Tibetans in prison for supporting rebellion, so we kept our noses clean and brought no photos. Many people pulled out little trinkets, charm boxes, and jewelry to sell or trade. We had been warned by Chang that our luggage would be searched when we left and any artifacts confiscated that we might be taking out of the country. I was hesitant to trade. I could see how the Sherpas had become such efficient traders; they were a part of the Tibetan culture. Before the 1950s I had read that Australian butter, English whiskey, and even Elizabeth Arden products were found in isolated Tibet!

We were swept up in the crowd circumambulating a large building with a ring road around it. In the center of this crowded way was the 1,300-year-old Jokhang, or House of Wisdom, the holiest temple in all of Tibet. The Chinese had just reopened the temple to active worship in 1980 after thirty years of closure. Earlier there had been 300,000 monks in Tibet, but after the Chinese takeover only 2,000 remained, mainly working as custodians. The Chinese controlled the opening and closing of these remaining temples daily; the monks were directed by the Chinese officials. Tibetan Buddhism itself seemed to be on display as in a living museum. Even our interpreter told us, when referring to the Tibetans, "But you know, they are peasants, just masses. They are ignorant and dirty."

This elaborate ancient system and culture, with detailed medical scripts, a college, highly developed psychology, and devotion to peace and nonviolence, was reduced to this bigoted view in the eyes of the Chinese overlords. We gave Native Americans blankets infected with smallpox to kill them. Were we any different from the Chinese? We had black slaves on plantations. Was this different from the Chinese imprisoning monks and nuns for remaining devout to the Dalai Lama? The guilt of dominance is widespread.

Outside the Jokhang, I noticed a crowd around Jim that seemed intent to push up his shirtsleeves and rub his hairy arm up and down with their hands and laugh. The Tibetans are relatively hairless, and they howled at the thought of Jim being such a hairy man. Jim was loving the attention, grinning from ear to ear as he was jostled in the throng.

The Jokhang had an electric energy in the hot, humid space. There was a constant droning of *o mani padme hum,* the most common Buddhist prayer, in the darkness lit by thousands of heavy-smelling yak-butter candles. The sweating crowd moved through, shoulder to shoulder, touching the holy shrines and laying offerings of money, scarves, and grain before them. I knew many of them had traveled perhaps hundreds of miles, prostrating themselves along the way, to be here for this moment.

The atmosphere was overwhelming yet not suffocating. All treated each other with quiet respect, knowing they were there for the same reason, looking to improve their karma or their spiritual standing for an elevated or improved rebirth after death. I had not experienced the power of belief, like this, before in my life. The meditation and chanting swept me away.

I had learned about Buddhism on the first half circle in Nepal and had read more since, because my original experiences in the Sherpa Buddhist culture had been so profound. The original Buddha, a prominent prince in India who denounced his status and went in search of truth, sat under a tree in final meditation and became enlightened. Once enlightened, he told his followers there were four truths, later becoming the basis of Buddhism: (1) life means suffering, (2) the origin of suffering is attachment, (3) the cessation of suffering is attainable, and (4) there is an eightfold path to the cessation of suffering—right view, right intention, right speech, right action, right livelihood, right effort, right mindfulness, and right concentration. Buddhism was making more of an impression on me as I grew in awareness.

We left Lhasa before daylight on April 22 for the three-day, 800-kilometer "drive" to Everest. The day before we had loaded the four-ton army "liberation truck" (designed in 1949) with all our food, camp equipment, and mountaineering gear plus two fifty-five-gallon drums of gas. Although we were driving to Everest, autos and trucks were still a luxurious commodity in China.

Losan, our liaison officer; Laba, our driver; and Chang, our interpreter crowded into the truck's heated cab; we bundled into parkas and windproof jackets and climbed over the tailgate and into the back, which was covered with a canopy tied over metal bars. Despite the heavy green canvas covering the overstuffed truck, a cloud of dust and dirt drifted around us as we put on white surgical masks to keep our breathing passages clear. The ride over the rough road was so bumpy that I found it was good passive exercise trying to keep myself from colliding with the guys and our packaged supplies. I felt like a dirtball bouncing in the belly of a vacuum cleaner. We all still felt queasy, like kids smoking their first cigarettes behind the barn, as we were heading ever up in elevation.

Rick still wasn't well and had been throwing up in Lhasa. He stoically kept to himself during the ride. Underneath our masks the air became hot, stale, and sticky, but if we tried riding without the masks we ate too much dirt. As we drove higher and the air became thinner we began to feel as if we were slowly suffocating beneath our masks. When I turned to look at Jim, I began to laugh. He was swaddled in down clothing to ward off the cold and snuggled up to the unwrapped dried sheep carcass that would feed us in base camp. He, like the rest of us, was coated in gray dust that had changed the color and texture of his hair and skin. "Bridwell, you dirtbag," I laughed. He just rolled his head toward me and returned my grin without a word.

We had three passes to drive over in these three days, all about 17,000 feet. We spent a couple nights in what amounted to concrete bunkers and used warm water from a thermos poured into a basin to wash the dust off ourselves at night. Each morning we were served tinned fish, a strange relish, and vinegar-soaked garlic; no tea was available. There was always frost on Mr. Truck, as we affectionately called our ancient, quirky vehicle, when we headed out every morning. The Chinese had built this road we were negotiating to supply their successful Everest expedition in 1960, when our friends Lao Chu and Wang had summited. But this road had been used very little since.

Initially, before this road was ever built, the maps for this area were created in 1921 (and still remained unrevised in 1980), when a month-long British expedition traveled 240 miles from Darjeeling, India, to Shegar in Tibet over the windswept plateau. A hundred mules carried provisions for nine Englishmen, still wearing the tweeds of London, as they trekked in to have a first look at Everest from the north in order to plan an expedition the following year to climb her.

Because we were acclimatizing as we rode for three long days, we drank gallons and gallons of water. Because Laba, our driver, wasn't keen to stop the finicky truck for such nonsense as relieving ourselves, we became adept at leaning over the tailgate to do our business. This became a comedy routine for me. The men could stand and face out the back, brace themselves, and see what they were doing. I had to sit on the edge of the tailgate, pants down, and hug a gasoline barrel so as not to fly off the back into the road on my head. If it was particularly bumpy I had to ask the guys to hold my legs down and struggle to relax my stomach muscles enough to let go and pee. It was either this humbling bladder-relief position or wetting my pants. So there I sat, bare-assed and clutching a barrel, the knife-edged tailgate cutting into my loins, while the guys regularly threatened to open the gate.

As daylight faded, our truck ground up the last incline to about 17,000 feet and rattled across a windswept gravel plain toward a cluster of tents pitched just below the terminus of the Rongbuk Glacier. Everest glowed like a great monolith above us in the alpenglow of the evening. This was base camp, occupied by two climbing teams, British and American, whom we had expected to find here. The truck stopped, and we jumped down to introduce ourselves.

Our camaraderie with the British was instantaneous. We rolled right into a party, which only gained momentum as the evening wore on. When I tasted the last sips of our sixth bottle of Hennessy cognac, I tossed my head back and laughed out loud, "The last thing I expected to find at Everest base camp was a fully equipped bar." "Just a minute, I'll hatch you another one," Joe Tasker said, grinning demonically. He rocked to the side of the large box he was sitting on, reached between his legs into the box, and pulled out yet another airline-size bottle of cognac.

"Ta da!" he sang proudly as he lifted the bottle over his head and twisted off the cap for me. The caps had mysteriously become more and more difficult for us to twist off as the night wore on. Joe was one of the four British climbers fashioning a route up the unclimbed, difficult East Northeast Ridge on Everest. They had carved out two snow caves for shelter and had run up fixed ropes above the higher cave at 23,800 feet but had returned to base camp for rest and replenishment. As they put it, "We're down here for four days to stuff ourselves with food, three huge meals a day." We had just driven in April 25, the evening following their return. The rest of the empty tents belonged to Lou Whittaker's American team members who were all higher on the mountain.

We staggered into our individual tents at 3 a.m. the next morning, and I felt no hangover when I eventually awoke. It was miraculous, or was I just so accustomed to feeling poorly I couldn't discern the difference? The men, holding their heads in their hands, were impressed with my drinking ability. Inside one of our tiny tents, unlike the luxury of tables and chairs in the giant mess tent the British sported, we began to pull ourselves together for our trip around Everest. Rick had retired from the party before the rest of us the night before, yet he seemed vacant and slow this morning. He still hadn't recovered from our constant gain in elevation, and though he tried to hide his discomfort, his dull eyes gave him away.

Rick and I set to sorting out food. Ned had his hands full with Losan, our liaison officer. Losan was short, stocky, and full of unabashed mischief. He was a climber himself and had gone quite high on Everest itself in 1975. Lao Chu, our liaison while we were on Muztagata, seemed to make everything magically and miraculously happen for us. Losan seemed inflexible, more like a roadblock to our logistics than a problem solver. We hadn't expected this.

Getting back to some sort of civilization after finishing our circle was becoming a challenge. Ned was looking for yaks and herders to come in to meet us; Losan was balking. Ned was frustrated because we'd paid a fortune to be here. All the while Jim was in his tent reading a good book. I was puzzled. He didn't seem like the old Jim I had known, making wisecracks and messing with gear. Maybe he was frustrated too, knowing he'd never touch the high rock and ice on this trip.

The ceaseless wind howled. There was nothing in this long valley to slow it in its path. I began to understand how the wind in Patagonia in South America was said to make people go mad. My tent was loud in my ears as the nylon shuddered and constantly whipped in the wind. The noise never stopped. We had to shout to speak with each other. The wind was exhausting. We all slept the afternoon away. The next day we hauled out the skis, bindings, screws, glue, heel plates, skins, safety straps, and other assorted ski paraphernalia for assembly. Rick took charge because it was his area of expertise. Although he was still having trouble keeping his food down, he gallantly directed the rest of us and did the bulk of the work himself.

"Hey you guys, these boots are going to need some modification if we're going to use them," I said, holding up an overboot as I clomped around on the moraine with a bare boot and ski on my right leg. "Well why don't you modify it then, Jan? I'm not going anyway without an overboot," Jim stressed. Jim's feet had been freezing on the summit of Pumori, and apparently the memory was still fresh. I figured out, by using a bit of "home ec," how I could get the overboot system to work.

I collected everyone's overboots, dove for my tent—out of the wind—and set to work. But sitting alone in the tent made me aware of just how much I was coughing. My throat was raw and dry from the parched, thin air. I thought for a bit and decided from then on to try sleeping with a dampened bandanna tied over my mouth to moisturize and warm the air before I breathed it in. Now I understood why the British team had designed a kind of hookah to inhale steam at night to soothe their parched throats and help them sleep.

I was delighted to hear the British had invited us for a picnic the following day, a day of relaxed pleasure, before they left to make their final push to ascend the peak. The event seemed in keeping with their civilized, hospitable style. At the site we ate delicate cheeses and various dried meats off real plates and drank sumptuous wine out of real glasses. The British knew how to travel. We had only our little plastic bowls, one each, to hold all drinks and meals. The early British expedition to explore this area as a base camp for climbing in 1921 was most likely equally, if not more, civilized than the current British expedition. We had this original exploration expedition in our minds as we picnicked near the ruined site of a monument including George Leigh Mallory, who had been on the 1921 reconnaissance and had died on his subsequent summit attempt on Everest in 1924.

Mallory is a legend for us all, not just the British, and was perhaps the first man to summit Everest. It is still not known if he reached the top of the world before he died, perhaps on the way down. His teammate sitting at 26,000 feet, Noel Odell, had spotted Mallory and his partner Sandy Irvine almost at the summit. Odell wrote, "I saw the whole summit ridge and final peak of Everest unveiled. I noticed far away on a snow slope, leading up to what seemed to me to be the last step but one from the base of the final pyramid a tiny object moving. . . . A second object followed, and then the first climbed to the top of the step. . . . I could see that they were moving expeditiously as if endeavoring to make up for lost time."[1]

A storm enveloped the peak, and it has been a mystery ever since if the experienced Mallory and young Irvine ever reached the summit of Everest thirty years before Sir Edmund Hillary, who has been bestowed with the title of the first man to reach the top of Everest in 1954. Mallory has since become world famous for his response of "because it is there" to the question he was repeatedly asked, "Why do you want to climb Everest?" It wasn't a curt, trite answer from a tired lecturer. The statement had more meaning than his audience perceived. For Mallory and his close friends *there* was a term denoting anything that had a mystical quality. In their letters back and forth certain books and paintings they valued were also deemed "more there." But for Mallory, personally, nothing was more there than the summit of Everest. Perhaps he meant that *there* is something felt in the heart, not seen with the eyes.

I woke up on April 30 feeling terribly tired and groggy. My knees had been an old problem, but this respiratory ailment was new and bothersome. I crept out of my bag and slowly began packing. "Hey, Jano, happy birthday!" Rick was warm and cheerful. His smile lit up the tent when he looked in, and his energy spurred me on. Rick had begun to feel like himself again. "Thanks, Rick, I forgot." I saw Jim's feet walk by my tent door, backtrack, and then his head poked in the door. "Happy birthday, old lady," he laughed and went back to packing. I was pleased they had remembered my birthday, especially since Ned had seemed to have forgotten it, and so had I.

By half past ten we had five yaks loaded with our skiing and camping gear and ready for our trek to the Lho La, the 20,000-foot pass we planned to ski. Three more yaks were all set to carry in supplies for a cache up on the East Rongbuk Glacier, a point farther along on our swing of the Tibetan semicircle. With whistles and time-honored calls from the drivers, the yaks poked out of camp like an old train trying to muster up steam. Ned, Rick, Jim, and I all brightened in spirit to be moving again en route to the border between Nepal and Tibet. We would be touching one end of our half circle completed the winter before in Nepal. I remembered Pumori vividly. When I closed my eyes I could still see its shape and envision our route. I looked forward to seeing the peak again, but this time I'd gone around the world and would be approaching it from the northern side.

We hiked for six hours along a lateral moraine of the Rongbuk Glacier. These residual rocks of varying shades of gray accented with black formed banks on either side of the long, white river of ice, which was covered with white and blue seracs resembling sails cutting the wind. The scene was colorless and dreamlike. The skies were absolutely clear, and the thin air heated so intensely that it smelled scorched. It felt good to be moving again, and my head cleared with the exercise. I could breathe again. I felt alive. Time spent in camp tends to dampen the spark of adventure: I'm never so aware of this as the day I depart.

The moraine was undulating, and the glacier curled and turned as a river would. When we reached 18,500 feet I spotted two tents large enough to stand up in. This obviously was the site of the American Everest team's advanced base camp. It was also the end of the line for the yaks and their drivers, because the terrain was too rough for them to go any farther. Two men appeared; they introduced themselves as Phil Ershler and Dan Boyd and invited us in. Rick's back was bothering him, Jim had a headache, and Ned was gathering information, so I got a couple of large plastic containers and lugged some water from the broken glacier below for tea and dinner.

"Happy birthday, Jano! I didn't forget," announced Ned as he handed me a wad of crumpled toilet paper on my return. I felt through the paper. There was something hard inside. I couldn't help it, I started to cry. Inside was a bronze medallion, a hand-cast Tibetan calendar. I stifled the tears as soon as possible so the men I just met wouldn't feel uncomfortable, hoping that Ned would understand how pleased I was. I had even forgotten again that it was my twenty-fifth birthday. Marking my birth near Chomolungma, Mother Goddess of the Earth, at the top of the world, was a great omen for me and metaphor for feminine strength.

In the morning I felt like hiking alone, so I packed up quickly and slipped off before the others were ready. I knew they would soon be close behind me. I was hungry to be by myself so I could absorb more of the richness of the surroundings. After I had meandered up the moraine a couple of hours I spotted some lumps that looked like painted turtles on the edge of the snow—the Americans' camp one. Two small figures emerged from the tents, and because I was so far away they seemed to be drifting over the snow on the path marked by the crevasse warning rods.

This surreal vision reminded me of the fantasy world climbers live in. Perhaps some of us are drawn back to the mountains again and again because we feel in control here. We can design our own destiny; make our dreams come true. The very limitations of life in the mountains make it a playground for the mind and a testing ground for the body. It's living a fantasy, vivid and exhilarating in a microcosmic world. Every time you walk into a mountain, it's a different mountain, reformed by weather and time. The conditions in this world are constantly changing, and those who survive are keenly able to adapt to change. Those who can truly survive in the mountains have learned never to impose preexisting patterns on new information. One must always allow new information about the mountain—snowpack, weather, wind, and so on—to reshape your thinking. This is not the mountain you saw yesterday; it is the mountain it is today, only.

On May 2 we rose early and hiked back up to our gear stashed at snow line. The weather was beautiful, and I wanted to be skiing, so it seemed to take forever to put on all the paraphernalia: ski boots, overboots, skis, harness, ropes, prussic slings (devices used to escape in the event of a tumble into a crevasse), and safety straps. Finally we skied off in a "Volga boatman" rhythm and stride, roped together to guard against falling into crevasses. I felt like part of a chain gang.

We stopped after a few moments to tie bandannas over our faces as protection against the harsh sun. During the process of covering up someone suggested we do away with the rope. "That's a good idea," Ned agreed. "We're running perpendicular to any crevasses, so we're pretty safe with our skis on. They're plenty long enough to distribute our weight over thin snow bridges." I was ecstatic about being able to ski freely, and I took off fast. Rick and Jim weren't as interested in endurance sports as I was, and Ned was busy snapping photographs, so I just left them all behind. It was so hot I could have been skiing comfortably in a bikini if it hadn't been for the risk of an outrageous burn. I did take my gloves off for a while until I noticed a blister rising on my right index finger within minutes.

I reached the crest of the Lho La, just shy of 20,000 feet, glowing from exercise. I could look right down the rocky cliff into Nepal and see directly into Everest base camp on the south side. To the west Pumori rose proudly, and my eyes traced our winter ascent. I could hardly believe I stood on top of the peak just a few months earlier. I remembered the strain and the cold. Our windy, frigid summit day contrasted sharply with the still, torrid weather today. Yet in January, and now in May, I'd touched the border between Nepal and Tibet. I saw the circle taking shape—our fantasy was becoming reality.

Ned skied up, "Hey, did you see the Russian's camp in Nepal?" When we looked we could just see the huddle of their orange and blue tents. Our eyes began combing the southern exposure of the peak, and after a few moments we spotted what looked to be seven tiny figures moving up. "There they are!" Jim's voice jumped into the silence. Then he boomed as loudly as he could between cupped hands, "Hey, vodka . . . vodka . . . Smirnoff," and began waving his right arm like a metronome over his head. Perhaps it was our willful imaginations, but we thought we saw them waving back! We laughed and laughed at Jim's proficient Russian and his imaginative leap of political barriers.

The slope we had just skied up was very gradual, gently easing over a mile back down to the Americans' camp one. My descent was free and effortless. I looked up and over my shoulder at the looming rock and ice masses and hummed familiar music to myself. I wasn't carrying any weight on my back, and my skis were carrying me. I was very content. Happiness smoldered deep inside me like a glowing coal. Hockey stop parallel turns weren't possible since my skins held my metal edges off the snow. But the smooth arc of the ancient telemark turn was perfect. The telemark turn, named after Telemark County in Norway, was used centuries ago in Scandinavia for turning the ten-foot-long edgeless wooden skis. By sliding one ski ahead of the other and genuflecting, you arc your skis in a swooping turn.

All during my descent I was entertained by Ned and Rick, who had torn the glued climbing skins off the slick bases of their skis and gotten in some good turns and some bad turns but also got more serious thrills. We collected at the bottom to pack our gear and skis to lug them back down to advanced base camp. The first skiing of the expedition had been a breeze; the weather had cooperated, and we had reached the border. It had almost been too easy. We ribbed each other about style variations and spills. Jim teased, "I don't really think we are going to be able to use this footage for much of anything. If you guys are supposed to look like expert skiers, you sure did a good job of hiding it."

After a long slog back to base Rick and I woke the next morning to an inch of snow on the ground while Ned and Jim were away, scampering up a small, neighboring peak. Rick and I scurried around camp getting yak loads together along with four pairs of skis, all in a heap, and motioned to the two yak drivers who had come to work. They came over to us waving their arms as if they were pushing something imaginary away and shaking their heads no. Eventually I got the message that they were telling us to get rid of some of the stuff, that it was too much for their four yaks.

Rick and I looked at each other and shrugged. We, of course, had thought we needed everything in the loads but figured we had to do something. We started opening up everything, asking each other if we really needed this or that. We soon got the loads down to a more manageable size—provided the two drivers carried small packs as well. The drivers refused at first, and then began demanding more money to carry the small amount on their backs.

I didn't want to delay our departure by quibbling with the two men, and I didn't want to antagonize the only two drivers we could get for the next three days. It was worth it to me to make them happy now so I could establish a good rapport with them and enjoy a hassle-free trek to the British advanced base camp. I ran to the tent and pulled out some of my own money and jewelry and offered it to them. They were delighted, and we were on our way.

I wasn't sure what Rick thought about the way I handled the situation. I wondered if he thought I was too soft because I had not only succumbed to but exceeded their demands. Or if he thought I was overbearing because I had taken charge. But he didn't register any complaint. Either way I intuitively knew what studies have confirmed: a woman will generally have more influence with her male peers if she is tentative rather than aggressive in speech.* This goes along with the idea that women are more prone to add tag lines, making questions instead of statements. As a man Rick might've made a firm decision about the drivers himself but might have wanted me to ask for his input before deciding.

Although Ned and I were coleaders of this trip, we hadn't indicated who was in charge when we split the group in two. I never gave authority a thought when Rick and I worked to get the equipment together, but I naturally came forth with a solution to get our drivers on the trail at my own expense. I was being that assertive female in speech and action.

---

*In one study cited in Janet Shibley Hyde's *Half the Human Experience,* a mixed-gender group listened to four recordings: a woman speaking tentatively, a woman speaking assertively, a man speaking tentatively, and a man speaking assertively. The group responses varied. The woman with tentative speech was *more* influential to men than the woman with assertive speech. The men, whether tentative or assertive in their speech, had the same influence on both men and women.

Although Rick and I had asked each other our opinions about how to pare the loads down for the trek, I sensed Rick took a slight offense to my self-assured negotiations with the drivers. However in reality I was the more experienced and a coleader and therefore, without analyzing it at the time, had naturally stepped up to make things move forward.

By early afternoon Rick and I had learned the drivers' names were Norbu and Turtup. Norbu was a scruffy, wiry old man, and I guessed that Turtup was his son. Turtup stopped the yaks at a predetermined campsite. The route up the East Rongbuk Glacier could be done in one long day hiking alone but would take two and a half days at yak rate. Norbu erected the tent we gave him near Rick's and mine. Shortly after we'd settled in, Norbu's face appeared at the door of our tent. His gestures indicated that he wanted something, and we finally figured out that it was scissors and a mirror so he could trim his beard. I had scissors on my Swiss army knife and a smudged one-by-two-inch mirror.

Then Turtup appeared, asking for some of our freeze-dried food. I knew that he and Norbu had plenty of tsampa, the ground barley that is the staple of their diet at home, but I supposed they wanted to experiment with our funny stuff in the bags, so I gave him a bag of stew. "I don't know, Jano. These guys are getting pretty greedy," Rick said as we looked at each other after this last request. Still we had to laugh when, a few minutes later, Norbu returned, obviously feeling quite slick and proud of his trimming work, brushing his shortened whiskers forward and smiling.

The requests continued all evening for this or that. We realized they were simply curious and would ask for anything that caught their eye, and we were no longer afraid that they would quit and leave us stranded. If the request wasn't reasonable we simply said no, and there were no repercussions. The following day during our midday break, after eating some nuts and cheese, I pulled out my little wooden instrument. As I played Norbu hopped up on a boulder and started to dance what looked to me like a jig. His expression was intent, and his dark, tattered clothing flapped up and down on his thin, dirty body.

From this time on I noticed that Rick began to droop like a plant without water, and I was afraid that coming up in elevation again might be giving him some trouble. We stopped for the day, and while Rick rested I looked for a spot to put up the tent. But as I paused at one site after another, Rick called out some reason why the spot wasn't appropriate. When I asked him where he thought the tent should go, he said he wasn't sure. Then I realized there was no way to please him.

"Why don't you just wait for a minute, Jan?" I could feel the tension in the air. I didn't want to say I was eager to put up the tent so he could crawl in. That could be misconstrued as demeaning, when I really had concerns for his condition. There was an awkward pause, and then I continued with the tent as if I hadn't heard a thing. I was baffled by Rick's attitude. I thought maybe he was frustrated at not feeling better. But I didn't want to stop what I was doing; we needed the tent up.

It was interesting being with Rick and assuming the forward-moving position. Jim and Ned were comfortable for the most part when this occurred, appearing to actually enjoy the effort and output on my part and the momentary easing on theirs. I was tossing around the idea that this difference in reaction by the males was about gender, or more precisely about being able to dismiss the focus on gender, allowing androgyny some room to move and breathe. Androgynous people like myself perform better in a wider variety of situations because they have a broader range of characteristics and can relate to and connect with a greater number of people.[2] The men who were not focused on the fact that I was a woman seemed to let things flow easier within the group.

I was beginning to surmise that older men had an easier time of it whereas the younger males I had worked with on expeditions—Allan and Tom in New Zealand, Rick here in the Himalayas—were more challenged by a female who was comfortable exhibiting male psychological characteristics like motivation, action, decisiveness, confidence, and so on. Earlier Rick had said to me good-naturedly, "Jan, you're not a man, and you're not a woman. I don't know what you are!" To me Rick displayed wonderful concern at times that would have been considered a feminine reaction. I laughed and thought we'd just been through a role reversal, Rick being particular about the tent and me being all business.

I was exhibiting male characteristics, and he perhaps feminine; maybe we needed to acknowledge our androgynous selves.

Androgynous means having both masculine and feminine psychological characteristics (not physical). In Greek *andro* means "man" and *gynē* means "woman." A person is perhaps considered well rounded and mature when he or she becomes androgynous, able to exhibit both male and female characteristics. When tested, androgynous people also seem to have higher self-esteem.[3] In effect, a woman who can hug and comfort someone injured then make the decision for treatment and set the wheels in motion for action, either by doing the job herself or delegating it to a more competent person, would be displaying both masculine and feminine psychological characteristics. She would be giving comfort and taking charge when each is necessary. A man in the same situation doing the same actions would be considered androgynous as well. Being male or female is not black and white in nature, from a psychological point of view; it is varying shades of gray.

The snow swirled down from the plateau below the East Ridge of Everest and stung my eyes the following morning. When we finally reached the British advanced base camp we had to push and pull the yaks through the deepening snow to an appropriate unloading site. Charlie Clarke, the doctor on the British expedition, must have heard the drivers' calls, because he came pushing through the frozen flurry. Norbu and Turtup were yanking off the ropes, letting bags and skis thud onto the snow. I rushed to the yak carrying the camera in time to catch the camera and set it gently onto the ground. I could see Charlie grinning under his balaclava as he came nearer, then he grabbed me for a big hug.

"Charlie, are Ned and Jim here with you?" "No I haven't seen them, but Joe, Pete, Chris, and Dick are all here. They're exhausted and going down to base for a rest before trying again. They did some amazing climbing and reached 26,900 feet." Charlie must have sensed my disappointment as he waved his arm up toward their advanced camp. "They'll be along. Come in for some tea."

"I'll be along in a bit, I've got to pay our drivers and organize our gear," I replied, trying to hide my concern. Ned and Jim should have finished their extracurricular climbing two days ago. I thought they'd be here before Rick and I arrived with the equipment. I could see Rick coming in the distance, and Charlie descended to greet him. This was our highest point yet on this half of the expedition, 21,000 feet and a new altitude record for Rick.

I said good-bye to Norbu and Turtup, then stacked and secured the bags. I took one long last sweeping look down the glacier, hoping to see two figures approaching. When I didn't I realized how concerned I was. Seeing the British boys huddled around their teapot hookah to soothe their aching throats was humorous and brought out a laugh as I entered their tent. They were all visibly worn and thin, noticeable just within the week we had been apart. One is always slowly dying at these altitudes we were inhabiting, and the higher you go the more concentrated the breakdown.

The Brits seemed to truly enjoy our company as a diversion perhaps, and as they left to move down to base they asked if "the party girl" might want to come down too. I took the party label as a compliment rather than an offense. They seemed impressed with my ability to drink and to have a good time. Rick and I were allowed to use their bigger mess tent, which seemed almost spooky without the Brits or our teammates, while we waited for Jim and Ned to turn up. My mind began running through many of the possible disaster scenarios that could have befallen our teammates, and I began the mental exercise of looking for them and deciding whether to carry on and complete the circle without them. This made the big, dark tent even spookier.

Rick rested after tea, and the silence drove me out to peer into the wind and snow for any sight of our missing mates. Unbelievably, two days later than expected, there they were, trudging in the distance. I suppose the feeling is like that of a wife on the widow's walk when she spots her man's ship coming in after a storm at sea; the relief from my imagined bad endings was palpable. I poured some hot tea, clumped down to them, and threw my arms around both Ned and Jim, scolding them in good fun for being late.

The next day, May 8, was spent in the British mess tent between naps. Rick was still altitude sick. Although he never complained, it was evident as he ate his food like he was eating dirt. Jim and Ned were determinedly mopey because of fatigue from their adventure and the realization that it was only passes not peaks from here on in. I was keen that any ideas about detours be let go so that we could complete the circle without any disaster. We still had the Lhakpa La and the Karpo La passes, 22,000 and 20,000 feet, respectively, to cross before touching the last border site between Nepal and Tibet. We were here to circle Everest, not climb every mountain.

We spent the next three days skiing under the north col of Everest. We had to maneuver between crevasses, seracs, and icy firn and lurch down wind-etched unyielding snow. Rick, finally able to perform his specialty, was masterful. He was feeling better, and a glint of pleasure was in his eye and a deep laugh after every good turn. "There is no doubt that we purchased the world's most expensive ski ticket for the world's worst skiing!" Rick exclaimed.

May 12 we loaded up eight days' worth of food into packs weighing about forty-five pounds each and trekked after noon for about an hour to the base of the Lhakpa La, which means "windy pass." By now the wind was roaring as always, so we made camp about one-third of the way up in a somewhat protected nook. We had to crampon over a crevasse field the next morning for about 1,000 feet but reached the pass and our last view, looking back, of the Rongbuk Glacier, our world for the past weeks on the north side of Everest. Clouds were piling up over us under gale-force winds, and we barely had time to see our descent route in front of us, down from our 22,000-foot ridgeline to the Kharta Glacier. We needed to move, to let go of our past and the friends in that realm. We had the adventure of seeing the dangerous, unpredictable East Face of Everest ahead of us, beckoning.

It was a straightforward rappel down a snow slope to the Kharta Glacier. I slipped down first, and when we were all down, we roped up in pairs to cross the glacier, which was laced with crevasses. Hopping the cracks took a lot of concentration, but it gave me something to focus on in the midst of the lowering whiteout. Even though Ned and I have traveled roped together countless times, our timing isn't perfect. I was walking behind Ned with a small coil of extra rope in my hand to play out or haul in as needed to keep the rope fairly taut between us.

Ned suddenly began to speed up. We'd been traveling over soft snow for quite some distance, but Ned had just reached a section of firm hardpack that sloped down. This made walking easier for him, but I was still working through the deeper stuff behind him. I gradually played out the rope over the next few yards but ran out of buffer coil just as I hit a crevasse. Before I could lift off my feet to jump it, Ned jerked the rope forward—and me with it—and I went right in.

I fell in right up to my knees, and Ned got a sharp jerk. "What's the problem back there?" he asked as he was turning around. We could just make each other out vaguely through the cloud curtain. It became obvious to Ned that I was sitting on the edge of a crevasse because there was no other apparent reason to be sitting in the snow. "I didn't have much choice," I yelled back loudly. "It was an involuntary crevasse inspection. Take it easy when you're in the clear. Remember, I still might be wading through some junk."

I could hear a faint chuckle as I extracted myself, brushed off the snow, and coiled a bit more rope. We wandered in and out of the white void that afternoon, gusts of fifty miles an hour shoved us along our way and sandblasted spindrift into our clothing. The blowing snow was so thick at times that it felt as though we were in the foam of a breaking ocean wave. We camped on the glacier just below 21,000 feet in the somewhat protected lee of an ice bulge.

The tents flapped wildly as we struggled to erect them, clutching the fabric for all we were worth so that our shelter wouldn't blow away before we got in it. Our "house" had the floor area of a dining room table, where we had to cook, eat, sleep, and take care of all other functions—including using a plastic bottle as a toilet during inclement weather. Even if you made the effort to be as gracious as possible, it was impossible to avoid the belches, farts, nose blows, chewing quirks, snoring, body odor, dandruff, and stinking feet of your partner. It's one thing to put up with the odors and dribbles of someone you like, but unbearable with someone you're not completely comfortable with.

It was apparent that life was a bit strained in Jim's and Rick's tent. They had been thrown in together, not knowing each other before the trip. Each made an effort at preserving the peace, but a slight chill hung inside their tent. It reminded Ned of a dissolving marriage: they were both determined to keep up appearances for civility until the end of the expedition. Ned felt responsible for the problem but didn't have a solution.

Early the next morning, May 14, I heard Jim's voice breaking into my dreams as he unzipped his tent. "What a whiteout out there. It reminds me of watching TV at four in the morning." Then I heard Rick in a silly mood, "Hello, campers! Another fine day! Okay, Jim, it's your move. I moved the pee can to the corner. You can move the pads." I was glad that Rick felt good enough to joke—especially since the previous night had been our highest sleep so far. The wind intermittently blew violent gusts so strong they seemed to shake our brains. During these bouts Ned and I would lie on our backs, pressing our arms and legs against the fabric on the top and walls of the tent as additional reinforcing rods so the tent wouldn't collapse. We weren't going anywhere today.

Between wind blasts I had time to attend to matters that often go neglected on an expedition, like taking my hair down, brushing it out, and braiding it tight again to hide beneath my silk balaclavas. I decided to change my socks as well. Because I like to travel as lightly as possible, I take only two pairs of wool socks. I wear only one pair, keeping the second as an emergency reserve. Because I wear only one pair continually, I slip into my bag at night with damp socks on, but they are dry again by morning. Jim's technique is to alternate with two pairs of socks. He puts the dry ones on to sleep at night, and dries the damp ones underneath his armpits in his sleeping bag. Ned has extra socks dropping and falling out of everywhere.

My socks had been getting pretty ripe, and when I did take them off, I discovered I had gardens growing between my toes. Quite suddenly

Ned bolted out of the tent door on all fours, screaming. Jim unzipped his tent immediately and asked with anticipation, "Hey, did you guys have a fight?" as Ned lay writhing in the snow clutching his throat. "No, Jan just took off her socks. I was being asphyxiated." Everyone, including me, burst into laughter.

We heard soft sounds of thunder throughout the day and also had occasional clearings, which gave us a view of Makalu and a couple of other smaller peaks. We were so close to the Arun Valley where we had finished our southern half circle his past winter, I could smell it. The next morning we were in the clear. Our immediate morning challenge was Kharta Glacier. Ned and I were keenly aware of each other's position and occasionally gave belays over short, sharp descents and large, gaping crevasses.

I looked down one hideous smile of a crack, wondering if I could see its bottom. I couldn't. I'd have to do a decent standing broad jump with a full pack on my back and land with control so I wouldn't twist an ankle from catching my crampons in order to call myself a competent mountaineer. "Okay, here we go," I cheered. "Watch me, Ned," which means give me an active belay. "Wait, Jano, that's a great shot." I waited and accepted my duty to model with chagrin. Just as I took flight, on Ned's signal, I realized Ned had both hands on his camera, not on the rope between us, which dangled down from his waist into the crevasse and lay on the snow right in front of me as it hung from my waist.

I grabbed the rope, midair, and flung it over my head to swing it away from the rope chopping spikes of my crampons. Ned shouted, "Hold it," while I was in midflight, as if I had the power to remain fixed in the air. Not only did I have no belay to arrest a slip or fall, but I could have chopped our rope in two with my crampons and dropped far out of sight below the surface of the glacier, not to reappear for centuries, until I was pushed out the snout of the glacier. Ned got a great shot though. The moral is: Never rope up with a photographer; the photo may be more important than your life.

The last stretch was a long, gradual slope up to the height of the Karpo La, our last pass in the circle. It was merely a matter of post-holing to the top, where we paused for water and chocolate and—in Jim's case—cigarettes. From here on the only way was down. As we stood on the crest of the pass, our last 20,000-foot perch, we looked into one of the most splendid, remote valleys on Earth, the Kangshung, certainly one of the wildest and most pristine in the Himalayas. There weren't even any current maps of the area, only the 1921 map, with this area in the gray not fully explored or drawn to scale.

From here Everest's East Face would shine at the end of the Kangshung Valley, if she wasn't veiled by white, vaporous clouds. Our rapture over the potential view was interrupted by a pragmatic discussion, "It's one—at the most two—rope lengths to rappel," Jim said curtly. "We'll be down and off in half an hour." He spoke as if we were people blind to the obvious. Ned and I as endurance athletes were willing to walk around this steep slope to an easier descent without relying on equipment. Jim, our techno expert, had had it with snailing along carrying a heavy pack.

Backed with two axes and a bollard for an anchor, we slid down the rope as a single line, not doubled as usual, at Jim's suggestion. When we reached the end of the second rappel without incident, Ned exclaimed, "Hey, we just won the freeze-dried delight sweepstakes, a trip to the Kangshung!" We all laughed with relief. Tension was released; our spirits were jovial and celebratory.

Still, I was bothered that Rick had given no opinion about which way to proceed on the pass. Regardless of experience, I think it's good to express how you feel, or just what you are thinking, for general consensus, even if you feel your voice will have little impact. I wondered whether it was our personalities or our experience on expeditions that caused Rick and me to react differently in group situations. I felt keen to express thoughts; Rick held back. I had noticed some androgynous characteristics in both of us before when we worked together with the yak herders bringing our gear up to British advanced base camp. I took the reins and made decisions and managed the gear physically so Rick could rest, because he felt altitude sick.

We worked our way down the Kangshung Glacier, picking our steps over the moraine, and camped on broken rock that had moss, sedges, and reddish flowers decorating it. It was awesome to see biological diversity again, color and plant life. It seemed like I was going from living in 2-D to 3-D. The lower elevation and heavier air made me groggy, and I drifted into an early sleep.

The women walking the brilliantly lit ramp were stylish and stunning. The hues they wore were so vibrant that they woke me up out of my dream. I was ecstatic to realize I had color in my dreams again. For a long time my dreams had been vague and muddy, but now that we had descended below 18,000 feet they were vivid and clear. Many times before I had noticed a flood of thoughts and ideas as I descended in elevation. It's as if all the sparse oxygen at higher altitudes had been used for basic reason and muscle output so that my imagination was starved and ceased producing until it had sufficient fuel.

I awoke from my dream at about ten o'clock on the morning of May 16, the day we would complete our orbit of Everest. We were in no hurry to move; we were savoring the peace that follows urgency. The scenery of this valley with all her peaks was so spectacular I felt I had broken through to a new world, almost like Alice in Wonderland. We were mere tiny black specks in relation to all the surrounding peaks. But we still hadn't seen the East Face of Everest, the only face we had yet to look upon, as it was continually hidden in clouds.

We crossed a frozen lake and hiked down a rocky gully to a soft carpet of moss and dirt. Here Ned and I sat on a rock, kicking the moss with our bare toes, a sensual luxury after months of continually wearing boots and protecting feet from frostbite. I felt very close to Ned as we sat, leaning against each other, silently absorbing our dream come true. The solitary moment was so powerful there was no need to say anything. Only Ned and I had endured every leg of the expedition. We hadn't failed each other. We had done what we set out to do.

To me, success isn't about elation, but a deep confirmation of self. Reaching a goal supports the ability take a vision into reality, reinforcing the notion; your imagination is your only limitation. I recalled my thoughts at age twelve: your life is what you make it, and the world is what it means to you. It still rang true for me. I didn't feel trapped by society's expectations in terms of gender or material wealth. I was still free to determine what was of value in this world and how to express myself without limitation. Life was good, if not unusual.

We chose a campsite a bit farther down valley where we caught the sweet scent of rhododendrons that were blossoming into spring. Everything was becoming so effortless and pleasant that I had the feeling that I had entered a fairy tale. If the East Face of Everest remained clouded through the next day we might never see it, which would be a great disappointment. Jim woke us early at the turn of day with a delighted shout, "Look at this: Everest is as clear as can be."

When I stuck my sleepy head out of the tent door, the view stunned me wide awake. The East Face of Everest was massive and intimidating. Avalanches shoved off and tumbled down with frightening irregularity. This place had the sense of being threatening for mountaineers. (This face was the last to be climbed, by an American expedition in 1983.) The East Face was wild, powerful, and unpredictable, like an untamed predator. I stared, mesmerized, anticipating the next thunderous avalanche, intimidated by the force and awesome power. Now I had seen all the faces and many of the moods of Everest, Chomolungma, Mother Goddess of the Earth, hidden to the south, bold to the north, and intimidating to the east.

Everest, Mother Goddess of the Earth, had become anthropomorphized to me. She was real, had emotions, a body, a spirit, and an intelligence. She made choices and communicated in her own way. I felt she was palpable. She had allowed us to circle her, unscathed, and I was grateful. By noon we reached a high yak pasture at about 16,000 feet. It was a welcoming spot, a pastoral Shangri-la. The idyllic nature of the place lulled us into an unhurried pace. As we continued to move down we lost the meager yak trail. A massive landslide had torn away an entire mountainside, leaving a three-quarter-mile wide chaos of giant boulders. The river below looked dangerous—if not impossible—to ford.

We faced roaring water, grinding ice, and tumbled rock. Rather than backtrack, we simply tackled the obstacles head on. We began a painstaking traverse across the landslide, a long battlefield of immense boulders, which we had to negotiate while encumbered with our loads. The rocks were sharp edged and tumbled against each other in such a manner that there were gaping holes to jump and small ridges to climb. My pack caught and hung up on protrusions, nearly pulling me off balance several times. We all picked our separate lines through the peril but shouted to each other now and again to make sure everyone was making careful progress.

As soon as we cleared the boulders we were faced with a waist-high sea of green juniper, which we virtually had to swim through to make any headway. I kept my arms and legs moving. I laughed to think my feet weren't even touching the ground, but despite how funny our mode of travel seemed, we were wearing out fast. The ease of the day before, our first day off snow, had vanished. Now we had to tackle increasingly difficult terrain and surging, swelling vegetation as we descended.

I began to wonder if this was the start of a new chapter of adventure, like the struggle after we had completed our first half circle in Nepal. Our circle had been well calculated and well executed—but once again, it was finding our way back to civilization that provided the severest test. Then I began to see why that was so. When we trekked into the mountains the route was obvious as the peaks we were headed to were visible. Your goal could be constantly viewed on the horizon for reference. But once the climbing was over we had to search, like sleuths, for civilization, clue by clue. In a sense this was the true adventure of the expedition: this mystery couldn't be planned for or prepared for; we had to rely on our instincts and our wits.

We stumbled upon a patch of juniper and decided it was a perfect place to lay our heads for the night. The clouds began to sprinkle snow lightly down on us. It was beautiful, but wet, so we quickly crawled into our tents and tried to find ourselves on the map. Our exact position was confusing. We could pinpoint where we had been at midday, Pethang Ringmo. Still, I wasn't concerned. It was warm, we were near running water, and we had food, so it couldn't be nearly as draining or brutal as when we had been lost in Nepal in the dead of winter with no food. I slept soundly.

The next day shone with liquid brilliance. All creases in the green rhododendron leaves held drops of melted snow that sparkled in the sun, and the ground was still elegantly dusted with white. When I went for a short walk to absorb the grandeur of the new day, I thought, money meant nothing in this part of the world. A million dollars was useless, barely enough paper to make a good fire. It couldn't provide the comfort and security it was capable of providing in the Western world. Here in the Kangshung Valley a person could be nothing other than the essence of himself, unaffected and unadorned. He had no wealth or power with which to shape or protect himself.

Ned had opted to hike to a nearby knoll to try to get a look at a trail he thought he saw above us, way above us, even though this trail didn't match the map's indication of trails, because all trails change over time, especially yak trails. While Jim, Rick, and I waited for a report on Ned's return, Jim took off without warning. I thought I heard him mutter something like, "I'm going to find that bloody trail." When Ned returned he was startled and annoyed to find Jim gone and saw no alternative but for us to go after Jim to keep us from splintering and losing track of each other. After a couple of hours of searching I started asking who had what for gear to determine just what Jim had on his person for support during his solo trek, considering it could be possible we might not see him for days.

We eventually came across some semblance of a yak trail, and in the wet ground began looking for footprints made by Jim. It was a stretch, as we had been traveling somewhat aimlessly for a couple of miles through pathless brush and had found this trail paralleling the river hundreds of feet up the canyon. As I bent over about the tenth possible tread mark, something caught my eye a few feet down the trail. It was a crumpled piece of cellophane wrapper from the throat lozenges we'd all been eating to soothe our raw throats. "Look you guys!" I called out. "Jim must have been here. Here's one of his wrappers." "Litterbug!" laughed Rick.

It was a strange coincidence that Jim had already passed this way.

I remembered my experience on my own, separated from the group in New Zealand, as we made our way out down the Rakaia River. Unlike Jim I hadn't chosen to go solo; I was left by the others. Yet I did find the trail without the map, and the others did not. I waited at our pickup site, not wanting to deviate from our last plan and cause confusion concerning my whereabouts. Where would Jim wait for us? We were looking, ultimately, for the settlement called Kharta but could only access it from the Kangshung Valley by finding and crossing the 18,000-foot Langma La pass. Down the trail we found a couple more lozenge wrappers, and we were sure we were on Jim's scent.

The trail stopped abruptly at what appeared to be some kind of campsite. We found fire rings and cut limbs in the matted juniper bushes. We circled like bloodhounds trying to decipher which way the Tibetans might have left camp, but there was no obvious route. Soon we spied some footprints in a melting patch of snow. Apparently Jim, as confused as we were, had opted to push on in the same direction the trail had been leading. A logical decision. We could follow Jim's prints only through the snow; after that he was impossible to track, which sent us back to square one again—no trail, no Jim.

"Why don't we just walk back the mile to the last campsite, or head down to the river to look for the disappearing trail?" I offered. Even this mild question was enough to trigger Rick's anger in his distress. "Jan, that's not going to do us any good. Why don't you be quiet." His comment was curt and out of line. This was *not* something he would say to either of the males on the trip. Ned and Rick had been making the decisions, just as Craig and Ned had been making decisions in Nepal, each time after Jim had left the scene. Somehow, I was surmising, Jim's faith in me had kept me integral. Craig came around to valuing me as a team member in time. Would Rick?

I chalked Rick's comment up to his anxiety and kept quiet. My influence in this situation was clearly about keeping quiet to keep the peace, not because he had convinced me he knew better. We began to push forward in silence. We were soon swallowed up by 20-foot-high rhododendron. The trees were so tightly packed that the only way we could move ahead was to crawl on our bellies, with our packs pushing our faces into the ground. A machete would have been useful, but we hadn't thought to bring one along. An ice ax just didn't cut it.

Because progress was slow we decided to work our way up higher to see if the forest thinned enough to spot where we were in this river valley. This was what I had hoped for earlier. Rick looked at me and ordered, "Ned and I are going up. You stay with the bags." He seemed so tense and distracted; I didn't argue. I suppose, because I had spent more than a year organizing the expedition and had been on every leg of the circle, I might have bristled at having Rick dictate to me. But I couldn't see anything that would be gained by arguing with him while he was in this frame of mind. So I leaned on my pack and relaxed as I listened to Ned and Rick rustle through the forest.

No Jim, no trail, no clearing. Darkness was seeping through the forest, and the only sensible thing to do was to retreat downhill to the river for fresh water and a campsite. The reality of Jim's separation hit as the evening began to fold around us, and we thought of him spending the night alone. I missed him and hoped he hadn't encountered any serious trouble. We stopped on the mossy bank of a small tributary shortly before reaching the riverbank, and I was listening to Ned and Rick discuss what to do next when I heard two very faint yells.

"Hey, I heard something. A voice. Maybe it's Jim." I could tell by their expressions that Ned and Rick didn't take me seriously, but I began yelling back anyway and waited for an answer. It came—indistinct but audible. Ned and Rick joined in with my calls. And a few minutes later Jim came crashing through the bushes. "Okay, Jim, where have you been?" I laughed. "We've been trying to track you all day. We followed you as far as the bog."

"I was up on the ridge watching you guys flailing down there, going in circles. There was no way you could hear me call, and there was no way I was going back into that bog—that was nowhere. I could hear Rick cooing later on, so I knew you were close. I figured you'd head to the river at the end of the day, and I'd case the bank until I found you. And here you are." Had Jim taken us on a wild goose chase, or a wild Jim chase?

The next morning Rick popped his head in our tent and apologized for having been curt the day before. I was glad to have the air cleared. We had a brief map consultation and started to think we'd trekked beyond the Langma La. It was almost impossible to know if we had because we couldn't trust the scale of the gray area. This gray area on the edges of the map was not calibrated like the colored, contoured main map. Still, I loved being lost and often said so. I think Rick thought I was losing it. I had been out too long to think straight.

He had never been truly lost before, so perhaps to him this situation seemed desperate. I was warm, fed, and well rested. To me this was the heart of a good adventure, a nonthreatening unknown. Rick hadn't experienced our epic last winter, starving in caves on our way out of the Himalayas on the first half of the circle, so he had nothing to compare our predicament to. Some movement caught my eye, and I grabbed Ned's arm and pointed in the direction of the movement. From behind us came two Tibetan men carrying full loads of lumber. They stared at us in wonder and were obviously apprehensive. I noticed that they gripped their axes tightly. It was quite probable that they had never seen Westerners before, and here I was with a bright red coat, a pink bandanna around my neck, a blue one over my hair, and dark sunglasses covering my eyes. I could have looked something other than human to the barefoot men with dark skin dressed in black.

Jim was tired of being patient and wanted to solve this Langma La mystery once and for all. He boldly approached the men and began speaking English very slowly and distinctly, as if they might understand. I began to belly laugh out loud at Jim's attempts, which startled the Tibetans. When they realized the laughter meant no harm they seemed to relax. He had repeated the word Langma La enough so the Tibetans realized that was what we were looking for. Jim pulled out our topographical map in the faint hope that they might recognize the river on the map and might possibly point out the pass in relation to it. It was a long shot—but why not?

Jim grunted and motioned, and the Tibetans returned the gestures. Jim and Rick went with the Tibetans down the river for a clear view and more specific directions. We crossed the river again as directed, on our own, and in about a mile came to a beautiful clear pond and a meadow, where we decided to camp among the yellow wildflowers for the night. The next morning, while everyone was packing up, I slipped off for a little exploring myself. In a grove of trees I found a path leading out from camp. It was well camouflaged but obviously well traveled. I was proud to announce to everyone that I had a strong hunch which way we should head. Once we were on the trail we lost it at the first large open meadow. We dumped our packs and scattered to find the trail leading out of the pasture. It took almost an hour before Ned cupped his hands and yelled, "I've found it, over here," and began waving to us.

We trundled back to our packs and joined him. From the ridge we could see that this trail paralleled the area we had been lost in for the past couple of days. We were heading right back to where we'd come from only much higher now and could only hope we were headed in the right direction. We toyed with the idea that the Langma La might be shown on the map as being farther downstream than it really was. If so, we were headed in the wrong direction. As we discussed this I mentioned this was the day I had calculated we'd meet the Tibetan porters Chang was sending to help us, if we had been near the Langma La. The big if! I wondered if the porters would leave if we weren't in the vicinity of the pass to meet them.

We pushed up the trail until dusk and put up camp for the night in another high meadow with a patch of snow we could melt for water. We were up high, above the jungle, even though we were backtracking. As we were finishing our hot drinks we heard thumping and bumping outside, along with excited voices. Small, smoky, black faces appeared in the door of our tent. After another grunting session we learned these were the Tibetan porters Chang had sent to greet us! What a stroke of luck. We were in the right place at the right time!

Once on our way to the pass the following morning we discovered these porters were quite unfamiliar with portering. They claimed exhaustion every few hundred yards and asked to take a rest. We would have made much better time without them, but we were sure they knew the way, and we weren't quite sure we did. As it turned out the Langma La was hidden, until we were almost on it. We trekked along a valley that looked to be a box canyon, but tucked behind some cliffs was a rocky trail leading steeply up and over the pass. High atop the 18,000-foot pass the wind blew tattered prayer flags, and the skies were gray and spitting snow. We did not stop trekking until six o'clock that night. The next morning we walked into Kharta and a reunion with Chang, Losan, and Laba.

Kharta was exotic and beautiful with its three-storied stone houses looking like fortresses with a few small open-air windows. On top of the homes were great, flat, open spaces for socializing, bordered by stacks of juniper branches. Fresh green sprigs sprouted in the irrigated fields of barley, potatoes, and mustard, bordered by rose and currant bushes. After the stark landscapes and biting winds on our Everest Grand Circle, this village was magical. The people were curious and welcoming. We decided to spend a few days meeting the locals who eagerly invited us into their homes to climb the ladders to their flat rooftops and drink chang while listening to the many birds. I especially liked all the coo-coo birds, which they told us were saying boo-coo, meaning "Plant rice!"

Almost no foreigners had been in these remote parts, ever, so on May 25 we were surprised to see a truck lumbering toward our camp because there were no motorized vehicles in Kharta. As the truck drew closer I recognized Chris Bonington and Charlie Clarke standing in the back. Ned waved and yelled an exuberant welcome, happy to see our British friends. They stood unmoving, holding the superstructure of the vehicle. Their odd frozen attitude was ominous. The truck pulled into camp and stopped. Without a word of greeting, Chris, looking terribly emaciated, said in a hoarse voice, "Joe and Pete are dead."

As the others joined us he repeated the wrenching words, "Joe and Pete are dead." We were stunned. What had happened? Peter Boardman and Joe Tasker, two of the best climbers in the world, had vanished high on the East Northeast Ridge of Everest in a courageous final effort to reach the summit. They had climbed as a team of two after Dick

Renshaw had suffered a mild stroke up high, and Chris began suffering from extreme exhaustion.

Our satisfaction with completing our circle dissipated instantly with the realization that we were only lucky, nothing more. The pain from the loss of our friends was devastating, confusing, and hard. Chris had come around to this yet unclimbed East Face of Everest to see if by any strange chance the men had to climb down the East Face to save themselves. Chris needed to ask if we had noticed any sign of Joe and Pete in the area. He doubted this would be possible, but he had to check every imaginable scenario to assure the families back home that he had tried everything to find the men, or their bodies.

Joe and Pete disappeared, in much the same way Mallory and Irvine had almost sixty years ago. It was mysterious, and questions remain unanswered. Both parties just never returned. It took this level of play for Joe and Pete to feel totally alive and thoroughly engaged in life. Anything less did not offer a satisfying reward for them. Stretching their limits fed them as nothing else could. It wasn't a death wish, but a life wish, to live life fully. But was this disastrous result worth it? Our Everest Grand Circle began from a drunken comment at a Beijing banquet after skiing Muztagata. I was becoming aware of just how easy it was for me to accept an adventure, like this circle we'd just completed. Maybe I needed to think about this while I was still in one piece.

CHAPTER 6

SKI, SKATE, SHOOT, FLY

AS I SAT AT THE TABLE loaded with press and sponsor dignitaries at a fancy, fancy restaurant in New York City, my damn ear kept itching and paining me on the back of the lobe. And then, to make matters worse, while I was being plastered with questions I suddenly blurted out, "Excuse me," and never even got out the "please," before bolting for the bathroom. Food poisoning works fast. After I violently emptied from both ends, I looked in the mirror. As I folded my ear to look at the back of my lobe, I saw the little, hellish culprit that was paining my ear. A tick had suctioned onto the back of my ear and had engorged itself with my blood. I pinched it hard with my fingers and ripped it off with a snap of my wrist, fortunately, head and all. After cleaning up the bloody mess and rinsing off my face and mouth, I sauntered back to the press conference.

We'd literally been picked up at the airport upon our return to the United States from our Everest Grand Circle Expedition and deposited at this luncheon while I was suffering the effects of remote travel. Being more than twenty pounds thinner, food looked good to me, although I still didn't know if I could keep it down or not. Funny how I was supposed to be a heroine to these people, and I was really somewhat of a wreck. Soon after we proceeded to do a more than twenty-city tour across the country, grilled by newspapers and radio and television personalities. We started right off with the major morning TV news shows, *Good Morning America* and *The Today Show* in New York City. It was amusing to think of me, a Vermont farm girl at the end of a long line of siblings, being picked up in limousines and ushered into green rooms for makeup.

After having set the record for high-altitude skiing with *National Geographic* on Muztagata, then completing the Everest Grand Circle, another world record, people were curious to see just what this female looked like who set records with all-male teams. I wondered if I disappointed the public by not being six foot two inches and 200 pounds and rippling with muscles. I was only five foot eight inches and down to less than 120 pounds from my fighting weight of about 135. I would work out to gain weight postexpedition, but it would take time.

Ned and I sometimes split up duty, especially when it came to the newspapers. Unlike radio and TV, where they needed to get us on and off within minutes, the newspaper people raked you over the coals looking for their angle. They seemed to take forever, because they had forever to talk to you. In one city Ned and I agreed on the plane that it was his turn for the newspaper interview so I could go to the movies. Suddenly, shortly after the movie began, I realized not only did I not know the name of the hotel we had checked into minutes before, but I didn't even know what city I was in! I had simply asked the cabbie to deliver me to the theater.

I ran out to the concession and asked for the name of the biggest local paper and got right on the phone to locate Ned mid-interview. He couldn't contain himself when I asked him what hotel we were staying in, then I sheepishly admitted I had had to ask the kid at the candy counter what city I was in. If I had missed Ned at the paper the only information I had was what plane to get on the next day. Ned would have had the police out looking for me while I would have hit some cheap motel until flight time. Although I had been dreading this tour, blasting through cities, sometimes two in a day, ended up a real adventure in its own right and an education in terms of the American public and what they want to hear. I think John and Jane Q. Public really are more interested in the bizarre and the gory than the spirit of achievement.

When we returned to Vermont, I was still wrestling with the death of Pete and Joe on Everest. Enough so that I had been unable to deliver this information at past interviews without becoming visibly upset, so Ned had taken on this part. I still had some big questions about expeditions in general and especially the high-profile, high-risk, high-altitude type. The statistics weren't good for those of us, like Joe and Pete, who went high often.

I recalled my sixth-grade teacher, Mrs. Oliver, who demanded to have me in her class because she was going to make a lady of me, only to side with me in the end, congratulating me for bloodying the nose of a boy who she said, "Had been asking for that for a long time." Mrs. Oliver taught us, as she did every year, a special class about odds. She didn't want any of us to fall prey to gambling of any sort and taught us how to figure out the math for the odds of anything. I knew my odds weren't good for staying in one piece or staying alive with the type of lifestyle I had been leading. As much as I loved my life as it was, I could hear Mrs. Oliver in the back of my head reiterating, "Know your odds and abide by them."

Because I did feel my life was what I made it, and the world was what it meant to me, I decided to see myself as another sort of athlete with different odds. I had been one of the top Nordic skiers in the United States, and I wanted to see where I could take endurance skiing again, yet I needed more, considering all I had learned and experienced through climbing. What I felt most intriguing on the rock and ice was the intense focus, often adrenaline induced, when embroiled in difficult climbing.

I decided to pursue biathlon, a fire and water mixture of the mental and physical, combining cross-country skiing and rifle marksmanship. Women were just being allowed to compete with the men in biathlon. Biathlon would allow me to see what I had for endurance and focus, tested in competition rather than an expedition. This was for me. I could work on the intense mental focus through the Zen of accuracy in target practice, and I could push my endurance limits training for skiing.

Bill Koch, a fellow cross-country ski racer and silver medalist in the

1976 Olympics, had designed extraordinary trails for early training in the mining town of Labrador City, Quebec. All the top cross-country and biathlon competitors would be skiing there in November, training to make the U.S. team, and I thought I'd join them. If I made the team, all I could possibly lose was a race, not my life.

The thoughts that were shifting my athletic focus, when I investigated them deeply, were born of pragmatism. Fear wasn't motivating me; I just found the odds not in my favor after four major expeditions. If one out of every eight is killed on this type of venture, maybe I was down to a fifty-fifty chance of being the next one. I did feel skill and judgment played crucial roles, but watching the avalanche fall the day after we climbed Pumori, right over our route, also taught me you can only be as good as your luck too. Who knew that glacial mass, that ice chunk, was ready to calve? The snow itself was unstable.

I purchased an Anschutz .22-caliber rifle and named it Sweetie. A local biathlete gave me shooting tips, and I went to the range to kill black circles. I was unaware just how addicting marksmanship could be, living in pursuit of the perfect aim. I became captivated, like the Zen archers who cleared their minds to be one with the target had been centuries before. By November I was ready to ski and shoot with the big boys—and girls. I was supporting myself meagerly with the articles I had written and photographed about my past expeditions and travels. This month I would only focus on skiing faster and shooting straighter; like an expedition, life boiled down to its simplest elements was extremely appealing to me.

Out on the snow there were mostly guys but still plenty of women, with great bodies all around. Big-dog coaches barked at little-pup racers as they skied by. Our wardrobes were limited because we had to lug rifles, ammo, cleaning gear, wax boxes, skis, poles, boots, wax irons, benches, ski suits, and plenty of long underwear and socks. So we all looked like we were right out of *Star Trek* most of the time in our one-piece, body-condom racing suits. Most of the biathletes were great characters. You've got to admit, it takes some type of imagination to want to push your body to the limit skiing and then pull yourself under your mind's control, slow your breath and heart, and start consistently dropping targets no bigger than your fist at fifty meters. I had scored well enough in the competitions in Lab City that I was being considered for the first official U.S. Women's Biathlon Team. The other ladies had been racing for years, but there had never been an official team, even though the men had been racing in World Cup and Olympic competition. I had fallen in love with racing all over again.

Then I learned from a friend that the people at Beaver Creek Ski Area near Avon, Colorado, were looking to put on what they called "one of the most brutal tests of mountaineering and endurance that the human body is capable of performing in one day." I decided to hightail it back to Colorado. The idea captured my imagination instantly, and it was also just a race, nothing death defying. Thinking back on my experiences with hard days of mountaineering, I recalled the day in 1980 when I climbed 5,000 feet to the summit of Muztagata in western China, to about 25,000 feet, and skied back down to 20,000 feet in one day. And I recalled the day in 1982 when I made the summit of Pumori in the dead of winter on the Everest Grand Circle Expedition. Could a race match those challenges? Fortunately I found out the members of the Beaver Creek organizing committee were still planning the contest; they were looking for guinea pigs to do a trial run to see how hard the route really was—and whether they could get anybody to enter the race in following years. Naturally, I volunteered.

When I got to Colorado, the next day was race day. I arrived at the parking lot at 8:30, a little late, and was instructed to dump my snowshoeing gear in one bag and my running gear in another; later, I was assured these bags would appear on the trail when I needed them. It was casual to say the least. I scribbled some wax on my skis and ran to the starting line. That was another surprise. There were only four guys there, and I had been expecting about twenty. It appeared that all the other entrants had suddenly found other pressing obligations.

I had hardly a moment to size up my competition before the starting gun sounded. Anyway, everyone was wearing dark shades, and I couldn't see their faces. Then I noticed a lovely lady in the crowd kissing one of the racers good-bye. I pegged him for a soft ladies' man, and nicknamed him the pretty boy. I figured I might have a chance to beat him. Being the only female specimen in this racing experiment made no difference to me. I found the thought of coming in last appalling.

At the summit of the first peak, after climbing to about 12,000 feet, I figured the ski run under Beaver Creek's ski area lift would be the most direct shot down. It was. But it was also slick and bump infested. I pitched and heaved on my skinny skis as the crowd on the lift yelled, "Point'em down! Get some air! Telemark!" By the time I reached the bottom, the guys were about seven minutes ahead of me. Even the pretty boy, who was a skilled bump skier, caught up with me as I changed into snowshoes. Drat! I could see he didn't fancy being beaten by a woman, and he could tell I abhorred last place.

He told me his name was Gary as we proceeded up our second peak of the day—a 2,270-foot climb. Neither of us was willing to let up. We drove each other into the ground. Somehow, working together on the toughest part of the course, trying to catch the lead pack, created a bond between us. But a race is a race. I didn't let any kind feelings prevent me from galumphing away from Gary on the long downhill stretch. When I reached Avon I donned my running shoes and began my 10K.

I waved "'c'mon" to Gary, but I had gained too much time for him to make up. Daryl, the winner, completed the course in 5 hours and 7 minutes—6 minutes ahead of second place and 12 minutes ahead of third. I sprinted across the finish line 6 minutes after that, with plenty of gas in the tank. I was pleased at finishing with the men instead of behind them. But the feeling was fleeting. It reminded me of the time I punched my sixth-grade buddy in the nose when he tried to make me sit in a mud puddle. I enjoyed the act while performing it but felt so sorry afterward—when his nose erupted in a Mount Vesuvius of blood—that I cried.

I enjoyed every minute of the hours I struggled to stay ahead of Gary, but when I actually beat him I felt sorry for bruising his ego. I kissed him when he crossed the finish line hoping to soften the blow.

Later, after a few beers and some time in the Jacuzzi, we all vowed to meet again next year at the starting line of the first official Mountain Man Triathlon. Meanwhile I got word I was on the U.S. Biathlon Team, which meant I was entitled to all their upcoming coaching and training camps. I was pumped up to race, race, race—now with a shot at the Olympics and the first official Mountain Man coming up the next winter.

I spent the summer training out West and living out of my car. When I returned to Vermont at the end of the summer, Ned announced he was going to row to Antarctica and wanted me to join the crew. *National Geographic* would like the story. Wow, I had geared up for two major competitions and was completely committed to training to see what I had in me. It was apparent there was a division of philosophy that had been developing between us. It came to light that I saw myself as a writer and photographer, and I went to the places where my story was. This was how I had been making my living. Ned saw himself, ultimately, as an adventurer, and he photographed and wrote about his adventures.

Perhaps this seemed too subtle of a distinction to make at this time, but it became more and more apparent. For me, my love of the mountains drew me into and up them. But to row in the world's most dangerous seas in a boat made to roll over and over with the people as contents, like clothes in a washing machine, didn't appeal to me. I had nothing to prove; it wasn't important to me to show that I could survive this event. I didn't need to be a great adventurer, but I did need to investigate a good story, one that deeply interested me. I was doing an article for *Outside* magazine on the Mountain Man, and one for *Powder* magazine on biathlon already. I was the one who had secured a publisher for the Everest Grand Circle book with a sample chapter, then invited Ned to coauthor with me. I was creating, writing, and photographing an ad campaign for The North Face. This is what I did. This is who I was.

Something else odd was occurring. Once during a conversation, Ned was complimented about the Everest Grand Circle article with big photos just out in *Powder* magazine, and he simply carried on, sucked up the praise, and chatted. As we walked away I bumped him in the ribs in a jocular fashion and said, "Gee, thanks a lot!" because it was my work, my article and photos. I had procured and completed that job solo. We loved to poke fun at each other, so I went along with the conversation, thinking it was all a grand joke, shaking my head and nodding as Ned glowed. When I noticed Ned wasn't really laughing good-naturedly with me, I sensed something awry. Now that I could outbike him upon occasion and sometimes whipped him on skis after training in Colorado, he seemed less happy for me and more frustrated with himself. I felt the ugly head of competition rearing itself.

I left Vermont for the Olympic Training Center in Lake Placid feeling a bit unstable in my relationship with Ned. Were we together as a couple? Partners on expeditions? A support for each other in our whirlwind lives? Just what were we to each other? Ned had wanted to marry, but with his nickname of "Ned Never-have-a-kid Gillette" and my desire to have children, I thought it best to wait until we could resolve the issue of having a family, or not, first. I could wait for family life, so we were coasting, letting the relationship wend its way along. We loved each other and that was what we clung to. But can a relationship survive long periods apart, different lifestyles, and, most of all, competition with each other?

My room at the training center was right next to the bobsledders. These guys were hysterical and took my mind off my relationship concerns. They were all my buddies, like big, I mean really big, brothers. All the athletes competing for spots on various winter sport teams for the upcoming Olympics were here, going through preseason training with their respective coaches. To me it was like one giant slumber party. Life was a gas. We trained, ate voraciously, and hung out laughing in the dorm. I could have college life all over again without the hassles of exams. I had competed in four varsity sports in one year at the University of Vermont, so this was like a walk back in time for me.

The bobsledders were a bunch of laid-back guys who always enjoyed a good belch, called each other penis breath, screamed like opera singers over Monday night football, and blasted heavy metal tunes down the hall. The other women athletes found them somewhat offensive, but probably all the tent time I'd spent with some of the most rugged guys on Earth while on expeditions had conditioned me to appreciate the nuances of this male behavior. I'd sit with them in the cafeteria just to watch them eat. The amounts were enormous. We had a good time, and these giant guys respected the fact that, although I was much smaller, I could shoot them between the eyes from fifty meters away, five times in about thirty seconds. And then I could get away because they could never catch me. Although if they did, they could crush me like a bug.

One of the most fascinating aspects of the Olympic Training Center was the special psychologist brought in specifically to work with the biathletes to help us train our unconscious, or as some say our subconscious. Our discipline of marksmanship was totally mental, and we needed to embrace that. I clicked with this psychologist, and she ended up being my roommate to boot. I reveled in the higher states of consciousness that she brought us to, and she told me I had an aptitude for it, tapping in to my own "electrical" system traveling up and down my spine. I could feel the energy moving throughout my body, my hands tingling and even the muscles of my face twitching.

In these deeper or higher states the goal was to train your mind to see the perfect target through your scope, with your eyes closed during meditation. As a result, on the range, your mind would have you pull the trigger when you saw the perfect target before you even had time to think, "I should pull the trigger now." Consequently I began pulling the trigger without really being aware, consciously, in my surface thoughts that I was going to pull the trigger. I often surprised myself that I had pulled the trigger before I even decided to do it.

Zen monks do something similar when training their minds through meditation for archery. When the archer no longer needs or desires to hit the target, then the way leads him there. Being one with the bow frees the archer from needing to hit the target; the bow does it for him. Between my private coaching in Tucson with Marie and working with this psychologist at the Olympic Training Center, I was improving my accuracy rapidly. I began to feel I might have a chance to make the top four biathletes in the United States and travel to the Sarajevo Olympics.

Although it was exciting to make the team, it was the best to watch, while my team rested, all my friends of different disciplines go through their Olympic tryouts. I had a gas watching the bobsledders do their thing, was amazed by the speed skaters, and stood at the top of the jump to watch the ski jumpers launch themselves off huge ramps out into the air and drop onto sharply steep landing hills. Human beings are amazing creatures, and the pastimes we create are surprising and weird—and I'm one of them!

Then we ladies received word that we were not allowed in the Olympics. Sounds dramatic, I know, but it was crushing. The world either recognizes you as an Olympic athlete or just another good athlete. This Olympic distinction may not seem like much, but it sticks. I suspect this had been brewing, but our coaches wanted to keep us motivated and waited until they received final word from the Olympic Committee before letting us know our status. Apparently we needed to have raced a World Cup Championships first before technically being allowed into the Olympics, even though the men's biathlon team had been competing on this level for years. We would, instead, compete with the best female biathletes from around the world, who would have been at the Sarajevo Olympics, in a World Cup Championships in Chamonix, France.

I immediately disappointed my coaches by announcing that I was leaving for the Mountain Man Triathlon in Colorado and that it would be a great thing for strength and endurance building for Chamonix. They let me go, with very quizzical faces, wondering, I'm sure, why they said yes. But things were a little different now that the pressure was off to get to Sarajevo, and it was taking time to organize the Chamonix competition. We female biathletes were not financially supported, and I had a story to write for *Outside* magazine about this winter triathlon, so I was really going to work, and they couldn't say no to that! The women's biathlon team would borrow funds from the men's team to travel to Chamonix, but everything else, all year long, had been paid for by each individual female biathlete herself.

On Mountain Man race day it was apparent that things had changed from the quaint little contest I'd had with the guys last year. This year there were about twenty entrants. The media had come, press packets in hand, and the racers were given turtlenecks and hats with the Mountain Man logo. All very professional. The course itself had changed somewhat. Specifically, it had been lengthened, and we would be speed skating instead of running. Granted this Mountain Man didn't have the mileage that the Iron Man had, but miles are counted in vertical and weather in the mountains, and we were racing at much higher altitudes to boot. The Mountain Man also required very finely tuned skills in skiing and speed skating. After racing big Californian summer triathlons in the past summer I found the winter triathlon more demanding in terms of technical skill.

I was still among the top ten racers when I got to the top of the first peak. The ski descent this year was a piece of cake compared to last year's episode. I reached the start of the snowshoe leg in good time, but a problem was looming. I had a sinus infection from a nasty virus I had caught at the Olympic Training Center, and my head was so plugged up that I felt like I was under water when I bent over to take my skis off. I couldn't hear a word anyone was saying until one guy screamed in my ear, "You're twenty minutes behind the leader."

As I crossed underneath the chairlift, stomping along on my snowshoes, a boy yelled down, "Hey lady, have you done the swim yet?" After that my head started throbbing from the infection. Two-thirds of the way up the slope, I heard another voice. It was Gary, the pretty boy who had been far behind me after the first peak. I was glad to see him but mad he'd caught me. Was this where I had to pull out the little white flag? Gary caught me a few hundred yards from the top of the bowl. I picked up my pace and stayed with him to the top. We slammed some Gatorade at the feed station there and began our pounding run down. "I'm glad we get to race together," puffed Gary. I thought for a minute.

"I'm not sure," I said. "We'll probably kill each other or die trying." We pounded down with galumphing strides to the lake and pulled on speed skates. I started running down the snowbank wearing my skates, until someone grabbed me and walked me down the path to the lake, and then I heard the crowd begin to roar.

Over the loudspeaker I heard "And it's John Dozier, coowner of the Ute Mountaineer in Aspen, Colorado, winner of the first Mountain Man Triathlon with a time of 4 hours and 43 minutes." Amazing. His time was somewhere between 1 and 2 hours faster than anticipated. I finished my first lap as Gary appeared on the ice; with that kind of handicap, he and I were about an equal match in the remaining twenty-seven laps I had to go. It looked like there would be a mad scramble to the finish. A few photographers began snapping pictures of me.

Then after the fifth lap something weird began to happen. My ankles started turning in and lowering toward the ice. It was such a surprise. I just stared at my feet in disbelief. I tried to muscle them up into position but nothing happened. After making a few more laps, I knew I was in for a long, rough skate. I had to let go of the thought of finishing with the big boys. I'd wanted to finish in the top five but would have been satisfied with getting in the top ten. Now it was a matter of just hanging on and finishing. I had energy to burn, but my ankles had just given out. With three laps to go, I wondered if I'd be crippled for life! All my weight was on those two useless ankles; my blades were worthless.

I was sliding on my ankles, my skate blades lying flat out, parallel with the ice. My speed was miserably slow; the leather on my skates was wearing through where they rubbed against the ice. I wanted to melt into the ice and disappear every time I slid by the crowd. Every lap someone would implore, "Don't you want to stop before your legs snap off at the ankles?" Photographers madly clicked away. I winced and blushed as a cameraman from *The Today Show* got down onto the ice for a close-up of my feet. I honestly admit I'd never been more humiliated in all my twenty-seven years. Several of the fellows I'd left in the dust earlier were now whipping by me laughing. "I'll teach you to skate if you teach me to ski!" one of them shouted.

The sad thing was, I'd skated this distance easily, but I'd never done it after five hours of hard mountain travel. Gary asked the doctor in attendance to get a wheelchair ready at the finish. I nearly died from embarrassment when I heard about the wheelchair.

I finished in eleventh place with a time of 6 hours and 24 minutes. The doctor pushed a folding chair under me on the ice, and I put on my wooden clogs and to my surprise simply walked away! My Mountain Man buddies were still there waiting for me, ready with hugs, kisses, and congratulations. Later I was given a dozen roses and a bottle of champagne. Also my name was printed on a bronze statue that stands at Beaver Creek Ski Area. I won for the women, but I still don't know if there even was another woman in this original race. It might have been just me being one of the guys again. This time right in the middle of the pack, even though I had a great calamity.

I headed back to Lake Placid and the Olympic Training Center. Because we were a small team of female biathletes, we were becoming bonded, which was something new for me, who had spent my life bonding with guys. I'd given all the girls rock star names for the people they not only resembled personality wise but uncannily looked like as well. Holly Beatie, our California girl, was Bonnie Raitt, a tough-stomping, hard-rocking kind of girl. With round red lips and long, light-brown hair, she was a heartbreaker to look at for the guys, and she reveled in that attention.

In contrast Julie Newnam from Washington state was Carole King. A songwriter for many of the most famous pop singers, she occasionally sang and recorded her own songs made famous by the stars and made them sound even better in my opinion. Jules (Julie) was humble, unassuming, and the funniest cynic I've met. I always leaned closer to hear just what she was saying under her breath, because it would break me up every time. She didn't look for attention but satisfied herself with knowing she had what it took.

Kari Swenson from Montana was pure and sweet Emmylou Harris;

a bit of a country twang, but with the sound of an angel. Kari was gorgeous but more conservative and retiring than Holly and less of a wit than Jules. Her long, thick, shiny reddish hair went to her waist and was always braided long, hanging beside her rifle on her back as she raced. She was sincere and hardworking and stopped people in their tracks when they looked at her gorgeous, pure looks. Me, well, I was dubbed Joan Jett. As different as we all were, we had a passion beyond words for the biathlon, a common bond that held us tight. Music, in training and in the dorms, also kept us together, pumping us up as we danced in the morning and firing us up for workouts, another reason I related us all to rock stars.

We had some training races before we took off for Chamonix, and lo and behold, maybe it was the altitude training, but I was winning, having the strongest showing over Kari, who had been our top competitor. We actually watched the men in competition in Sarajevo on TV at the dorm before we left, laughing hysterically when a commentator asked people on the street in LA what the definition of a biathlete was? Responses like, "Someone who combines swimming and jumping" to "Isn't that what Rene Richards is?"—a famous tennis player who had a sex change during competitive years. It was stark evidence of the anonymity of our sport in the United States. For the majority of the sports-viewing public, biathlon was still a conundrum.

After we arrived in Chamonix, France, and settled into a cheap pension in Argentiere, a satellite village of Chamonix, our first concerns were for pastries and chocolate, along with sleep. Later we wandered out to inspect the firing range and racetracks. Things were shaping up, and it appeared we could begin training the next day, provided our missing baggage arrived with all our equipment. Four rifles and about twenty pairs of skis were in airport limbo, somewhere on one side of the Atlantic or the other.

Soon gear arrived and training began. I felt complete to have my rifle on my back once more. I slid onto the range and began loading five rounds to each clip. During competition we used one clip to hit five targets, one bullet per target. Hitting all targets was called cleaning them, as the round black dots closed over with a white cover. It even looked clean when the five black circles turned all white when you didn't miss. This way spectators would always know instantly if you hit or missed your targets. The air was clear and calm, creating a near perfect day to zero our rifles. Zeroing is the precise process of aligning the delicate sights on your rifle to be able to group your shots onto a paper target.

Ideally you would have all five shots go through the same hole at the center of the paper target. While in a prone position I should get five shots within the size of my thumbnail in the center of the target. Sometimes your group of shots would be consistently off—high, left, or right. You would know you were shooting straight, but the wind, your body position, or something else was affecting the bullets or your aim, so you would readjust your sights until your group was in the center. Ammo is often erratic in cold temperatures. Once I was so focused on zeroing my rifle in weather well below zero that I actually froze my toes. They blistered, turned black, and peeled. I had always been too aware when climbing to let this happen. I just never thought it would happen during a sport, but zeroing is such a meditation that I lost the connection with my body just a little too long.

As I skied over to the firing line I looked up and saw the mountains leering at me, almost sneering at me for toddling around in tracks and fussing over finicky, fine points in the valley. I had traded my life in the high mountains for the complicated intrigue of biathlon. I laughed at the personal irony of my being in Chamonix, a town drenched in mountaineering history and centered on 16,000-foot Mont Blanc, the highest of the peaks in the Alps, and also the site, down in the valley, of the ultimate in biathlon. Here I was at the gates to an amazing world of climbing ascents and skiing descents, and I was forbidden to enter.

Each morning life was like a grand circus. All the shooting points were littered with well-toned bodies in tight, bright suits. There was often quite a wait for a turn at the shooting gallery, so I'd ski around meeting the other teams. I particularly liked the Soviets and sang the kid's song "Good Morning to You" to them in Russian, which got a good laugh out of them. As we'd never competed against one another before, we were all anxiously awaiting the first race to see how everyone would size up and which countries would dominate. It was interesting—as women we bonded as friends, regardless of country affiliation, yet we still kept the competitive moxie.

Finally I got my turn at the firing range. Things clicked and targets fell easily. I looked around, and the others on my team were knocking down targets like crazy. I swelled with pride. We were hot.

The morning air on race day was quiet and still. I had the dubious distinction of receiving bib number one in the draw. It was a distinction to be the first in the world to compete in the birth of a new sport for women. It was dubious, however, because racing later would be better, as the tracks got faster. All I could do was pour it on, regardless of where I was in the lineup.

I noticed some fellow racers were plagued by a persecuted feeling that crept up on them before a big competition, as if they wished the race were already over. But I was happy because being number one meant I didn't have to wait a minute to start. I loved competition. Marie, our rifle coach and the only female coach on the circuit, accompanied me to the start to observe the formality of the officials weighing my trigger. Time was fleeting; I had but a few moments to stretch and warm up my muscles before the start of the ten-kilometer race. As I stood in the starting gate the coaches tried to convince me to tuck my necklace of pearls inside my uniform. I laughed, as the World Championships was the only event at which I would wear them. I skied the first loop, cruised on to the range, flopped on my belly, and cleaned all five targets, then slung my rifle back on and took off in fifty-nine seconds. I was making good time and having so much fun.

Yellow, green, yellow, blue were the loops and were to be skied in that order. I tucked a small downhill and hammered up a small incline. As I glided down the backside my eyes popped open in shock. I was approaching the end of the blue loop. I had beaten the marshals to the cut-off point, and they were not there to direct me onto the correct loop. Being number one had its disadvantages if you were fast. I turned around and skied by them pointing to my bib. They had to record me on the green loop or I would be disqualified. I shot two more times and skied two more loops.

When I finished the race I rushed to our tent for results. The times were confirmed, and our team member Kari was fifth, behind four Soviets. She'd outdone all the women from the other ten nations. I laughed to hear Julie say, "Here's some results for 'em"—in reference to all the officials in the United States who demanded results this first year or women's biathlon would become instantly extinct.

I finished in fourteenth place; I'd missed only three of my fifteen targets. Only three women in the world had better shooting scores than I did that day, but I paid dearly for skiing an extra minute or so because the marshals were not out directing the course. My coaches figured I would have been in seventh place just behind Kari when they subtracted my extra ski time. Still, ifs and buts don't count; mistakes do. And even though I had made a mistake, I was still alive, knowing what I was capable of rather than dead in the big mountains where any mistake can be critical.

We had a couple of days' reprieve between races, and I used my precious time for the essential things like buying French pastries, perfume, and champagne. I was desperately tempted to ski high in the mountains during this downtime, but I knew my coaches would have kittens if I did. I felt as if I were torn between two love affairs, one with the mountains and one with elite competition.

For the five-kilometer event I drew the number seven, lucky seven. My coaches still didn't move me up in the ranks with the better athletes, even though I was number two for our team out of the four of us in the first race. They stuck with the original tryout order no matter what. It was strange but unshakeable.

I made up my mind that I wasn't going to get into any mix-ups in this race like the previous ten kilometers. I skied out fast and cleaned my first five targets in fifty seconds. I was excited. I skied my next loop with good speed, and as I approached our team timer at the side of the track, just before the shooting range, he yelled, "You're in second place behind JJ!" JJ was the nickname I'd given to my buddy, a tall, lanky Soviet who I had traded watches with earlier.

JJ had taken second place in the ten-kilometer event two days before. I knew she was a strong contender. If JJ and I were close, I knew at that point in the race I was in the winners' circle. But anything less than first place is like kissing your brother—nice, but no big thrill.

This is when I made my second big mistake. I thought if I were ever going to go for it, this was the time. I skated onto the range instead of coasting. Normally I glide on, mentally working to lower my breathing and pulse. I had my rifle in position in a flash, positioning it in exactly the same spot I shoot from every time for complete, consistent accuracy. I began blasting away at my targets.

Marie told me later that she winced when she saw me flying onto the range so fast. She knew what was going to happen before I did. Instead of lapsing into my usual concentration as I faced the targets, a voice of inexperience began beckoning in my mind. Myriad hurried thoughts coursed through my brain. I was thinking about JJ, thinking about shooting faster, thinking about everything when I shouldn't have been thinking about anything at all. Not only that, my pulse was sky high from skiing in too hard. Throughout the championships I had been shooting well and faster every time. Not knowing my own limits I'd pushed myself beyond my own capacity. I hit only one target out of five and spent two to three minutes skiing four penalty loops for missed shots.

Still it was a calculated risk, because I knew I was one of the fastest biathlon skiers in the world. Luckily the penalty for misses was added loops not added time. I knew I would just have to ski like the wind to make up for my mistakes. If I had taken a risk and gone beyond my capacity in the mountains I could have easily died, so biathlon was the place to exceed myself. I slipped to sixteenth place but still I knew what I was capable of. I wanted to see just how aggressively I could ski and how fast I could shoot and still be accurate. I found out the hard way at the wrong time. But I was alive.

Returning to the States I threw myself into training for the Mountain Man. Specificity would be my key to excellence and good skates too while training for my Mountain Man comeback. I was getting some stiff-booted speed skates made to the mold of my foot by an expert in Canada. I also mounted some speed-skate blades onto some stiff, plastic hockey uppers and created a hybrid speed-hockey skate, in case my special-order speed skates failed me.

I had to laugh at the sign of the times when actor Jack Nicholson was quoted as saying, "Women today are better hung than the men." Daryl was the only one of my original Mountain Man buddies still racing, and we bonded over trying to prove who was better hung every day in training. We ran up and down every mountain in the Vail area on a daily basis. Daryl was in the winners' circle last year, and I wanted in. I won for the women, but it was the men's circle I wanted to crash. Race day was beautiful, and Daryl and I ran it pretty much together. He wouldn't let me by him on penalty of death, for both of us. The best part was running after Daryl, catching him as he took a leak sideways while running on his snowshoes. He didn't dare stop but couldn't pee moving forward without wetting himself, so he loped sidelong, peeing out and away, facing across the hill instead of down it. When I'd catch him he'd hold his yet undrained member out in the cold air and run like hell, only to lope sideways again and resume peeing. My belly laughing doubled me over and kept me from passing.

The skating portion of the event went without a hitch. My personally molded skates, which the pros wear, did just fine by me, and Daryl and I were just about elbowing each other for fourth place. I was crawling up his back, drafting. He couldn't shake me. I think he truthfully would have tackled me if I made a move to pass, so Daryl and I pretty much tied but were fourth and fifth, respectively, overall. This was good enough for me, to be within the top five men in the country. I could hang up my racing bib with satisfaction.

I also felt content that I was among the best women biathletes in the world, even with my mistakes. I didn't feel I needed to race another four years for the next Olympics; I knew my ability, and there was so much else to do in the world. I had a living to earn and a life to live. Although Ned and I met soon after to put the finishing touches on the Everest Grand Circle book, I knew we were living separate lives by now. I helped Ned christen his rowboat, built on the East Coast of the United States to row the perilous Drake Passage from Chile to Antarctica. Ned still held out hope that I might continue with him on the project. But I was committed to my own adventure; I was committed to flying over Everest.

By another stroke of luck, coincidence, or fate, I'd had a call when I arrived home in the states from Chamonix.

A heavy Australian accent from a male voice blasted out, "G'day, mate. Wanna balloon over Eeeverest?" "Sure, when we leavin'?" was my quick, curt reply. An astonished, "Well, you're certainly game" came back to me over the phone. This mystery male initially thought he'd take me by surprise and would get a rise out of me through shock value by just blurting out his intentions. But quite the contrary I shocked him, because I assumed this was one of the guys on my many past expeditions yanking my chain, having some fun with me before they entered into a conversation to see what I was up to.

After Ned came over to race the world's largest ski marathon with me, the Swiss Engadin, which followed the Chamonix races, we stopped over in London en route home. It was there that something quite coincidental happened. While Ned went into a boardroom to talk with a company about making a film of his future row to Antarctica, I sat in the lobby talking with the secretary. When she served them coffee in the boardroom she found out about Ned's intentions and queried me about my plans. I explained we had done the Everest Grand Circle Expedition together, but I was enthralled with racing and didn't plan to do this row. She seemed fascinated that I had circled Everest and wanted to talk about this.

Shortly after, when the boardroom was occupied with another adventure film opportunity presented by a wild Australian, the secretary served coffee again. As she listened they began to talk about needing an American on this balloon expedition over Everest so that the film would sell in the United States. "Americans don't buy films without Americans in them," someone proclaimed. Then another piped up stating, "We need a woman on this expedition. We have only men from Britain and Australia involved." "But we really need a mountaineer familiar with the Everest Region. These balloon pilots have never even camped out in the snow before, let alone climbed in the Himalayas," replied another. "So we need a female, American mountaineer, intimately familiar with the Everest Region, with the time and compunction to fly over Everest in a hot air balloon. No problem!" one fellow said cynically. Softly, the secretary spoke up in between pouring coffee into mugs, "Well I know who she is. I've met her. She was just here in the lobby. I can get you her phone number if you like."

And so, out of the blue, I was called and invited to fly over Everest. The timing was great for me. The timing was not good for Ned though. He did not get accepted for a film of his row, but I was invited to do a film with the same company for the Everest flight. Not him. This didn't help the subtle, growing competitive vibe.

Esquire and *Ultrasport* magazines had just done articles about me, and *Outside* magazine put me on their cover because of the article I had written about the Mountain Man Triathlon for them. I was also invited to raft in Africa for a film, and Ned wanted me to ski a peak in Chile with him while he continued to work to get the row organized in South America. It was enough to make a girl's head spin. But I was solid, with my head screwed on right and my feet on the ground, calculating risks and brushing off the media attention. Although I had taken to competition to minimize risk, I felt that to soar over peaks high in the jet stream, which I had climbed in the dreadful winter season, just couldn't be missed. I couldn't find it in myself to say no. I made the choice for me and for no one else or any ulterior motive. I made the choice to go for the pure adventure of it, to fly over Everest in a balloon. I couldn't help myself.

Before I knew it I was headed to Australia to begin skydiving the day I landed. They let me have an afternoon of instruction before they took us all, the Australian balloon pilots and me, up to bail out of a plane for our first time ever at 10,000 feet. Skydiving was our only line of retreat if the Everest balloons failed. Right off, we jumped out of the stalled plane and fell 4,000 feet at 120 miles an hour in this Accelerated Freefall Course. We had no static line, a cord that automatically pulls your chute so you never have to make a decision or free fall.

This first skydive ever was a gas, jumping right out into thin air and falling free. We pulled our own chutes and steered under the canopy to the dirt pit. Following my teachers' instructions to a T, I traversed back and forth losing altitude, tracking it on my altimeter, and landed with one foot on the little dinner-plate-size white, plastic disc in the middle of a huge gravelly circle maybe fifty yards across.

My instructors, who had bailed out with me in case I got into trouble, hustled over to me on the ground, yelling, when I landed. I was confused. I thought I had done fine, until I could gather what they were saying. "That was really stupid, a very inappropriate joke! How long have you been skydiving? You should have told us. It was dangerous, and you were making fools of us!"

"Wait, wait, you guys. You are such good teachers. I just did what you said, exactly, and it worked. This was my first jump, honestly. It was beginner's luck that I hit the dot." They thought I lied to them, because apparently it is really tough, even in competition, to land on this dot, jumping from 10,000 feet. The fact that I yelled Geronimo and laughed when I bailed out didn't help. We were expected to do an "on your mark, get set, go!" before jumping. The instructors lightened up and congratulated themselves for their work when they were quite confident I'd never skydived before.

We were training to fly along the Himalayan chain in Nepal, ascending above Everest in two hot air balloons designed and built in Australia. Chris Dewhirst, creative director of Peregrine Adventure Travel Down Under, had dreamed of ballooning Everest ever since he gazed at the Himalayan skies over the peaks and contemplated what was possible. Now he was pushing his dream into reality. The expedition was a joint Australian/British endeavor. The two other Australians were Aden Wickes, a Qantas pilot and balloonist, and Phil Kavanagh, the designer and builder of our balloons. The two Brits involved were cameraman Leo Dickinson, who is wild about skydiving and has written and filmed many a true adventure, and Brian Smith, who is a world authority on airships and balloon design. I was asked to fly as trip writer, photographer, and mountaineer. It was my responsibility to take charge when my balloon landed, wherever that might be.

Unfortunately I received this communiqué from Chris Dewhirst shortly after returning to the States:

EXPEDITION REPORT NOVEMBER 16, 1984: The current political situation in Nepal: In September 1984 General Rana, chief of the Army, placed a temporary veto on the balloon expedition. No official reason has been given for this veto. I believe that the unofficial reason relates to the British aid program to Nepal. Apparently British aid to Nepal in 1983–84 was less than British aid to Sri Lanka, a smaller country. This was bitterly reported in the press just prior to the military veto of our expedition. This information was discussed during a dinner conversation between Colonel Ongdi (the balloon expedition agent) and Brigadier Rana (director of military operations in Nepal). The implication was that it affected our expedition.

I have undertaken two further courses of action: 1. Approached the Governor General of Australia to ask Prince Charles to intercede on our behalf. 2. Sent feelers out for a flight in Bhutan, another Himalayan kingdom east of Nepal.

Poor Chris. He was wrestling with government bureaucracy at the highest level: planning, organizing, and straightening out extremely complicated logistics for a record-breaking expedition, while holding the hands of irate film investors who didn't care what heads rolled as long as they got their award-winning film. It was enough to make any mortal commit suicide, but not Chris! He now had lodged separate requests with Nepal, Bhutan, and China to fly over the Himalayas, whether Everest was included or not. He'd been pressured by sponsors into becoming a desperate man.

Despite all this adversity, a few months later Chris purchased a Bedford truck from Harvey's, a plumbing company in Sydney, Australia. The truck had never left the city limits, yet it had serviced more than 100,000 miles worth of leaky faucets and plugged toilets. Harvey the truck had 500 miles to go from Sydney to Melbourne, where it was loaded onto Chandridas, an Indian shipping lines vessel. Then it had to persevere 1,000 miles more, from Calcutta to Kathmandu.

In late September 1985, Chris received three telexes three days in a row telling him that his three tons of equipment, including a ton of high-quality propane, had arrived and was about to be dumped overboard in Calcutta Harbor because it was classified as hazardous material. Brian immediately flew to Calcutta and had the *Chandridas* unload the cargo onto a floating raft, thus technically keeping it at sea while the paperwork was done. Brian brought with him all kinds of ribbons and seals with wax to forge whatever papers he might need—the more colorful the better, apparently—and ended up doing a fine job of creating everything on his portable typewriter. This allowed the *Chandridas* to turn around and kept the hazardous cargo off the dock (where it's only allowed ten minutes before being thrown into the harbor).

Brian left a trail of toilet paper across India as a result of a bout of dysentery but reached Kathmandu in time to meet the rest of us. In mid-October our balloon team convened in Kathmandu. The weather was a disaster. The storms were the worst ever recorded in Nepal for October. We took a few scenic flights in Kathmandu to bide our time while the weather settled. We flew out of a tiny square surrounded by 1,500-year-old Hindu temples in Bahktapur, the oldest settlement in the Kathmandu Valley. There was just enough room to inflate both balloons, the *J&B* and *Zanussi,* named for our sponsors, and not enough room for the five thousand spectators who aggressively attempted to be flight crew.

Flying out of the square was tricky. The slightest breeze or mistake could spell disaster. Chris said for a moment he had a vision of standing among the ruins of the most priceless and ancient temple in Nepal—a vision only exceeded by the actuality of the temple keeper assisting on the opening of the balloon during inflation and holding up the envelope with his right hand, while his left hand held a ceremonial beheading sword. The first flight was smooth, and the ground crew ready for retrieval. We thought we ought to fly for the Buddhists as well and made a sunrise flight over Bodhnath, the classic stupa with the all-knowing eyes. The cameramen and the film director were very happy with getting as something as gorgeous as these flights in the film can and felt a little less jumpy about getting what they needed to make a film.

The mountains cleared, allowing us to trek to the Khumbu with an army of Sherpas carrying our balloons wrapped up in canvas like long, white sausages and lugging our wicker flight baskets, which were broken down into sections. This trek gave us expedition members time to get to know each other. In Kathmandu we were in hotels and for the most part only ate together, each focusing on his or her specific job during the day, which, in my case, was organizing climbing, camping, and emergency gear. Phil, Aden, and Brian were responsible for the fuel, burners, and balloons; Chris dealt with the bureaucracy; and Leo tended to his camera equipment and film. I had skydived with all the other lads in Australia, except for Leo, who already was an expert. Leo was interesting for me to get to know.

I was still naive about the way other countries viewed Americans, and I hardly thought it applied to me as an individual working with other individuals. But both the British and Australians on this trip had preconceived ideas about pushy, aggressive Yanks. And not only was I the only American, I was also the only woman. I was always under scrutiny, especially from Leo.

Leo was a small man, smaller than I, and of a macho persuasion. He seemed confused about how to relate to me—more so than any other male I had worked with. On the androgynous scale for personality traits exhibited, from very masculine at one end and very feminine at the other, Leo would fall toward the very masculine. Fortunately Leo was in the *J&B* basket with Chris and Aden. I was in *Zanussi* with Phil and Brian.

In ancient myths, such as Adam and Eve in the Garden of Eden, the male is the normative and the female, Eve as the rib of Adam, is the subset. Some say men created these myths out of fear of women to keep them in their place. I figured Leo liked this myth. By contrast, some of the earliest creation myths were of Mother Earth, a feminine image of power and creativity. Biologically the female is the normative, and when testosterone is added, the male becomes the variant of that female normative. The female XX chromosomes are the normative, and the male XY is the derivation.[1]

Chris and I would often have a laugh over some comment Leo would make to me, casting aspersions about how inadequate I was or might be, as I ran circles around him trekking into the Khumbu. Chris was a beautiful, fun-loving bonus on this trip. I was used to Ned's intensity when we co-led the Everest Grand Circle Expedition in this region, but Chris was positive to the point of being a lifelong dreamer; nothing, no matter how politically or personally daunting, seemed to set him back. It was a joy for me to be just a cog in the wheel of this expedition, only needing to do my job well. I placed great faith in Brian and Phil, my pilots, and although Leo wouldn't want to depend on me, these two fellows were prepared to trust me with their lives, once they landed the balloon.

Brian was so delightfully eccentric and at the same time pragmatic. He flew to the Himalayas on his own to see if this whole thing would be feasible and decided it was okay to fly. Phil was our only family man, with his wife and two boys along on the trip. He was strong, gentle, smart, and unassuming. Aden was a bit of an enigma, very gregarious but clever as a fox, with something always cooking in the back of his brain. I remember him saying, as he jumped out of the plane to skydive his first time, "Why pray?" as we all laughed. "You don't expect God to take care of you when you jump out of a perfectly serviceable airplane do you?"

Yes, Aden was a balloonist and learned to skydive, but he really was an airline pilot first and foremost. He had trouble acclimatizing, so he got himself in the good graces of the other airline pilots and flew all over the region, leaving the trekking and acclimatization to the rest of us. He felt it was more important to fly in planes around the region to prep himself for the flight, regardless of Chris's disappointment. Chris was a bit afraid that Aden would want to "bomb it in early" if there was a threat of a high-altitude landing because of Aden's difficulty with the elevation. Chris and I had a running bet that whichever balloon made it closest to Everest would owe the other a good bottle of Bollinger champagne, and he didn't want Aden to stand between him and the bubbly.

We took two test flights in the 12,000-foot valley of Kunde and near the Thyangboche Monastery to get the feel for the morning up-valley winds, which we would have to land in at the close of our high-altitude flight. These test flights, snaking up the Khumbu Valley, were spectacular. I felt as though I could reach out and touch the peaks I had climbed during the winter. We were a bit stunned by just how fast the updraft winds began; as soon as the sun's light had warmed the peaks, the air began to move, then boil. The rockier the peaks, the more heat was created. We knew we needed to be landing early before the air turmoil began in earnest or risk being thrown up in the air while trying to land.

We returned to Kathmandu to roll out our 200,000-foot, high-altitude balloons (our test balloons were half this size), and we packed the parachutes and tested our oxygen equipment. We had five days before Martin Harris, the British meteorologist working with us, was due to return to Britain. He was the only one who could operate the satellite monitors. Martin's equipment was so sensitive that the readings on his screen, taken from Soviet and Japanese satellites passing over Everest, could tell us if there was even a plume of wind off the peak.

After only two days of waiting and preparation, Martin said we had a forecast close to what we were looking for: jet-stream winds varying from 250 to 290 degrees. A flight to Everest was along a 256 trajectory from Kathmandu. We hoped to fly up to 30,000 feet and right into the Khumbu over Numbur Peak and land before smacking into Everest or crossing any international borders. We were expecting 60-knot winds and minus 40 degrees Fahrenheit. However, if the winds were blowing close to 290 degrees, they could blow us into Tibet and big, big trouble. Takeoff time was 6:15 a.m., but we didn't leave the ground until 6:40 because the film crew didn't have enough light to film our ascent. The delay was a mistake we didn't realize until we attempted to land.

The film crew had the two balloons rise simultaneously. Another mistake. Three hundred feet above the ground, our balloon, the *Zanussi,* hit a 180-degree wind shear, and our basket collided with the balloon fabric of the *J&B*. Phil leaned out to hold the fabric away and prevent it from tearing; Brian was burning on all barrels, and I was photographing like mad. It's amazing how safe and removed from disaster you feel behind a camera.

Leo was filming and Chris was hanging on to the prayer flags yelling, "You guys will do anything to win that bottle of Bollinger!" Luckily the *J&B* didn't rip, and both balloons rose at 750 feet per minute. We whooshed through the 500-foot cloud bank and were blasted by dazzling sunlight. When we hit the open skies we rose so gently we could hardly feel it. You never notice any wind in a balloon because you're being carried with it. *J&B* reached 22,000 feet before they were able to raise us on the radio to find out why *Zanussi* was lagging behind.

"Brian, can you read me? Brian, say mate, what are you having for breakfast?" came Chris's voice over the radio. I loved these guys; they could have died, and they're still cracking jokes. Phil didn't miss a beat, "We're just finishing our cornflakes, but Jan spilled the milk. It went thousands of feet. By the way one of our oxy [oxygen] leads came loose. We'll be catching up soon." We had leveled out at 17,000 feet. In two hours *J&B* had reached 28,000 feet and was flying above Gaurishankar Mountain, and we were close behind looking one hundred miles into Tibet. It was so warm from the radiant heat from the burners that I was handling three cameras without gloves.

We could sit on the edge of the wicker basket and dangle our legs over the world. I had more oxygen in my mask than I could breathe, and my parachute on my back made me feel falsely secure. I stopped looking through my cameras to absorb where I was and to gaze at the Himalayas, which looked like bright, white teeth. I remembered climbing to the summit of Pumori, daughter peak of Everest, in the dead of winter. That had been severe. This trip was incomparable. I was feeling something I'd never felt before.

My euphoria was broken when we saw the *J&B* dropping out of the sky. We couldn't raise them on the radio. They fell 11,000 feet before we heard from them. Their pilot lights had gone out because of the finicky oxygen feed at altitude. They were able to light them again about 1,000 feet above a lead into the southwest ridge of Cho Oyu, a 26,906-foot peak, much too close for bailing out. With 85 percent of their fuel gone and fifteen miles short of our objective, *J&B* landed in the only clear spot in the snow-dusted forest for miles and miles.

We thought we were terribly clever and sailed over their ridge to the next valley, hoping to float down valley and avoid the long walk out. We were smug because we could almost taste the champagne we had won. But we'd taken off late, and the sun had been working on the east-facing slopes for three hours, creating a savage up-valley wind, now hard at work. We were caught in an updraft that threatened to pin us under an overhanging cliff. Brian and Phil launched into a full-scale argument about when to vent and pull the top out of the balloon with a rope to begin somewhat of a controlled crash. Their version of disagreement began something like Brian: "Vent." Phil: "No." Then progressed to: Vent now. No. Vent, vent. No. Vent, vent, vent. Okay. Vent like fury! No swearing, only the necessary words. It still sticks in my mind how succinct and to the point these two were in a crisis.

True survivors manage their fear; they are not overwhelmed by it. Much like elite athletes, competition inspires; it does not impede.[2] Control lies in the mind and is as much or more a natural trait than learned. Phil and Brian, even in the heat of the moment of being pinned under a cliff and collapsing our balloon, were calculating the exact moment to pull the plug and give us the best chance of landing without peril. Judgment would be impaired in a panic, but we were all very present, in the moment, and keenly aware.

Brian grabbed the rope, ripped out the top of the balloon, and we dropped into the forest. We snagged on a tree momentarily, and Brian exclaimed, "Jesus, how are we going to get out of here?" Not being a climber, it looked desperate to him. "Don't worry, Brian. I can get you out of here," was my simple reply. "Look out my side of the basket!" was his retort. I knew I could set up a simple rappel, clip each of the men in, and get them down to the ground without injury. "Geez, how am I going to get my camera?" I wondered aloud. The camera hung from some rigging I had set up so that I could photograph us with a remote while we flew inside the basket. "All this woman is worried about is her bloody camera!" Brian exclaimed incredulously. I could see Brian was showing a different side when things were out of his realm of expertise.

Before I could assure him, we heard a crack, and the basket hit the ground and rolled, pinning us all underneath. I had been trained by the pilots to shut off the gas tank nearest me by turning the handle in the event of an emergency landing. But when we hit, flames flew up immediately inside the overturned basket. I could hear the crackling of a fire outside and all around us too. Brian was tangled and tied up in the rip line, unable to move, and Phil was trapped by a pack. I couldn't turn my face to the flames or else risk being terribly burned. I clawed and scratched my way from under the basket, still encumbered with my chute, and beat the flames out with my blistering hands as the guys yelled, "The fire! Get the fire out!"

What seemed like forever happened in an instant. I recall struggling, in barely a flash of a moment, with the instinct to run when I was free of the basket when I realized that the gas tanks could blow up. Oxygen and gas tanks don't blend well with open fire, or should I say they blend too well—into a huge explosion. Somehow the other two gas tanks didn't get shut off in the turmoil, and the flames from the burners caught instantly in the dry forest undergrowth. But I didn't run, and I extinguished the fire in enough time, my hands feeling no pain, perhaps because of the adrenaline. If I had run, there's a good chance my pilots wouldn't have survived the blowup.

To this day Brian and Phil still think I was thrown from the basket. They say there was no way I could have made it out from under that fast. When I showed them the melted hood of my parka, explaining that the flames under the basket were right by my head and I couldn't turn my face, they just shrugged. But I know that I too was trapped, and though it took effort I managed to extract myself. Maybe I had that kind of burst of strength you hear stories about, like mothers when they lift a car off their child, but I think I just had an opportunity, a possibility, and I made it work.

When we collected ourselves and our smoldering gear we saw that the guys had done just what they had threatened to do in jest—gift-wrap a tree with the balloon. Suddenly Chris's voice cracked over the radio. We assured him we were all right, and he let us know they were all in good shape, and Aden had plenty of oxygen left over to have as a cocktail when needed. Then he laughed, "We may not have planted the champagne bottle on the summit of Everest, but we've done the highest bloody alpine flight in history." I set up camp and got some food going for the guys. There was no need to climb or trek out. A helicopter was coming in a day or two to airlift the gear out, and we all could hitch a ride.

CHAPTER 7

CROSSING
THE NANGPA LA

THE SUN WAS SETTING, casting a long, low shadow over the great Chang Tang, or salt plateau, of Tibet, set at about 12,000 feet. Caught in a maze of deep, icy blue crevasses, I had to choose between continuing through the puzzling maze, often retracing my steps in the oncoming darkness, spelling an almost certain disaster; bivouacking on the ice with no shelter or provisions, here at 18,000 feet; or trying to climb the crack in the ice wall in front of me as if it were rock, without crampons for my feet or an ice ax to use.

From an existentialist point of view I was responsible for exactly where I was in the world right now, whether or not I liked it. By trying to pin some blame on another person or circumstance or deity I would be sidetracking what was important, dealing with the situation at hand as only I saw it at this particular point in time. My life was what I had made it, and the world was what it meant to me, and a real conundrum of a world it was at this moment.

Alone, with no one to confer with or to get emotional or physical support from, I chose to climb the crack of ice as if it were rock, using my hands and feet directly on the ice. I knew if I could get through the crevasses by climbing this crack I would be able to move up onto the ice shelf, too high for me to jump onto, and get onto the moraine on the edge of the glacier like a good survivor.

If I had had ice tools and crampons I would have hammered my tools into the frozen surface, kicked the front points of my crampons into the ice wall beside the crack, and climbed up easily and safely. Instead I moved with slow, strong movements, placing a foot in the crack and twisting it to the left, making my right hand into a fist, pushing it into the crack, and also turning it left to hold me as I committed to putting my second foot in the crack above the other and twisting right, as if to pry the crack open, then doing likewise with my left fist above the right. I moved deftly, but quickly, so that the warmth of my hands and feet wouldn't melt the ice. About thirty feet below me was a pool of water, probably 1 degree above freezing. The least bit of melting would slide me right out of the crack and to my death in the frigid pool, surrounded by thirty-foot walls with no escape.

Calmly, deliberately, I placed one foot then one hand above the other as I moved upward.

I breathed as in biathlon competition during target shooting, moving in the pause between breaths with total focus. In my mind there was no pool below, there was no melting ice, there was only my hand or foot pulling or stepping up in the crack, one appendage at a time. This hyperfocus is a meditation, as it squeezes every other thought out of the brain. Again, just like on the shooting range, what seemed to take a long period of time actually transpired in a few quick moments. The perception of time is altered in this zone of focus, stretching out as every detail is perceived separately and precisely in the mind.

I pulled one hand free to rest it on top of the shelf, then moved up one foot, slapping the second hand on top in order to mantle, push my upper body up far enough to swing up a leg on top and roll onto the shelf, allowing myself to lie panting with relief. If I had ever truly projected myself into the actuality of a solo crossing of the Himalayas over the Nangpa La pass and imagined myself in scenarios like this, I wondered if I ever would have come alone in the first place. My own father had looked me in the eye when I left home and instead of saying good-bye said, "I didn't raise you to do these things," then turned and walked away. I wondered what possessed me, once again, to do something like this. What was it in me that thought always about what I could do and seldom, if ever, about what I couldn't do? Was this a good thing or twisted?

During the Everest balloon flight I had met a mountaineer, Pete Athans, who had helped out as ground crew while we flew test flights in the Khumbu. He told me stories of the Nangpa La, the highest trade pass on Earth, an ancient salt-trading pass set at about 20,000 feet high, crossing the Himalayas from Tibet to Nepal on the shoulder of one of the highest Himalayan peaks, Cho Oyu. Later, using the rare, antiquarian mountaineering books held in special reserve at a university library, I scraped together enough information to write a short proposal for *National Geographic,* asking them to send me to this area to do a story. *National Geographic* gave me the green light and the funding, saying they didn't even know that this pass, the Nangpa La, existed.

It seemed fitting to me to do this project on my own because I had co-led the Everest Grand Circle Expedition the first time to the Khumbu area, then was in charge of climbing and survival for our balloon team during my second visit to the area. Now it was completely up to me to make it all happen this time around. I was in charge, but more than that I was researching what meant more to me than the other previous expedition events. I'd record the people of the area and their indigenous culture in as pure a form as could be found at the time. I would explore the doorway, the Nangpa La, which the Tibetans had passed through hundreds of years ago to enter into the mysterious Khumbu of Nepal, where they eventually settled and came to be called the Sherpas.

When first settled the Khumbu of Nepal was a lush, thick, green forest where many animals, including large cats, leopards, and tigers, roamed. For the Tibetans coming from the Chang Tang—where the winds ruled the high, dry plain-looking desert—entering the magical world of plants and animals of the Khumbu forest was a great, wild mystery. When the monsoon clouds coming up from India hit the high Himalayas, they dropped their heavy rains in Nepal, leaving Tibet high, dry, and barren.

Because the temperatures on this Tibetan plain, the Chang Tang, are low, the rainfall is sparse, and the rivers have no outlets, salt has become very abundant. The land is so brackish, salt can be scooped right up in your hand, directly off the ground. According to legend the Rai people of lowland Nepal were cannibals. Buddha promised them something tasty if they would abandon their gruesome diet. He prepared a feast seasoned with Tibetan salt, which delighted them so much they foreswore cannibalism. From then on Tibetan salt was brought south, over the Nangpa La to Nepal. This centuries-old trade had perhaps more prosaic roots. There are no natural salt deposits in Nepal, and barren Tibet needed the grain brought up from the fertile Rai country in Nepal's lowlands. Eventually trade through the years over the Nangpa La broadened to include Nepal's rice, raw iron, handmade paper, dyes, butter, dried potatoes, unrefined sugar, cotton cloth, water buffalo hides, incense, yaks, and cross breeds for Tibet's wool, ritual objects, sheep, goat furs, dried meat, tea, tobacco, carpets, and Chinese silks—all carried by yaks or on individuals backs over some of the highest, most dangerous terrain in the world.

I trekked into the Nepalese Himalayas for my third time in early May 1986 to join the Sherpas with their spring yak caravans traveling along this fifty-mile salt route from Namche Bazaar, the cultural center of the Khumbu, to the town of Tingri on Tibet's windswept, 15,000-foot plateau. This high-altitude trade seemed destined to disappear within a generation because of the ongoing construction of a heavy truck route from Kathmandu to Lhasa and because of the trans-Himalayan cargo flights set to begin.

Namche's outdoor bazaar bustles on every Saturday morning, despite the weather. Everything is laid out on the ground for sale or barter: meat, soap, cough drops, batteries, dried bat wings, you name it. Namche is a crossroads in time, where ancient shamanism and the twenty-first century are displayed on the same woven mat. My mission for *National Geographic* magazine was to procure some rice at Namche's Saturday market and carry it over the Nangpa La to trade in Tingri, Tibet, just as traders had done for unknown hundreds of years, maybe more. I was apprehensive when I heard that it had been a particularly harsh winter and the snowstorms had lasted late into the spring. Moreover, the hay was all gone, and the normally green pastures of the high country were still white with snow, leaving the yaks weak and unfit for travel and certainly not strong enough to cross the Himalayas over Nanpa La's glaciated pass.

As I waited for conditions to improve I slipped into the rhythms of the Sherpas' life in the mountains. Almost everyone arises at first light from common family beds, nests of woven yak hair blankets laid out on the floor. Days are spent driving yaks to greener pastures, working the sparse potato fields, or leading treks. At the day's close everyone huddles around the open fire inside their one-room homes for their evening meal of potatoes, yak meat, and chang. I stayed with Anu, my Everest Grand Circle sirdar, who helped me to pull information and logistics together.

Anu introduced me to Kanjo Chumbi, a seventy-four-year-old Sherpa whose family had made its fortune from trade brought over the Nangpa La for centuries. Kanjo's father walked trade from China to India over the Nangpa La before the time of ships from Calcutta, India, to Chinese ports. Only the most precious items made the entire distance—Chinese silks and Tibetan bear musk, Indian coral and amber. The Himalayan mountain people were crucial to this extended trade: only people used to living above 12,000 feet could endure the continual hardship of such a high glaciated pass, the Nangpa La. For us Americans, climbing Denali in Alaska set at 20,000 feet is an expedition; for these Himalayan traders, crossing the Himalayas at 20,000 feet is merely a job.[1]

The weather remained stubborn and stuck in a dark mood. No one was willing to negotiate the pass with their weakened animals in these stressful conditions. So I spoke with Anu's Sherpa friend in the village and convinced him to let me hire three of his healthiest yaks to travel only as far as the moraine set at 18,000 feet at the base of the Nangpa La. I would not attempt to take the animals over into Tibet in the harsh conditions up on the pass. I wanted to set up camp by the pass and position myself to watch for any traffic crossing to photograph as soon as conditions improved.

Saturday arrived, and at sunrise I went out to the Namche market with Mingma, Anu's wife, before any supplies could be depleted. She was a bargainer extraordinaire. She taught me how Sherpas had made a living this high in the mountains as traders, before the time of treks and expeditions. She knew every price, how much it was up or down from the previous Saturday, what to buy now and what to wait on. I swear she would be a millionaire on Wall Street if she had been raised in the United States. With a mind like a calculator she knew what to buy to turn over into a profit or supply her lodge at a price that would benefit her. And if she wanted to negotiate a price, heaven help the seller. As tough as she was, every bout of the give and take in her strong voice was punctuated with her hearty laugh. It was all part of the game. Mingma was the CEO of her kitchen. Although cooking may have been her cultural role, she ran her kitchen with authority and humor, always compassionate but firm, as she fed many trekkers from around the world and managed a crew of several people around her open-fire hearth. Perhaps Mingma and I were such good friends because, regardless of our different cultures, we both found balance between our masculine and feminine characteristics. As a matter of fact I dedicated my book, *Mother and Child,* to Mingma.

In the cool air of the morning, the Dakre, or basket carriers from the lowlands, were wrapped up in their cotton shawls, huddled on the ground beside their wares: bags of grain, hot peppers, baskets of live chickens, meat hunks from recently slaughtered water buffalo, and so on. Tibetans wrapped in sheepskin coats had Chinese wares of green canvas army shoes, tea, handwoven Tibetan wool rugs, dried sheep meat, and more. Then there were the bizarre things, similar to the meteor Steve McKinney had found: dried ingredients for shaman potions, sacred and valuable Tibetan Buddha figurines, probably from a temple razed by the Chinese, and jewelry made with dzi stones—some valued into the tens of thousands of dollars when Westerners were buying.

It was shoulder-to-shoulder people. Some had traveled days on foot to get here and were therefore bartering for a week's worth of supplies, for some even a month's worth. All goods would travel back home on the shoppers' backs or that of their yaks. The market buzzed like a swarm of bees as negotiations were going on all around and items were measured, weighed, and exchanged. I thought of our grocery stores and their impersonal presentation. There was no connection to where our food came from in its sanitary wrappings, thus no connection to our bountiful Earth, which gives us food and life.

At this time Nepal was the world's third poorest country. The inequity of our world smacked me in the face. I shook my head as Mingma dragged me over to the bags of rice most often used for making chang, their local beer. She pushed me forward to do my own bidding, to garner some rice to carry to Tibet to trade in Tingri at the market called Gangar. She knew I wished to travel as an actual trader over the Nangpa La, not just as a bystander taking notes and photographs. Negotiations completed we headed home to her lodge, bearing our load.

The packed goods I tied onto my yaks'* backs were largely provisions for myself and the yaks, because their nurturing pastures weren't green enough to feed them. The salt trade route up the Bhote Kosi, or Tibetan River, winding through our route up the Thami Valley, had only sparse potato patches and no stocked food supplies for purchase anywhere. My rice for barter was hardly any consequence in the entirety of the loads for my journey. This Thami Valley was closed to trekkers and without teahouses or markets like Namche in the Khumbu Valley, so old traditions and customs were holding fast here in Thami, without the interference of tourists and the outside world. These traditional ways were just what I had come to see and experience.

Before the police checkpoint to enter the Thami Valley there is the Thami Monastery. I sought out some of the eldest in residence to ask a few questions through another young local Sherpa wanting to learn and practice English. We found a monk willing to give me some time.

---

*I refer to all yaks—*naks,* which are female yaks; *dzos,* which are nak and bull mix; and *dzomos,* which are yak and cow mix—as merely yaks.

The monk was most likely in his seventies, but he hadn't been counting. He had come from Tibet originally where he had received his training. Inside a small dark, almost cavelike building built into the hillside, he sat in his red robe wrapped in a heavier, dingy, yellow robe, near a small fire, which he flared up occasionally with a handmade bellows.

As we drank copious amounts of tea, he responded in a quite matter-of-fact manner to my questions. The communication barrier took some back and forth, but eventually I was turned inside out by this old monk. Something struck me, an "ah-ha moment," after several different tries at translation of one particular question: "What do you think of us foreigners visiting your land?" I learned that, although he didn't blame us, we were young societies, like adolescents. We hadn't matured yet, and we were still unaware that our motivation was all important for absolutely everything we do, not the act itself: "Your intentions make up yourself." Call me a simpleton, but this hit me like the trite ton of bricks. Being raised a Catholic, so much attention was focused on what you did or didn't do; we never learned as a child, or as an adult, that it is what you intended to do that defined your effort, not the outcome.

I was impressed by this monk who had spent his life studying and practicing Buddhism for the benefit of all beings, not merely for himself. Buddhists are not dualistic as we Westerners tend to be. Rather than seeing us all as separate beings, a Buddhist sees us and all sentient beings as one. A true Buddhist can empathize with his enemy because he does not even see himself separate from his enemy. He sees himself in his enemy. This allows compassion to grow. We Westerners, or those of the first world, cling to wealth and possessions and therefore feel pain when what we cling to is gone: a house, a job, money, a person. Buddhists are aware of impermanence. Nothing will remain constant; the only constant is change. To eliminate the suffering and pain caused by clinging, a true Buddhist will practice nonattachment, acknowledging impermanence. Nonattachment may sound cold, but backed by compassion and heartfelt intention, a Buddhist is always engaged with care and concern yet willing to let go when an action has been taken, to let the chips fall where they may instead of clinging to the expected outcome. From my point of view if Buddhism had a gender, it would be female, compassionate and dedicated to service to others.

The moment I truly understood motivation was paramount. Buddhism seemed to take me one level deeper into everything I did and into analyzing everything I had done in the past. So I meant it literally that this monk, in a sense, turned my inside out. What I felt motivated to do internally became exhibited externally by my actions. Yet, the outcome of my actions was not as important as the reasons for my efforts. Call me strange, but this gave me great peace of mind; it was like taking the pressure off. I did not have to be super successful at all that I attempted. I just had to be who I was, what my intentions were. My reasons counted, not my results.

This was a bit of a twist to my past "ah-ha moment" at the age of twelve, which had been my background premise for my point of view: your life is what you make it, and the world is what it means to you. Now my life was becoming what I intended, and I should not be attached to the results, because what transpired would be impermanent! Wow, I should just live intending to "do the right thing" and then just watch what happens? Instead of climbing another peak I was exploring an internal realm as opposed to an external realm; social rather than physical.

It was time to move up valley and cross the police checkpoint. I was a small caravan, with little for trade, so Gurmi, my Tibetan friend and owner of the yaks, drove the animals through the checkpoint while I snuck over higher ground to meet up on the other side, undetected. Although I had looked into paperwork to be allowed up this valley legally, the police in Namche told me there was no paperwork to be had. They also quietly indicated that if they didn't know of my whereabouts they were not concerned, but they were also not responsible for my welfare. The Thami Valley ends in the Nangpa La pass, which is a passageway, difficult as it is to traverse, to Tibet. Since the Chinese occupation of Tibet the trade over the pass had been regulated and at times completely shut down. Sherpas who lived on both sides of the pass along the trade route had been expelled from Tibet and their

Tibetan residences confiscated. *National Geographic* had wired China's Travel Association money for my permission to travel into Tibet, yet the Chinese hadn't responded to any of my telexes since I reached Nepal, therefore I couldn't get a legal Chinese visa from their consulate in Kathmandu.

My only choice was to travel the salt route as I had planned over the Nangpa La and to also get my passport stamped with a legal Chinese entry while going over the brand-new Kodari Road, the new truck route from Kathmandu to Lhasa, still under construction. This way I would have legal paperwork for being in Tibet and spare *National Geographic* any embarrassment of an author of theirs having been in a country illegally to get her story. Now faced with another illegal entry of sorts after slipping by the Thami check post, I leaned on the advice and encouragement of the locals.

Anu's father, Ang Dorji, who had traded goods in Tibet and crossed the Nangpa La for more than forty years, had told me, "Sometimes there is travel at night, past the check posts, hiding sheep fat and wool in the salt." Even the locals were up to bending the new politically imposed rules slightly. Ang Dorji had carried on through the new Chinese regulations, and managed to carry on trade in the old fashion, despite the political upheaval.

Our first day on the dusty trail past the check point and up the Thami Valley, we stopped for tea at Marulung, which, at 14,000 feet, is the last place potatoes can grow. Throughout the day, we had woven our way through the stone-walled pastures studded with stone huts. These *yersa* settlements are high, summer grazing fields owned by Sherpa families living down in the villages of the Khumbu. Gurmi spoke with a Sherpani, Nimg Dorma, tending her yaks. He bartered for some potatoes, and a roof for the night was thrown into the bargain. Delighted, I offered Nimg Dorma my ski hat as a gift, and she smiled, thinking, I'm sure, that she got the best of the bargain while I was thrilled to be accepted as a trader like the other locals who would have been offered a place to stay for the night. All doors to huts seemed to be open to travelers and commerce up here, no matter how meager the accommodations might be.

After unsaddling the yaks we settled in the dark, one-room hut for a bowl of strong tea and boiled potatoes. The chimneyless room was filled with smoke from the dung fire, sacks of hay and potatoes filled the back of the room, and the yaks were nosing in the doorway. Nimg Dorma and I sat on the only furniture, a Tibetan wool rug laid on the floor by the blaze. She told me herself, through gestures, Gurmi's help, and my map reading, that she had once carried a heavy load of water buffalo hides, used for making Tibetan boots, on her back over the Nangpa La.

I had learned that there were two types of traders traveling over the Nangpa La: household traders like Nimg Dorma, carrying goods on their own backs and making a yearly expedition over the high pass to barter for their family's personal needs, and those who traded as an occupation like Anu's father Ang Dorji, dealing in large sums of Indian, Nepalese, or Chinese coin. These professional traders often made several stops, buying and trading goods all along the way. Their border trade between Nepal and Tibet served as a major flow for more distant trade at either ends of the route, extending from China and India.

But interestingly enough no matter how complex or multisided the trade deals were, they were negotiated and run by individuals or a small team of men, or kinsmen, pooling resources. I was beginning to experience for myself, sitting together with Nimg Dorma, the brotherhood of barter, which has been lost to us today in our first world of impersonal purchasing through money only. As long as I was trading, I had a place to stay, a meal to eat, and the company of a local person who was eager to barter and connect with me as an individual. There was an unspoken acceptance and code of behavior, which seemed to be well respected and not abused. This is how culture is created, learned behavior passed down from generation to generation.

From what I had learned from Kanjo Chumbi and Ang Dorji and what I had experienced on my own, it seemed wealthy trading families did not dominate whole communities among the Sherpas. Good faith and integrity were more important among these trading societies. I had stepped into a world governed unlike the one I was from in the states.

Here, in the Thami Valley, life was still focused on small communities that sometimes ignored the regulations forced on them by the larger, occupying governments in favor of their ancient, local agreements. This handful of Sherpas and Tibetans I had been searching for were living a way of life, perhaps a thousand years old, and I had the unbelievable privilege to share it with them before it vanished in this last generation. At daybreak Nimg Dorma spread the ashes from the fire over her fields, I suspected to fertilize the potatoes. She added some sheep fat, which the locals say stays "good" for three years, to my packaged breakfast noodles. It tasted like cheese, and it greased the cracks developing in my lips, probably doing a better job than my petrochemical, commercial lip balm.

Gurmi instructed me with the expedition English he had as I lifted the bags to the saddles on the yaks' backs. "Little up, little down" was all he would say as he tied the yak hair ropes over the bags and through the hand-carved wooden saddle, which rested on a yak hair blanket covering the yak's back to prevent chafing. We had about eight miles to caravan to reach Gurmi's good friend's yersa settlement, situated just before the moraine leading into the Nangpa Glacier. Gurmi whistled to encourage the yaks along, just as we used to whistle and give calls to our cows on our dairy farm when I was young. We walked along at a lulling gait, soaking up the scenery as the valley walls began to narrow in on us, as we continually moved up in elevation toward the mountain peaks.

Gurmi felt the yaks needed to rest and chose to end the day at 2 p.m.; early I thought, but he knew best. Perhaps it was because his good friends lived nearby, and I was beginning to suspect that this trade was almost as much social as it was financial. Again we were readily invited in, and the night was spent together in much the same fashion as the night before, although this yersa home was even more spartan, at about 16,000 feet. Ang Pemba was the name of the strong Sherpa who hosted us, with his young son Phuti, maybe five years old.

Inside the mud-brick, low building, Phuti came and curled up in my lap of his own accord, although he remained wide eyed and appeared apprehensive. I gave him some of my peanuts, which delighted him, as he slowly ate them one by one. We let the fire die out and the cold seep in. They wrapped up in yak blankets with only Tibetan rugs for a bed, and I snuggled into my down bag with an air-filled Therm-a-Rest to lie on. Gurmi was the ultimate of efficiency, using the blankets from the yaks' backs to warm him and make his bed. Piles of dry dung and juniper branches sat in the corner of the one room for building fires, which seemed to house the many little rodents that I could hear swishing over the nylon of my sleeping bag all night. I tucked my head deep inside and closed the bag's opening to keep the little furry creatures from investigating me inside.

While bedded down I thought about all the millions watching TV at home in the States, where advertisers put out their best work to manipulate our emotions to keep us focused on endless desires: better skin, faster cars, thinner bodies, tighter dresses, better makeup, more electronics, cooler gadgets. Without ever stepping aside to reflect, how could any American escape the endless cycle of desires we are continually programmed for? I could sense what the monk had been telling me. This ignorance of the process of desire keeps us greedy, but material possessions cannot give us the satisfaction of connection with others and our natural environment.

Although I was in a very meager abode, the warmth of this man and his son, who had taken Gurmi and me in and shared a meal and stories with us, created a bond among us in a way a TV never could. Regardless of the mice, my experiences in the Thami Valley were palpable and clear. They were not imagined, and they would be etched in my psyche forever. This was all part of what I came to call the brotherhood of barter, commerce as connection.

That evening we had a classic meal of *sen* for dinner, which is balls of grain sometimes mixed with potatoes, and for breakfast the next morning we had rice porridge with dried yak meat before Gurmi and I loaded our yaks and continued up the trail. The food was good basic fuel for our long days. Gurmi and I took turns whistling and singing behind the yaks as we drove them over the last remaining grassy ground cover on our way to Lunag.

Vaguely, I heard voices through the thin curtain of falling snow. "Yaks peoples," Gurmi said quietly as he cocked an ear. We approached Lunag, which was a small cluster of four stone huts with no windows and not quite head height. We had to stoop to enter the lone doorways. These huts did, however, provide protection from the snow and wind. We were beyond all grass; there were only rock walls and rocky moraine now, thus the name Lunag, which means "black country." Some Tibetans with a couple of big shaggy yaks had just finished loading up and were intent on moving along. We could smell their recent yak dung fire, which was still smoking. I snapped a few photos as the Tibetans carried on with big grins. I felt disappointed we hadn't time for tea and perhaps an exchange or two. I had plenty of scarves and some small gold and silver pieces of jewelry to trade at a moment's notice.

Part of me wanted to leave Gurmi and follow the Tibetans back down to Thami. What if this was the only troupe I'd see traveling through? Shouldn't I meet and trade and photograph them? Shouldn't I see what they would do at the next Saturday market in Namche? Gurmi would be confused, I knew, if I left. He had stuck with me and already had taught me so much about running a yak caravan, taking me into the yersas to meet the locals and sharing their fare. I decided I needed to relax and hope the weather would clear for my own passage over the Nangpa, permitting me to bargain with others on the far side of the pass in Tibet. This would provide me with enough to photograph. As much as I wanted to enjoy myself, I never forgot that I was here to do my job.

It became difficult in the afternoon to keep the yaks on track over the rocks. Gurmi taught me how to take a stone and toss it to one side or the other of the yaks, and the clattering of the stone would turn them toward the direction of choice. I had sung to the yaks enough now that I had figured out what they liked best: blues, the slower the better. I found it strangely funny that their favorite song, the one they moved along best to, was Gershwin's "Summertime"—when the livin' is easy. Life can be a paradox. In one of the harshest climates on Earth, where it is never summer, a song of summer motivated the caravan.

Suddenly I had the feeling someone was staring at me. It was that feeling you have at a party, as you turn just in time to see someone fixated on you. Although you hadn't heard a sound, you felt the attention. Having this feeling now disturbed me enough that I paused to look around me. It was Gotaya. I looked up and saw a jagged rock formation on the skyline in the shape of a horse's head. Along with the Yeti, my Sherpa friends had warned me of Gotaya, the guardian of the Nangpa La. My friends had told me that Gotaya protects Sherpas and Tibetans in this dangerous high country and over the Nangpa La, but they didn't know if this protection would apply to a foreigner.

Odd, I had not been tracking the peak shaped like a horse's head on my map, but as soon as I was below it, I felt its presence. The sight of Gotaya did not bring on this feeling; it was born purely out of the feeling of being watched. Gurmi noticed I had stopped and caught my gaze upward. "Gotaya, Gotaya!" he shouted to me, giving me the thumbs-up signal. I carried on, hoping Gotaya was with me instead of against me. I was fascinated by this Gotaya story and all the mystery and folklore that surrounds the Nangpa La itself, a sacred place to the Buddhist people of Nepal and Tibet. Eleven enlightened monks, I was told, ordained by Buddha himself, are believed to have become protecting deities manifested in eleven peaks and holy places, one of which is the Nangpa La.

I recalled the stories of the Kirkiz at the base of Muztagata and the sacred garden at the top of the peak, tended by gods in white robes, which perhaps represented the snows and glaciers that fed their streams and nourished the land. With this notion of gods and gardens, their water becomes sacred and cared for, not desecrated or polluted. In a sense I felt these stories about the sacredness of the Nangpa La could also have been created to encourage the respect and reverence the place deserves, so that safe passage would become in itself a sacred pilgrimage. Myths were perhaps early environmentalism, a way to ensure protection of important or wild places and environments.

I shrugged off the chill as I stood under Gotaya and called my yaks to move on. As we walked alongside the jumbled rocks of the moraine, two men came into view. These two appeared to be carrying quite heavy loads by the look of their encumbered gait, although the bags on their backs weren't unusually large. With that density it must be salt I mused. We nodded to each other in recognition, as travelers and traders both on our way. They continued down toward Thami, and I toward Tibet.

Not long after Gurmi and I set up the tent and gave the yaks the last of the hay. I woke late that night and listened. I heard the bells tinkling around the necks of the yaks. A comforting sound to hear, realizing how dependent I had become on my animals. After tomorrow's trek Gurmi would take his yaks back down to the yersas while I set up camp alone, under the Nangpa La. Gurmi and I woke the earliest yet the next morning, and although the sunlight was bright on just the tips of the peaks as the sun rose, creating an incredible alpenglow all around the gray rock and white glacier, I felt that high-altitude sludge in my brain slowing me down, here at close to 17,000 feet. I had a pounding headache and was suffering from little sleep, all common acclimatization feelings I had felt so many times before.

I was low to the point of feeling grumpy until I sang the song "You Are My Sunshine" to Gurmi, which he loved. It prompted him to grin wildly and start his own calls to move the yaks together for loading. Yak carcasses were bleaching on the rocks; the wind howled. I remembered reading about the first ascent of Cho Oyu, which forms one sharp side of the Nangpa La, back in 1954. Swiss expedition leader Herbert Tichey was referring to this area when he wrote, "We had to cross a few moraines, as unearthly and awe inspiring as a lunar landscape. We could never have found our way out if it wasn't for our guide. The path could only be guessed by occasional yak droppings and a slightly more even surface discernible here and there among the wilderness of stones."

I felt like I was walking on miles and miles of rolling bowling balls as the moraine shifted and moved continually under my feet. The yaks, however, seemed surefooted, although Gurmi and I had to sandwich them between us so they wouldn't wander off the route. Needless to say the going was rough, and my yaks began dragging their hooves. I felt as though I were being microwaved under the sun. I had been told that if my animals became sluggish, I should brew up an entire brick of strong

Tibetan tea and push their noses into it to make them drink. My yaks perked up after tea and a rest.

But I was still uneasy as I recalled my conversation with a forty-nine-year-old Sherpa, Wangu from Namche who has been trading since the age of seventeen. He told me he makes about 5,000 rupees or $1,000 in a year from trading, but profits have been cut over the years because he has lost more than one hundred yaks during his many arduous journeys from Namche to Tingri. I understood why, as the Nangpa La came into view, bordered by sharp rock walls powdered by avalanches and guarded by a cascading icefall at the tongue of the glacier.

Gurmi hastily unloaded the yaks, as I knew he wanted to boogie all the way back down to Lunag and the beginning of green grass, just off the moraine and glacier, so the yaks could graze while he slept for the night. The animals were getting noticeably tired. I knew Gurmi didn't fancy his yaks getting too weak to continue, on account of not reaching nourishment in time and becoming carcasses like those we had passed. I got my tent up pronto, before Gurmi had completely unloaded, and we brewed some tea to support him for his journey back down.

I saw some men coming up the trail behind us. I was glad that Gurmi was still with me to help me understand the men as they joined us for tea. I learned that some Tibetan traders had gotten their yaks stuck in the deep snow on the glacier's edge on the other side of the pass. These Tibetan traders had to drop many fifty-kilo bags of salt in the snow in order to dig out their yaks' legs and free them so they could return back to their Tibetan villages to wait until the snows and storms abated and crossing the Nangpa La would be safe.

These Sherpas were planning on crossing over the Nangpa La on foot and trading with the Tibetans who remained with the salt, right there on the edge of the glacier, and bringing the salt back into the Thami Valley on their return, trading it all along the way down to the Namche market. They could barter for a better price for the salt by going to the drop site on the Tibetan side of the pass rather than wait for the Tibetan caravan to bring it over when the weather improved. I suddenly envisioned the Tibetan traders as cowboys and the yaks as their "doggies." This whole trading valley was a bit like the Wild West, where things were open for interpretation in terms of rules and expectations. Every day was a new adventure. It certainly wasn't a nine-to-five existence, like that of a bond trader in American society. The two Sherpas who had passed by us a couple days ago, with the elder chanting his prayers with every step, must have been up and over the pass already to get a jump on bringing this "first of the season" salt to market.

After tea all the men went their separate ways, including Gurmi with his yaks. I was right where I wanted to be, yet had never felt so alone. I knew more would be crossing the pass as the weather cleared, and I'd hardly be alone, but the sounds of the glacier like a whip cracking and the avalanches rumbling around me seemed to increase in volume as the deafening silence in my tent surrounded me. During the night I read by headlamp different letters friends had written to me before this journey. I felt strong, determined, fragile, and insecure all at the same time. Human beings are complicated I thought, as I tossed in my sleeping bag.

I packed my gear into my backpack: nuts, raisins, water, chocolate, ski boots, bivouac sack for an emergency overnight if need be, extra clothing, headlamp, climbing skins, and such. I slid my skis and poles down the side panels on the outside of the pack and put my cameras in a fanny pack worn backward around my waist. Fully loaded, I headed up to reach the height of the Nangpa La, just to see what I could see, like the line from the children's song, "The bear went over the mountain to see what he could see." I tottered along under my load, balancing on awful, shifting moraine. Memories of the Everest Grand Circle came back to me as I smelled my sweat building under my heavy pack.

I could follow a few, sparse cairns, which blended into the rest of all the other rocks, stones, and boulders of the moraine. After four hours I reached the height of the moraine and looked around. I was out of the stone trenches. I had that unacclimatized feeling, spacey and a bit dizzy in my hypoxic state. I knew there wasn't anyone to come looking for me if I wandered off route. Once on the ice of the glacier, I skied easily over crevasses about one and a half feet wide.

Then came the whiteout. By this time, in my unacclimatized state, my head felt strangely separate from my body and my thinking was slow and unclear. I had to watch myself. I focused on the snow below me, keeping close track of the footprints left by the Sherpas. According to my map and its calibrated distance I was minutes away from the height of the pass, but in this whiteout I knew I would see nothing but my hands in front of my face and even they seemed like they belonged to someone else.

The British account of their 1921 reconnaissance in Tibet wrote, "Traffic could be kept up over the passes all year, though only with much difficulty and great danger, whole convoys being sometimes wiped out by blizzards when trying to cross, as the powdery snow is blown down into their faces from every direction, and they finally get suffocated by it." I realized with the weather the way it was this probably wasn't where I should be alone, and not running on all cylinders I also realized I would reach the height and not even know it because everything was obliterated from view by the whiteout.

I decided it was prudent to turn and ski back down and make my way back to my tent before the weather worsened and I was indeed spending the night in my bivy sack up on the pass. I took care to put out only about half effort. It was vitally important not to sweat, to stay hydrated. These are simple survival principles. It is usually the gung-ho macho types who die first in emergency survival situations—putting out too much effort, thrashing about, wasting precious energy. The best survivors, surprisingly enough, are those under six years of age who tend to curl up and stay warm and behave in more instinctive patterns.[2] Comforted, as I drank tea in my tent, that I had at least been up on the pass, I felt as if I had arrived. I couldn't stay awake and snoozed because of the effort I had put out and because I had some nagging virus that seemed to worsen as I got higher. The physical strain on my body left little energy to fight this Himalayan flu. I was so congested that when I coughed up the glop, it nearly choked me. I had food and gas enough for my stove for about another four days. I thought I would lie low for a day and maybe feel a little better when the weather cleared and the trade traffic resumed. I thought I could then ski over to the great salt load on the edge of the glacier on the Tibetan side and trade my rice there. Whether I went all the way to Tingri or not depended on how closely the Chinese patrolled the border.

I met another Sherpa, Ang Neima, when he crossed the path where my tent lay while helping the expedition on Cho Oyu clear out higher camps on the mountain. He had crossed the Nangpa La many times. He said his yaks had jumped 3 foot crevasses carrying loads, and that he usually traded *dzomos* (animals that were a yak and cow mix) and water buffalo hide for Tibetan meat, tea, salt, wool, sheep fat, blankets, yak cheese, and tsampa. I was feeling so low from my virus, wondering how I'd carry on because I was sleeping through the day, so I asked Ang Neima if he might like a job.

I felt perfectly safe with Ang Neima. He exhibited honesty and integrity, and he wasn't any bigger than I. The interview and hiring process took less than five minutes; trust was nearly instant, and we were a partnership, sharing our different strengths. I was becoming comfortable with the ease with which people met and collaborated on this route. In my life in the States, it was rare to meet someone and instantly not only work together but share a tiny living space, food, drink, and responsibility for the task at hand. I could hardly imagine picking up a hitchhiker at home in the States and in moments agree to doing a potentially life-threatening event with him in order to write a story for *Geographic*. But here in the Thami Valley, on the rough salt route, this was life, not only accepted but normal. With my health flagging, this type of society was welcome and very appealing to me.

We woke early the next morning before the sun turned everything to knee-deep slush. I was coughing and hacking so much I couldn't get down the granola I had brought. But Ang Neima ate it, enjoying the change in his diet, while I drank copious amounts of hot Tang like a good astronaut. The wind was at our backs as I skied up, and Ang Neima traveled on foot. The crevasses were obvious now that the snow from the storms had settled. We reached the summit about noon, and at the very height of the pass, at about 20,000 feet on the Nangpa La was an auspicious pole of prayer flags. Most all those who passed by would hang a flag or a *kata*, which is a ritual scarf of white cloth.

I hung my kata given to me by Sherpa friends in Namche as a blessing for my trip and tied a yellow ribbon from a thirtieth-birthday present that some friends in Kathmandu had given to me. I had turned thirty on April 30. Today it was May 21. As I looked deep into the browns and violets of the broad, flat horizon of the Chang Tang of Tibet, I thought, what a way to spend a transitional birthday, on the salt route to Tibet, crossing the Himalayas on my own. I was joyous, and satisfied. The wind was now blowing about forty miles an hour, and we had to brace ourselves as we worked our way into it and down the glacier, me arcing telemark turns and Ang Neima on foot. We had no provisions with us for a longer journey, and I was still quite sick, unable to shake what had taken hold of my respiratory system.

All traffic seemed to flow through the Kangshung Valley, where I had pitched my tent. I returned to the tent while Ang Neima headed off to get our bag, which we had left behind, a stash of food and equipment hidden in the rocks. I fell asleep between coughing bouts while the water was boiling, only to cough up a couple of balls of glop, each the size of a walnut. I thought I was going to choke. I was getting worse. I couldn't even make tea; I just drank hot water. Ang Neima returned with his eyes glaring, screaming for my headlamp. Our bag was gone, and he was going to see who had stolen it. I fell asleep, unbothered. I was too tired to care.

I was woken up by the excited voices of other traveling Sherpas and Ang Neima. They had decided the bag was taken by some Tibetans who had just passed through, and if they left immediately they could catch them at Marulung or Thami. I was too groggy to grasp the situation. I just listened and felt my spirits sink, as I gave the last of the food to Ang Neima, hoping there was enough gas in my cylinder to still melt snow for water. I didn't know if I could get up; I didn't try. One of the three other Sherpas jumped in my tent. He had decided to stay while the other two accompanied Ang Neima. I rolled over and slept the next twelve hours straight.

In the morning it all began to come into focus for me. All my possessions were gone, about $1,200 worth of food, camping gear, clothing, electronics, and camera equipment. I truly had to be like the locals now. I realized the elements were so harsh here it was best to tuck your hair away and never wash or reveal your tender skin in any way. A good coating of natural oil on my face was protective. The locals only wear one set of clothes all day and night, for days at a time maybe months—if they are on caravan, who knows? I wouldn't concern myself with changing clothing. It would be good to eat, however, but I was sick enough to forfeit food too. The one concern was having enough gas to melt snow for water, but I was sure to find some yak dung around if I felt well enough to get out of the tent and make a fire like the Sherpas had taught me.

Maybe this twist-of-fate type of loss was for the best, to truly have me experience the salt route as the locals do—simply and efficiently. They seemed to travel for days with just the clothes on their backs and the food in their pockets, driving yaks or under heavy loads, possibly up to seventy pounds. They didn't have waterproof coats, down parkas and vests, different pairs of long johns, mittens, moisture cream, and so on. They were all minimalists with one sheepskin coat to wear and sleep in and maybe a yak hair blanket to wrap up in or lie on and sheep fat for their lips and face if need be. They moved completely over the pass in one long, well-calculated day and slept in the first stone huts on either side, like those at Lunag. From there on in, you visited the yersa settlements on the way down to Namche or Tingri.

My visiting Sherpa's name was Passang, with a bright round face and clothes in very poor shape. He showed me a count on his fingers to let me know he was twenty-one. I was amazed how these Sherpas had forgone their trade work and, along with Ang Neima, had taken up my cause without even my asking. I was sleeping! Perhaps any poor behavior such as stealing needed to be addressed by anyone who encountered it to ensure that the route was always safe and the people traveling through trustworthy. This would be a way for the salt route to regulate itself.

Next a couple of Tibetans showed up and started rummaging through my things outside my tent in search of a pot. I realized most people shared gear on this route and wasn't offended, just surprised at their somewhat brash manner. They were actually quite friendly in a harsh way. They pushed some of their roast barley at me, the same tsampa I had fed my yaks. I hadn't eaten for more than a day and had no food of my own, so it tasted good. These Tibetan guys reminded me of the tough bobsledders I used to hang out with at the Olympic Training Center in Lake Placid. Both were in your face, friendly and aggressive at the same time, but with good humor. They all fell, I would guess, on the more masculine end of the male-female scale, but I felt comfortable with them.

When I looked out of the tent at our visitors, I noticed this was the third day of good weather. This was perhaps the beginning of the common stretch of good spring weather before the summer monsoons hit and the pass turned to slush in the summer temperatures. The fall has a short window of good weather, too, when the glacier hardens up again before the harsh winter snows and winds set in. Most all trade over the Nangpa La happens during these two windows of time, only a few weeks during the entire year.

The Tibetan traders were cooking up some of their chang in the pot over a yak dung fire, reminding me of guys at hunting camp in the States. Maybe it wasn't just the trading or the hunt that mattered, maybe partying with the guys was just as vital to the trip as shooting an animal or making a great deal. I realized, even in another culture, it seemed to be me and the guys again. I know Sherpanis had traded over the pass, too, from the stories they told me, but I assumed it was rare, especially since the Chinese intervention.

It was okay with me. I wasn't looking to be with the guys; they just seem to frequent the same kinds of places that I do! Now I could see that these Tibetan guys were like all guys, regardless of cultural nuances. The women, the Sherpanis I spoke with, used our conversation, whether with words or hands, to connect, to be intimate. The Sherpas, the men, whether I could understand everything they were saying or not, used their conversation for status and independence. The struggle for hierarchy was palpable. Guys are guys in every language.

Young Passang watched me take out the camera I still had with me, with my longest lens attached, and look up on the pass. I drew him some pictures of a yak herd, and he got the idea that, that was what I was looking for. He knew some expedition English and called my telephoto lens a "big look" and kept asking for the "big look" throughout the day to see if there was any caravan activity. Now I had eaten only a little Tibetan tsampa in three days and was even out of tea, and I wasn't getting any better. Passang had no provisions with him either. Ang Neima and the other two Sherpas had taken all supplies with them, thinking they would be rescuing the gear and us.

I had just roused myself to pack up and try to struggle down the trail in defeat and retreat when Ang Neima and the other two Sherpas returned late on the fourth day. In a bit of a tizzy, Ang Neima approached the Tibetans who had been using my pot. He grabbed a rotten prayer flag, left by someone in passing, and tore it up to wrap two stones, one marked with a tiny mark of charcoal and the other not. He threw juniper branches over the fire and waved the two stones over the smoke.

I knew both the juniper and the prayer flag were sacred and wondered if this ceremony could be a Himalayan version of the game truth or dare. I thought perhaps this version was only about the truth when he first handed the stones to one Sherpa. The Sherpa held the stones over the fire and turned one over in his hand: it was unmarked. Next one of the Tibetans held the stones over the juniper fire and turned up the marked stone. Ang Neima delivered some harsh words and stormed off in a huff. I assumed this stone-turning ceremony proved the Tibetan was the marked man. I'd had it by now and started tossing things out of my tent and shoving them in my pack.

Just before I collapsed the tent to retreat to who knows where, as I could hardly walk, Ang Neima returned, motioning for me to follow him. The two Tibetans were going to show us where they had buried my gear in the rocks! It all seemed like a big, understated joke to the

Tibetans. They showed no remorse nor did they show disappointment at giving up my things.

Did they just want to see what I would do or see what I was made of? Is that why they did this when Ang Neima and I skied up to the Nangpa La that day? Had they been nearby watching all along to see if everyone would leave when Ang Neima and the other Sherpas left in search of them? Had they been waiting for me to leave too, or were they just toying with me? Is this why they stuck around and showed their faces, rummaging through what I had left and using my pot? I also wondered if they intended to take my bag back to Tibet, or if they planned to take it to Namche. Or did they always intend to give it back anyway? Was it Ang Neima's stone ceremony that frightened them into giving it back for fear of inciting the protecting deities' wrath upon themselves? These things I'll never know, but I certainly felt integrated in the trade world now. Every Sherpa far and wide already knew of my plight through Ang Neima, and soon the Tibetans would be passing on this story faster than any society with telephones.

I woke the next day to a brewing storm. All the Sherpas and Tibetans were gone; there was just me in my tent, whipping in the wind in this empty expanse. Ang Neima told me he would return with yaks, but I knew this might be unlikely. Yaks were hard to employ as most were involved in the trekking business now. I had sunk pretty low and was wondering if my father's curt way of telling me I shouldn't be here was right. I felt foolish, as if I'd failed. The day slid by. In the night as the snow fell, I turned on my headlamp to read my friend's notes of inspiration as I severely doubted myself and my abilities. Why did I think I could do this and on my own? My light caused my tent to glow orange in the blackness, and suddenly someone unzipped my tent door!

There stood the two men we had passed earlier on the trail and another young fellow. They were Passang and Tsa Wong, father and son who had gone back to pick up more salt from the Tibetan side, which they were carrying on their backs. It had gotten late, and their timing was off. They faced a night out in the storm with no extra clothes, no yak hair tent, no blankets, no nothing. When they saw my tent glow in the dark, it was like a miracle to them. I wrapped their shivering bodies up in my sleeping bag and parka, and they brewed up something for me that began my healing process, after they listened to my incessant coughing, spitting, and near inability to talk. We were actually taking care of each other to get through the night.

The next morning I knew this new snow would delay the Tibetan caravans that had been waiting on the other side to cross, and feeling somewhat improved from the Sherpa brew, I asked Passang if I could trek down with them. They invited me to their home. All of this was done with grunting and hand signals and such, as we didn't have a common language other than gestures. They fed me tsampa in the morning and shared tea and roast potatoes from the yak dung fire farther down the trail at Lunag. I was eating only the local diet, and it seemed to be helping. When we entered their small yersa home, I met what appeared to be the grandfather.

Three men of three generations caused me to wonder where the women were. Passang indicated that his wife had died. I supposed the grandmother had as well; the grandfather was looking quite elderly. Maybe there were no women left in their family? I wondered if this might be why they had taken such good care of me. I may have represented what they were missing. I spent the night feeling like a queen as they offered me countless cups of tea and tsampa. My health was also rapidly improving. Whatever they had brewed for me the other night in my tent had gotten me on my feet and down the trail. I began to see a shift in my attitude. I felt as though I could still accomplish my mission. Yes, I would go back to the pass, resupplied, and wait for my story to unfold with a real yak caravan crossing over 20,000 feet.

I found Ang Neima the next day, and he had indeed procured yaks for the journey to collect the gear left up in Kajung and was surprised to see me up on my feet again and down on the trail. On our way back up we stopped to find a wild jamboree at Lunag. Forty or fifty yaks and their Tibetan drivers were scattered about, resting, eating dried yak meat and yak stew, and making strong Tibetan tea over the thick smell of yak dung fires. Again, it reminded me of a wagon train or cowboys and their herd in the Wild West. This swarm of Tibetans must have come through yesterday when I left with Passang and Tsa Wang. The stew was a great feast for me, and no one seemed to care that I was photographing. The word was another yak caravan was coming in a couple of days. I felt a surge of desire to be there and to capture this incredible event that most probably would not continue into the next generation.

We made it straight to Dzampa, at the base of the glacier the next day, exhausted but geared up for the next morning's excitement. The place was home for the night to a bunch of Sherpas with loaded baskets on their backs, which hung from their heads by a tumpline, like a Canadian guide would carry a canoe. I was amazed at the dexterity of these heavily laden Sherpas, carrying over one hundred pounds, as they made their way through snow-covered moraine. Not only was it impossible to judge the stability of a rock in this moraine rubble, it was more likely that you would slide off the darn thing anyway because of its slippery snow covering and crash disastrously. I think Sherpas are some of the most dexterous athletes alive. They are strong, flexible, and quick. They seemed to float across the disheveled, snowy rocks under loads that would kill the rest of us.

I was so eager for morning to come, like a kid waiting for Santa, that I had to take a few shots of the Nepalese Khukri rum to put myself to sleep that night. The high peaks paralleling this valley of moraine and converging at the height of the Nangpa La blocked the early morning light and kept it from falling on the glacier on the morning of Friday, May 30. This gave me time to watch the Sherpas load up then for me to get into position on the glacier to catch the yak train when the light hit, assuming my information was accurate. Once on the glacier I heard the whistles and calls of the herders, and along came a train of twenty to thirty yaks, all moving in an out of the caravan so that it was impossible to count them. They had bright red prayer flags tied to them and were loaded with goods in traditional yak hair bags, woven in brown, black, and white , the colors of the yaks. The young yaks for barter were in tow, scampering along to keep up and staying close, which kept them out of gaping crevasses. I'm sure a few had been sacrificed to the ice in the past.

The herders themselves wore sheepskin coats with the curly fleece on the inside. They wore their hair braided with red yarn woven through and wrapped up around their heads. These were Khampas, known for being some of the strongest and wildest Tibetans. The herders wore a funny array of ancient and new sunglasses and glacier goggles they had no doubt traded for over the years, coming initially from climbers and trekkers. Snow blindness was a very real hazard on this pass. I was determined to photograph this event, the yaks crossing over a glacier at nearly 20,000 feet. I must have looked pretty unusual on skis and wearing a long skirt like the Sherpanis. I figured that being a foreign woman, alone and on skis, was enough to make them skeptical of me. The least I could do was dress as much as possible like their women to make them more comfortable with me.

But what I learned was that nothing really fazed these guys; anyone unusual just meant they had potential for something unusual or valuable to trade. My fingers were frozen, my legs fatigued from fifty-meter sprints at nearly 20,000 feet, but my heart soared. This moment encapsulated what I had come halfway around the world for and what I had lain alone, sick in my tent, anticipating. The first of the group had already settled in to Dzampa to brew tea before heading down on a long day to Lunag to sleep and graze their yaks. As I approached the Tibetan fueling the fire with dung chips, our eyes met. This fellow showed more amusement than surprise. His gorgeous, dark, strong face, lit by the red yarn in his hair, exhibited a playful intelligence.

I thought quickly. I needed something to trade, to engage him, rather than just sit or take photographs. I had fingernail clippers in my pocket. That was it. I bet he hadn't seen those before and what a handy tool for cutting all kinds of things, not just nails. And the way the top swivels around to open and close it was so cool, an ingenious, simple design, really. I had been trading wool hats, scarves, or jewelry because these things are small enough to carry and they aren't electronic or gadget trash, something that will break or is not congruent with their culture. I didn't come to change things or impress them with modernity.

I merely wanted to record what was there before my eyes before it vanished from our repertoire of humanity.

In all my determination to photograph, I didn't think about trade opportunities, but the clippers would do, I hoped. The fellow extended his hand holding a cup of tea and gestured that it was for me. I smiled and sat by him accepting the cup with gratitude. I at least knew hello in Tibetan. "*Tashi delek*," I said with a grin. He appreciated my effort to speak his language. My immediate acceptance illustrated a world that has nearly disappeared, a world where those such as Marco Polo thrived, a world open to connecting complete strangers in search of interesting trade goods, a world unlike ours today where we shy from strangers or anything we perceive as odd or different.

His face showed he expected me to reject the strong brew, laden with yak butter and heavy with salt. It was Tibetan tea. My body must have craved the fat and the salt because I had lost so much weight through my physical efforts, lack of food, and sickness. I had also sweat tremendously throughout this whole time period and must have needed salt. So instead of the tea being unpalatable, it was just what I craved because I had been living like he had.

I'm sure If I tried to drink this brew at home in the States, I'd have trouble choking it down. I slid my hand in my pocket, pulled out the clippers, and opened my palm to show him. He took them and held them up in the sunlight, looking a bit puzzled. I took them, and while he watched, showed him how to flip the top around and clipped one of my nails. He brightened, grabbed them for a try, and laughed out loud. He fished around in one of his bags and pulled out an old cloth with some Tibetan tsampa tied up inside. I smiled and took it with gratitude.

I began to envision these Tibetans would probably barter or sell much of their wares to middlemen, who would be sitting at the market in Namche Bazaar come Saturday. There would be so much trade going on all around. I realized I could never keep track of it all! Tibetans would be in the street, bartering hunks of dried yak meat still on the bone. Other Tibetans would be in Mingma's kitchen, selling Tibetan rugs, and then going all over town, as sort of door-to-door salesmen. I thought about how multisided deals got cut in New York City or Hong Kong or Moscow—over lunch, at the theater, at the country club, or any club at all. In Namche Bazaar it was the same, deals happening everywhere over chang, in the street, at a trekkers' lodge kitchen.

It was time to see the trade from the Tibetan side. Ang Neima went down the valley into Nepal packing all the gear on his yaks to give as gifts. I kept only my pack. That is how I got myself into trouble, all on my own en route to Tibet.

Searching for a way off the glacier on the Tibet side of the Nangpa La, I saw a crack in the ice wall that I could climb. If I slipped out of the crack, I was faced with a plummet thirty feet down into freezing water surrounded by smooth ice walls. I would have died in minutes from hypothermia. I climbed the crack by sticking my feet and warm hands into it. I moved fast enough that the heat from my feet and hands didn't melt the ice and slip me out. When I got to the top of the crack I lay on the flat ice knowing I was lucky, very lucky. As I looked around the beauty of the place seemed intensified to me, as if the colors had just deepened. Survivors are known for seeing beauty, even during their crisis. It has been speculated that a crisis opens people up to opportunities for survival rather than closing them down in fear.[3]

On the moraine's edge on the Tibetan side of the Nangpa La, I met Dawa. His name means "Wednesday" in his Himalayan language. Many are named for the day of the week they are born on. He beckoned me to have tea with him as he was just brewing up. I'm sure he anticipated great trades, seeing my down parka, which I let him try on, my flowered wool scarf, my pearl earrings, and my indestructible plastic cup. His open concern for me warmed my heart and soon his tea warmed my stomach. When I repeatedly said Gangar, the name of the Tibetan market, to indicate that's where I was headed, he offered to hoist my load onto his horse to balance his. In great appreciation I gave him a couple of scarves and some money before we worked our way down to some stone huts, much the equivalent to those at Lunag on the Nepal side of the pass.

It was very cavelike inside the hut, which was still one-third full of snow, but Dawa's candle created a warm glow to the place. These low, windowless stone structures were built beside the first of the grass, off the moraine, which accommodated the horse. The stars were absolutely brilliant in the dry atmosphere of this high-altitude desert set at 15,000 feet. This side of the Nangpa La was just a great, flat plateau, about thirty miles straight to Tingri, the home of the Gangar market. Dawa and I shared my food under the stars, and exhausted I crawled into the stone hut to sleep in my big, snug down bag. Dawa had only yak blankets. I hoped he was warm enough, but then again these people had been doing this travel for hundreds of years. They could take care of themselves, I was sure. They were certainly taking good care of me.

I felt like I'd been hit by a sledge hammer the next morning at 5 a.m. Fortunately, just down the trail, sheep herders offered us strong tea, which helped me to put one foot in front of the other. On the way down the valley, Dawa was bent on teaching me Tibetan and continually rambled on with tales about who knows what. He made sure I knew our division of chores: he was taking the horse, which he called Da, to the river, *chu,* to drink and get tea water, and I was lower in the pecking order and expected to have the dung collected and prepared when he returned to light it, using his handmade bellows. By 8 a.m. the wind had risen at times up to about thirty miles an hour, sweeping across this flat terrain with absolutely no windbreak. This was noisy and nasty travel, and although it was cold we were still under intense sun.

With our heads down we walked probably fifteen or so miles to Kyabrak. The rubble looked like the ruins of a series of trading huts, which probably once belonged to the trading Sherpa families. I assumed the huts were razed by the Chinese when the Sherpas were expelled, following the crackdown on trade in the 1950s and '60s. We had traveled along the Tingri Chu, or Tingri River, during the day, crossing the path of some of the first Tibetan yak herders I had recognized from the caravans in the Thami Valley, en route to Namche. Now they were returning back to Tingri after having traded for *rigi shakpa,* or dried potatoes, and the little three-year-old *dzomos* that were scampering along.

I knew this group had crossed the Nangpa La and back. They had the only all-white yak I had ever seen. Some of the men grinned at me in recognition, and I waved furiously in greeting, but our passing was brief. This chance meeting brought the salt route together for me. I had photographed the same caravan on either side of the pass, proof to the outside world that the salt trade still crossed the amazing Nangpa La. For us in the States this fifty mile journey, crossing over a 20,000 foot glacier, is considered an expedition. For these rugged fellows, it is just a job. As two people with a horse carrying our loads, Dawa and I were much faster and left the caravan behind.

Twenty-five miles later, and drooping like plants without water, we reached Kundepu to stay the night. Within a couple of hours of heading out the next morning, we were back in Dawa's home in Tingri. His young children were excited to see him and ran around us as we unloaded our packs. Inside, his warm, gentle wife served us tea. What a wonderful scene to be brought into and accepted in. As strange as I may have seemed to them, my presence was just another occurrence in the wild world of trade.

Dawa kept shaking his head disappointingly whenever I would mention Gangar. I dug my rice out of my pack and repeated, "Gangar?" At last he relented walking with me to my requested destination with his daughter of about five years holding fast to his hand. They left me to investigate. I wandered around the empty wooden stalls of Gangar. It was painfully closed, a ghost town. A man signaled to me, the only other person there. I came to know the man as Li Ming. Although he was Chinese the locals liked him well enough because he was a surgeon who would also travel out on horseback to treat the sick. The Chinese government either had given some big bonus for him to come here, or he was sent for duty as some governmental punishment. All Chinese people I spoke with on my previous Everest Grand Circle trip did not choose Tibet; it was chosen for them.

Li Ming scratched his head in disbelief, wondering where I came from and why I was here—a foreign woman alone who did not speak the language, had no weapon, almost no money, and no horse. I tried to explain as best I could—with Li Ming speaking bits of English and through using gestures—that I was here to work and trade with the locals and travel as they did on foot so I didn't need much money or a horse. I had chosen never to travel with a weapon because if I lost it or dropped it that weapon could be used on me. Li Ming unzipped his medical bag, which was just a nylon, carry-on bag for traveling, and showed me his tiny pistol, letting me know that he was a well-liked man who spoke the language and traveled on horseback and he *still* wouldn't be here without a pistol. I got his point, but it didn't change what I had just done.

Sadly, I dragged myself back to Dawa's home. He had known all along I had this bag of rice I was determined to take to Gangar for trade, and he had always known there was no trade at Gangar. I stood, drooping, clutching my rice, and Dawa disappeared. When he returned, Dawa, my traveling companion who had also become my teacher and my friend, held my hand securely in his two rough hands and grinned after he set a beautiful, small, hand-turned bowl made out of a reddish wood in front of me to offer in trade. I had to blink back the tears as I looked into the bowl and saw in it all the mystery, cold, harsh weather, illness, fear, satisfaction, determination, and raw beauty that had shaped my journey over the Nangpa La.

In the dim firelight I placed the pouch of grain in his hands, and his wife poured more tea, this time into my new bowl. I hadn't planned this exchange, but so much of my journey to this portion of the Himalayas had not complied with my plans; it had been a journey with its own plan of discovery about an ancient way of life and about myself. I couldn't have devised a better plan than to trade my rice from the market in Namche Bazaar, at the end of the route in Tingri, with a wonderful new friend.

Next, to my surprise, I was confronted by a Chinese soldier outside. The soldier drew a line in the dirt and kept pointing to Nangpa La. I assumed he was telling the growing crowd I had illegally crossed the border. Then more soldiers with more red bars and gold stars on their lapels starting surrounding me. I was attracting the big brass. I tried to stay calm as they became more riled, fearing I would be arrested and knowing full well what had happened to suspected anti-Chinese journalists in prison who had previously been arrested in Tibet. I grabbed from my pack a bag of hard candy I had brought from Kathmandu and placed candy into the hands of all soldiers, superior and subordinate.

The brass seemed confused. This took them aback, as I sat back on my pack, literally in the middle of this circle of military men. The subordinates ate the candy with appreciation right away, asking for more, and the brass shook their heads, looked at each other, and walked away. What caused me to offer candy I'll never know; it was a gesture. A Toyota Land Cruiser was only a dust storm in the road on the horizon. I grabbed my bag and ran directly into the middle of the road waving my arms, crossing them back and forth over my head. They had to either run me over, stop, or go off the road. They stopped, and I aggressively put my hand right on the door handle. It was locked but the driver came around and took my pack as I jumped in, saying, "You need to save me. I need to leave!"

At the time I had no idea if these men could even understand me, but I was sure my tone conveyed my need. The driver answered me half-heartedly, saying "no fit," referring to my pack. I almost screamed "drop it" but remembered I had money in it that I could give them. I leaped out of the cruiser, grabbed my pack, and shoved it in, falling in behind it. In my rising panic I cried, "Go! Go! I'll pay." The men took this all in stride and sped away to quiet me. They told me they were businessmen from Kathmandu on their way home after negotiating the sale of Nepalese vegetables to the Chinese to accommodate foreign tourism newly opened in Lhasa. Vegetables over this new road from Nepal were far cheaper than those flown in from lower China. Their English was quite good.

For long hours I sweated over the border guards being alerted by the military that a single foreign woman would be trying to cross the border and should be detained. I knew the military had plenty of communication here, even if the locals didn't. I explained my situation to the men, and at the border they let me lay low in the Cruiser. They took my passport with them, telling the guards I was sick and couldn't leave the car. I clenched in fear, but the men returned with my passport stamped as exiting the country. I was joyously legal on paper and relieved of a fear I have never experienced before as we drove away, back into Nepal and all the way to Kathmandu. I was a free woman, with a long story to tell to *National Geographic* magazine.

CHAPTER 8

AN EXPEDITION
ACROSS CULTURES

GOING SOLO OVER THE NANGPA LA working for *National Geographic* magazine on a project of my own creation and design was a step toward recognizing my own androgynous nature. I relied on both my masculine and feminine qualities. This trip was a celebration of doing it all alone. The famous psychologist Carl Jung said that both animus, masculine characteristics, and anima, feminine characteristics, reside in all of us.[1] You truly mature when you recognize the opposite gender—your animus if you are a woman and your anima if you are a man—inside yourself and accept it with a big, fat embrace.

After my Nangpa La work with the Tibetans and the Sherpas, I went to Samiland to travel with the reindeer herders in the Arctic above Europe, and I traveled on a camel caravan with the Tuareg in the Sahara. I also did the first-ever one-day ascent and ski descent of 17,000-foot Mount Ararat, which allowed me to live with the Kurds, who had been divided up into many subsequent nations—Iraq, Iran, Syria, and Turkey—after the dissolution of Kurdistan. The Kurds had suffered dispersion much like the Kirkiz I had visited while climbing Muztagata, who were spread through China, Afghanistan, Pakistan, and the former Soviet Union. I also took a hot air balloon, which was a replica of the Sydney opera house, across Australia in a competition with my pal Chris Dewhirst.

But the corresponding articles I had written for these trips, which had been slated for publication in *Smithsonian, Reader's Digest, National Geographic,* and *Sports Illustrated,* were rejected, after having been accepted. And now I needed back surgery. As my body was breaking down, my savings were dwindling because I couldn't work, and the rejection slips just kept coming in. Just when I thought I could keep a bag packed by the door, ready to depart at a moment's notice to cover another fascinating story, my house of cards had collapsed.

So I dove inside myself for clues as to why this was happening. I couldn't shake the feeling I was missing my true direction, that if I discovered and followed my true calling all would be well again. Whether naive, hopeless, or sound, whatever my reasoning, I didn't question my reaction; it felt right. For a couple of months I lay relatively still to avoid the pain and worked with my mind through dreams and questioned my deepest motives and intentions, Buddhist style.

The initial philosophy I had come to in the night when I was twelve years old ("Your life is what you make it, and the world is what it means to you") seemed to play out for me. I was a female mountaineer and the world's highest mountains were my playground. Yet after my time in the Himalayas in the Buddhist culture, I had learned a new twist to my initial philosophy: motivation or intention was the key to everything I thought then acted on. In the Buddhist sense one should strive to diminish suffering. Although I felt my life should still be what I made it I needed to use whatever talents or gumption I had to alleviate the suffering of others. By launching into living with indigenous tribes around the world, my intention was to give them a voice, to let the world hear them and hope that those affected by my work would see the value in the indigenous way of life. We all stand to learn so much from these tribes who are our ancient selves.

To those around me I would not look any different, but internally, just as I skipped beyond gender roles, the Buddhist view had allowed me to skip beyond myself and speak for someone else. It was a personal paradigm shift. I still felt my world was my creation, but I was motivated to do it for the benefit of others. Immersing myself in ancient life, still existing today, I became acutely aware of our past connection to Earth, her natural rhythms and cycles, and to the creatures living in her many varied environments. All indigenous cultures, on all continents, lived this way. We are obviously one human family. I had the privilege of experiencing life as it had been for most of all of time for human beings. The way we live today in modern society is not even an eye blink in the entirety of the human experience here on Earth.

Surgery became unavoidable as nerve damage was occurring and my foot was dropping; I couldn't hold it up when I tried to walk. Most nerve damage is reversible until it hits a point of no return, and I was entering that zone. During recovery, postsurgery, I continued to search for what my path should be if I did receive all mobility once again. I was willing to wipe the slate clean and move in any direction, if it was possible for me to move at all. What kept coming to mind and to heart and was confirmed by my dreams was that I had a strong connection with the indigenous peoples I had met in my travels—the Tibetans, the Sami, the Tuareg, the Kurds, the Kirkiz.

I felt that if I was able to be functional again I would like to do something with and for them. Their voice was a dying voice in our world, and I felt they had so much to say. The way they connected with and respected their natural environment and each other was something I felt we were losing in our society today. We are all descendants of these original people; these are the races that have civilized our own. I had made my way as an independent in the world, setting up projects and expeditions on my own, so I was confident that I could do it again. But how? I still had to make a meager living.

My roommate in the farmhouse I had moved into when Ned and I parted ways was a gem. She agreed to take me along on her trip to New York City, with her front seat laid perfectly flat because I couldn't sit, so I could visit with editors at a few different children's publishing houses. Even though I had a book out for adults and I had always written my articles for adults, everything was telling me it was time to work for the indigenous voice and to deliver the words to children. This was how I truly felt I would be the most effective because adults find it difficult to change but working with children can shape our collective future.

As it turned out all the editors kept saying, "Please take a seat," as they looked at my plastic sheet of slides, indicating the types of photos I would take to do a book series for children about indigenous life around the world. There was no way I would tell them I couldn't even sit down, when I was asking them for an advance to send me to the Himalayas and the Sahara to live with the locals and travel on yak and camel caravans across some of the world's most desperate terrain. They would think I didn't have my screws in tight. So I just said I'd been too cramped in the car and needed to stretch my legs, and they bought it, both the books and my white lie. The advance rolled in and I rolled out the door.

To supplement the cost of my newly contracted children's book series, I created a new expedition goal. I convinced a magazine to take a story about a ski descent I would pull off on one of the new "trekking peaks" in the Himalayas. I got a ski company to donate skis for a mention and photos in the story and set out to climb 23,000-foot Mera Peak with Mark Streuli as my climbing partner. I had gleaned through my many other expeditions, climbing trips, and training with men that the genders do in fact speak and communicate differently. I was aware that I might need to jump across the gender gap to a place of understanding. I felt it was better for men and women to try to interpret each other rather than to change each other. In the ten years that had passed since my first expedition with men in New Zealand, I had come to feel more comfortable with my own thoughts and ways of being, realizing they were okay and just as valid as those of the men I worked with. In many ways I had come to see what Jim Bridwell, the most accomplished climber I ever worked with, meant when he said he liked working with a woman because he felt she "monitors things."

I reflected on being invited to New Zealand on my first expedition with three men and following their lead and then running my expedition over the Nangpa La on my own and now inviting a male partner to ski a Himalayan peak in a new style with me. As a woman in what is typically thought of as a man's world, I felt that this world belonged to me as much as any man. It was a world we shared equitably.

Each expedition I had taken part in had been successful, even the first one-day ascent and descent of Mount Ararat. I had gone up a second time to make the summit rather than leave after our first, failed attempt as a team. Many of my expeditions were not well known because, as Ned would say, "we did too good of a job." He felt only the tragedies became big news. If you were successful, as we had been, it was of lesser note. So I felt we weren't risk seekers but rather good planners.

Ned would say, "familiarity breeds out risk." But I never saw myself as a thrill seeker, I saw myself as familiar with my workplace—the mountains—and making sound choices, not simply choosing to seek the next thrill. Anyway, whether I had less dopamine circulating in my brain or fewer neurons in my amygdala, which makes me sound like I'm working at a deficit, I felt like a complete woman, comfortable in her work again. There would be a new ski story for a magazine and a new book to kick off my new series for children, even after major back surgery.

While creating my Vanishing Cultures children's book series, I lived with several indigenous cultures where there were no political boundaries or ownership of the land and where there were only extended family groups with no other hierarchy other than respect for elders or the healing shaman. I visited these groups hundreds of miles from roads, power lines, and phone lines. There was no such thing as a written library, only songs, poems, and stories recited generation to generation. I realized that this is the way human beings have lived on Earth for hundreds of thousands of years. There was a certain psychological stability to this life; things were done as they always had been before. Today, with rapidly changing roles in society, blending of societies, and ever-advancing technologies, keeping pace with the changing definition of ourselves and our roles on this Earth is stressful. I noticed indigenous people, through daily life and the brotherhood of barter, have to connect with each other to survive. We in modern society can insulate ourselves from one another while working, shopping, or being entertained, and we're suffering a backlash of isolation, competition, and stress. Depression is more widespread than ever before.

When I was climbing hard and regularly, life was about my immediate surroundings and the two or three men climbing with me. Life was difficult yet simple. We had our own tribe and our culture of mountaineering, complete with our own language, dress, and rituals. In this microenvironment I distilled the difference, as I saw it, between me as a woman and the men. By immersing myself in these intense expedition events, I was able to leave gender expectations behind and choose my role and my actions as they suited me as an individual personality. For this I will always be grateful. I see myself as a woman with any ability that a man has. I also see and accept that I may choose to use my abilities with my own signature, my own way, even if it differs from the way a man might choose.

The guys and I had different chemistry in our brains as our hormones flowed through, and this seemed to me to create instinctual types of behavior. I'd have a tendency to nurture because chemically I was primed for that as well. I cherished our differences and saw that they could indeed complement each other if I was aware enough to appreciate the nuances. Ultimately men and women are much more alike than they are different. Although mentally I'm considered androgynous* (my masculine and feminine sides are nearly equitable with just a whisker of a hair tendency to be more masculine than feminine), physically I'm all female with my 36-26-36 build and the way my body responds. But psychologically I'm able to find a balance between nurturing, community-associated feminine qualities and decisive, motivated-associated masculine qualities.

And still my life continues to be one of the guys, for sure, with my family of males, after giving birth to two sons at home. I do the best I can to effect change as I raise my two boys and spend time working in

---

*Janet Shibley-Hyde's *Half the Human Experience* provides a test to find out how masculine, feminine, or androgynous you rate.

schools teaching environmental sustainability and cultural appreciation, using the twenty books I have created. My motivation or intention is clear, as I work toward creating cultural and environmental awareness among our youth with hopes for a brighter future. I still strive to make my life what I choose it to be as a part of our familial whole, and the world is still my playground as I work to serve through education.

Will my life and my words have any effect on our national psyche, on our process as a political entity, which leads the way in this changing world? Who knows? As a woman with world records and published books under her belt, can I impress upon the male-dominated political and corporate world that we need more of a balance between men and women in these positions of power and influence? Can I encourage women to value their natural tendency to nurture community and to recognize that their ability to create dialogue does not represent a lack of confidence but rather a striving for connection and unity? It will benefit us all, men and women alike, to appreciate our differences and use them to encourage balance. All I can do is hold the intention dear and try.

NOTES

CHAPTER 1. SOUTHERN CROSS EXPEDITION

1. Hyde, *Half the Human Experience,* 474–76.

CHAPTER 2. AMERICAN FRIENDSHIP EXPEDITION

1. Hyde, *Half the Human Experience,* 253.
2. Ibid., 104.
3. Ibid., 154.
4. Ibid.
5. Ibid.
6. Gonzales, *Deep Survival,* 179.

CHAPTER 3. FAILURE

1. Hyde, *Half the Human Experience,* 22.
2. Gurian, *What Could He Be Thinking?* 47.
3. Hyde, *Half the Human Experience,* 99.
4. Ibid., 104.
5. Ibid., 103.
6. Ibid., 103.
7. Ibid., 105.
8. Gonzales, *Deep Survival,* 242.
9. For more on this notion, see Tannen, *You Just Don't Understand,* 76–77.

CHAPTER 4. WHAT GOES AROUND . . .

1. Hyde, *Half the Human Experience,* 209.
2. Ibid., 240–41.
3. Ibid.
4. Ibid.

CHAPTER 5. . . . COMES AROUND

1. Norton, *The Fight for Everest,* 130.
2. Hyde, *Half the Human Experience,* 153–55.
3. Ibid.

CHAPTER 6. SKI, SKATE, SHOOT, FLY

1. Hyde, *Half the Human Experience,* 294.
2. Gonzales, *Deep Survival,* 41.

CHAPTER 7. CROSSING THE NANGPA LA

1. von Fürer-Haimendorf, *Himalayan Traders.*
2. Gonzales, *Deep Survival,* 170.
3. Ibid., 195.

CHAPTER 8. AN EXPEDITION ACROSS CULTURES

1. Jung, *The Archetypes and the Collective Unconscious,* 124.

BIBLIOGRAPHY

Gonzales, Laurence. *Deep Survival: Who Lives, Who Dies, and Why*. New York: W. W. Norton, 2003.

Gurian, Michael. *What Could He Be Thinking?: How a Man's Mind Really Works*. New York: St. Martin's Griffin, 2003.

Huffington, Arianna. *On Becoming Fearless . . . in Love, Work, and Life*. New York: Little, Brown and Company, 2007.

Hyde, Janet Shibley. *Half the Human Experience: The Psychology of Women*. 3rd ed. Lexington, Mass.: D.C. Heath, 1985.

———. *Half the Human Experience: The Psychology of Women*. 7th ed. Boston: Houghton Mifflin, 2007.

Jung, C. G. *The Archetypes and the Collective Unconscious* (Collected Works of C. G. Jung). 2nd ed. London: Routledge, 1991.

Kaza, Stephanie, ed. *Hooked!: Buddhist Writings on Greed, Desire, and the Urge to Consume*. Boston: Shambala, 2005.

Norton, E. F. *The Fight for Everest: 1924*. London, Longmans, Green & Co., 1925.

Tannen, Deborah. *You Just Don't Understand: Women and Men in Conversation*. New York: Quill, 2001.

von Fürer-Haimendorf, Christoph. *Himalayan Traders*. London: John Murray Publishers, 1975.

Young-Eisendrath, Polly and Florence Weidemann. *Female Authority: Empowering Women through Psychotherapy*. New York: The Guilford Press, 1987.